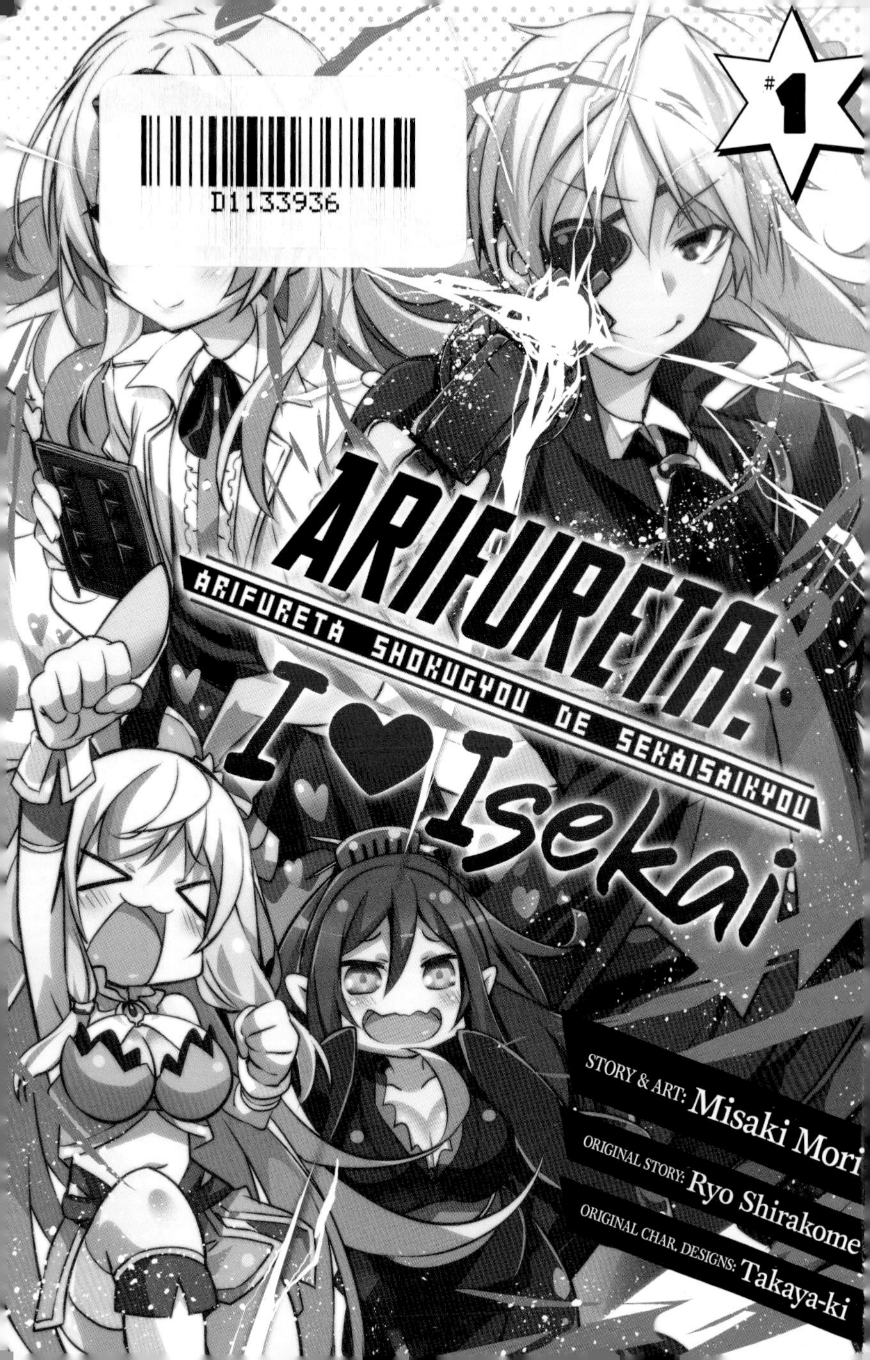
#1
ARIFURETA:
ARIFURETA SHOKUGYOU DE SEKAISAIKYOU
I ♥ Isekai
STORY & ART: Misaki Mori
ORIGINAL STORY: Ryo Shirakome
ORIGINAL CHAR. DESIGNS: Takaya-ki

TABLE OF
CONTENTS

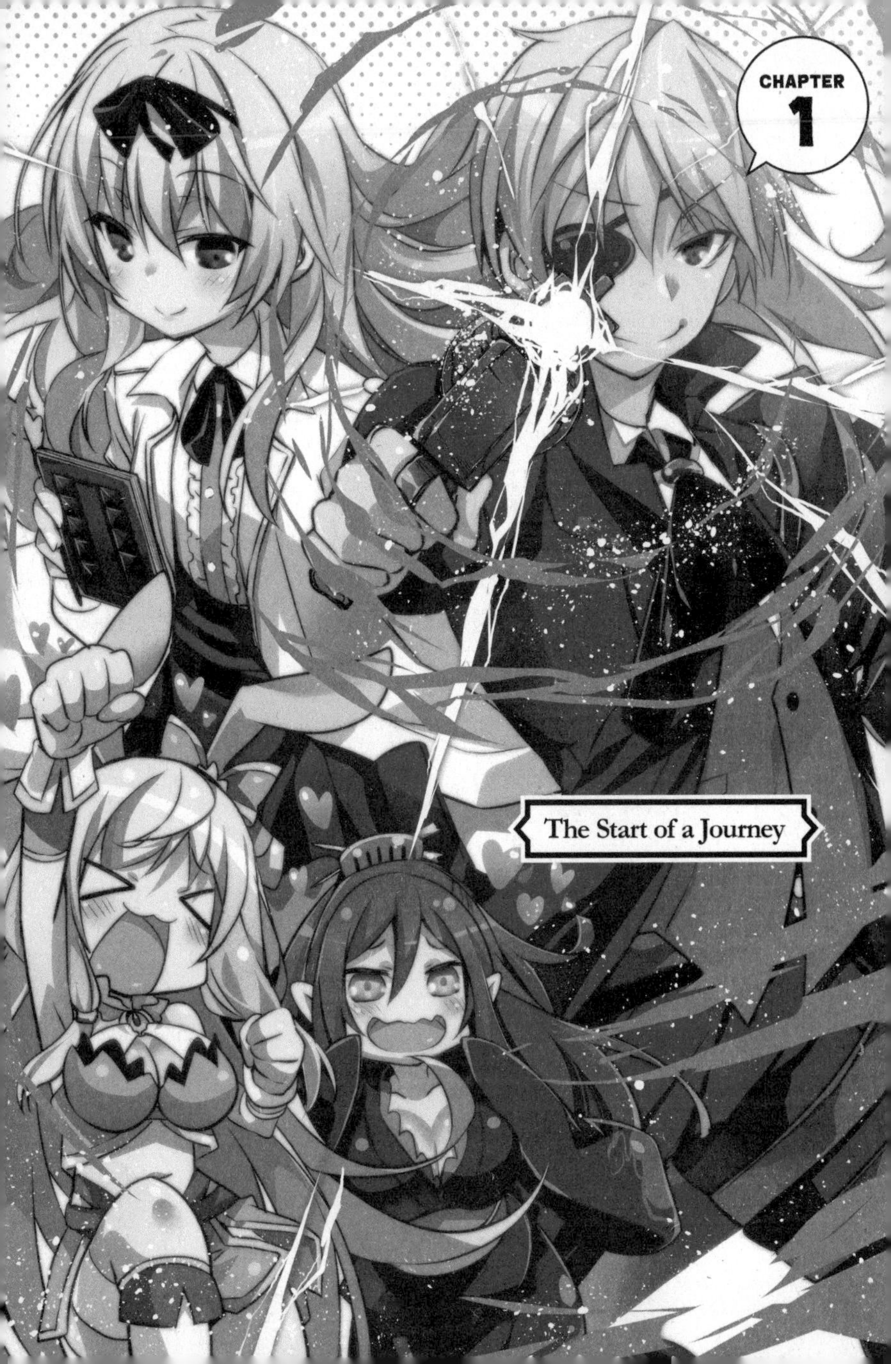
CHAPTER 1
The Start of a Journey

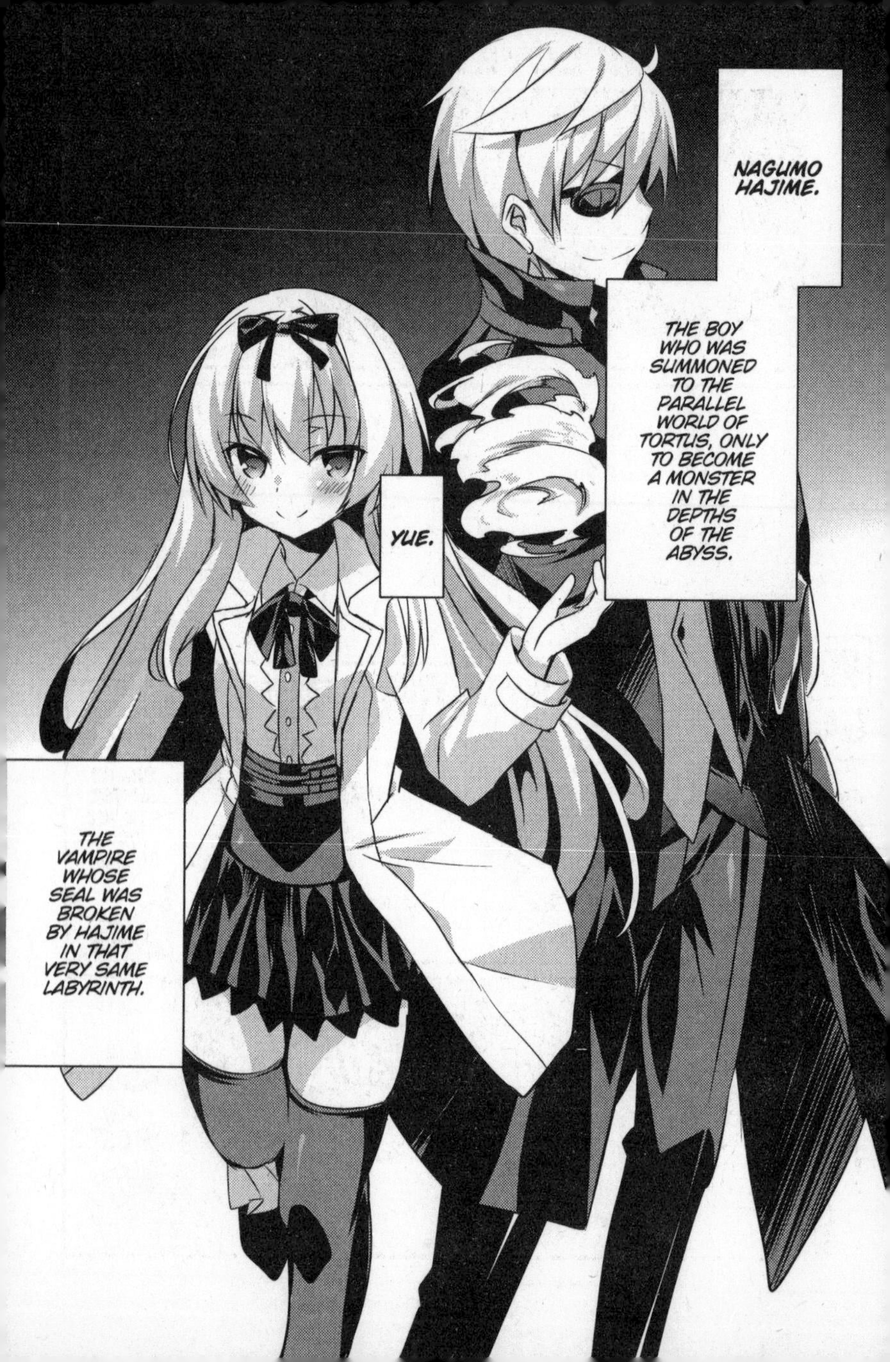
NAGUMO HAJIME.
THE BOY WHO WAS SUMMONED TO THE PARALLEL WORLD OF TORTUS, ONLY TO BECOME A MONSTER IN THE DEPTHS OF THE ABYSS.
YUE.
THE VAMPIRE WHOSE SEAL WAS BROKEN BY HAJIME IN THAT VERY SAME LABYRINTH.

GETTIN' LOVEY-DOVEY IN HELL

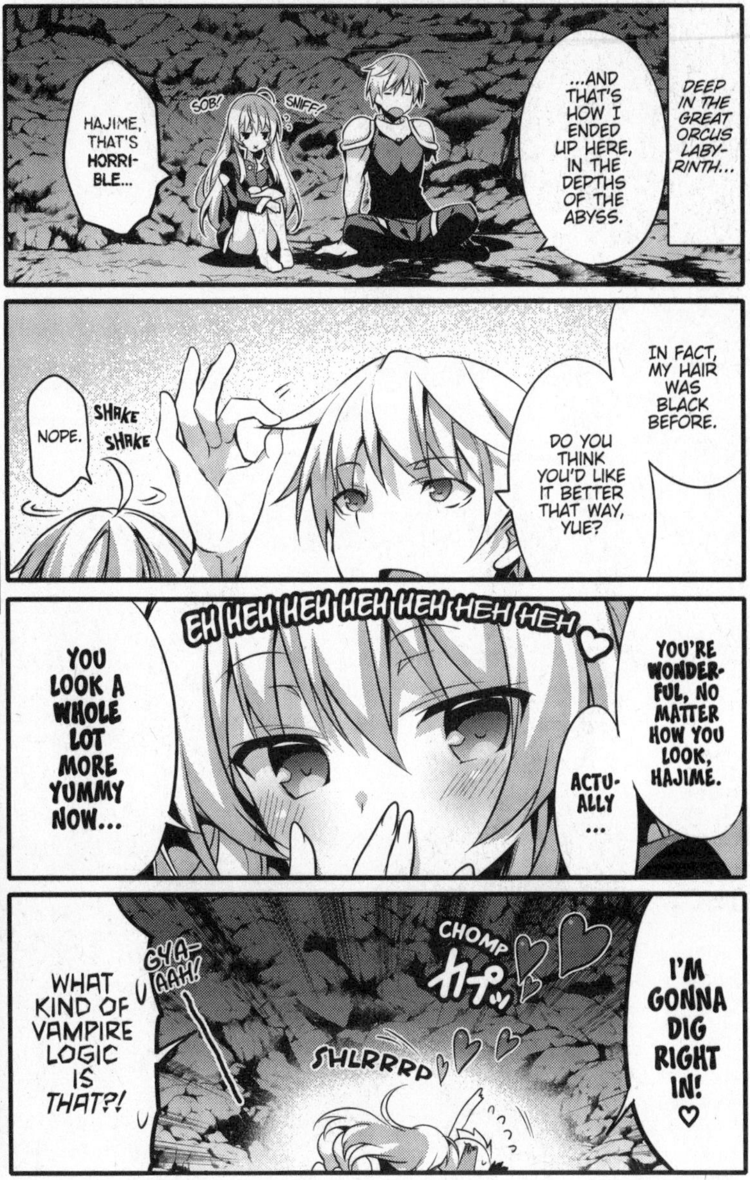
DEEP IN THE GREAT ORCUS LABYRINTH...
...AND THAT'S HOW I ENDED UP HERE, IN THE DEPTHS OF THE ABYSS.
SNIFF!
SOB!
HAJIME, THAT'S HORRIBLE...
IN FACT, MY HAIR WAS BLACK BEFORE.
DO YOU THINK YOU'D LIKE IT BETTER THAT WAY, YUE?
SHAKE SHAKE
NOPE.
YOU'RE WONDERFUL, NO MATTER HOW YOU LOOK, HAJIME.
EH HEH HEH HEH HEH HEH HEH ♡
ACTUALLY...
YOU LOOK A WHOLE LOT MORE YUMMY NOW...
I'M GONNA DIG RIGHT IN! ♡
CHOMP
カプッ
SHLRRRP
GYAAAH!
WHAT KIND OF VAMPIRE LOGIC IS THAT?!

ED

HERE IN THE DEPTHS OF THE ABYSS LIES A SPECIAL KIND OF HELL...

COOL POSE

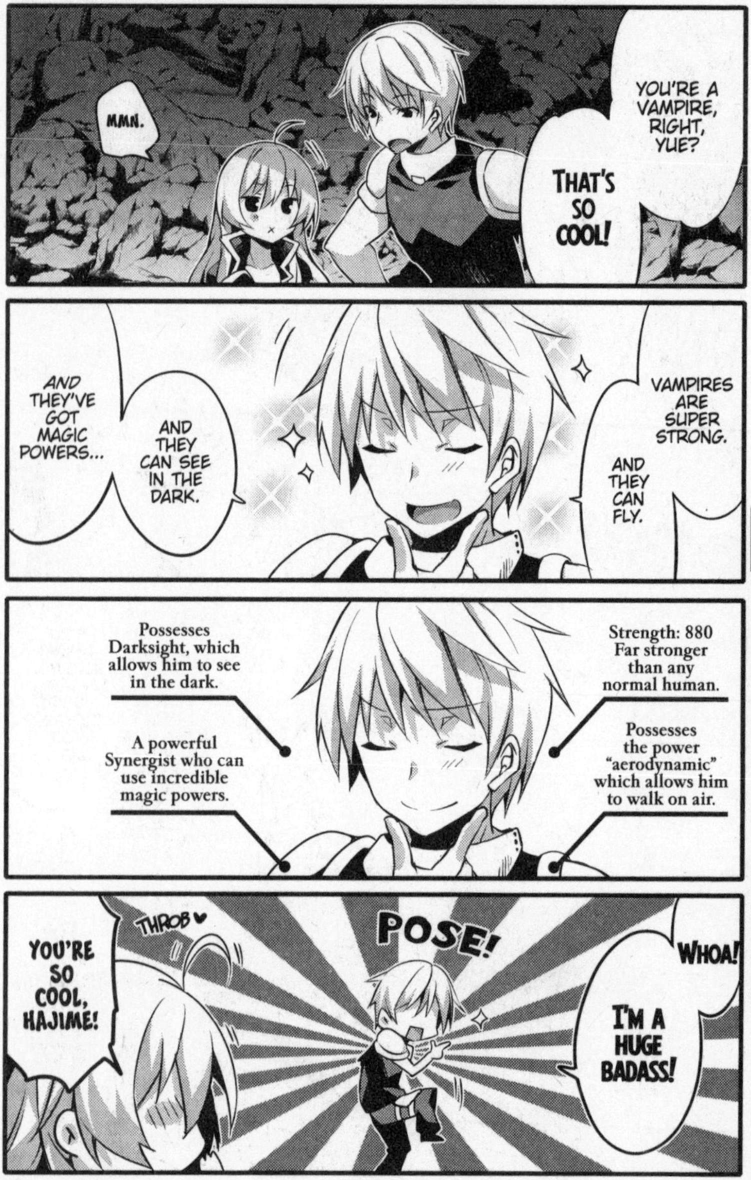
YOU'RE A VAMPIRE, RIGHT, YUE?
THAT'S SO COOL!
MMN.
VAMPIRES ARE SUPER STRONG.
AND THEY CAN FLY.
AND THEY CAN SEE IN THE DARK.
AND THEY'VE GOT MAGIC POWERS...
Strength: 880 Far stronger than any normal human.
Possesses the power "aerodynamic" which allows him to walk on air.
Possesses Darksight, which allows him to see in the dark.
A powerful Synergist who can use incredible magic powers.
WHOA!
I'M A HUGE BADASS!
POSE!
THROB
YOU'RE SO COOL, HAJIME!

SHIRA KOME

I APOLOGIZE. I JUST LOVE DELUSIONAL, CHUUNI GUYS.

(BUFF) CHEERLEADER

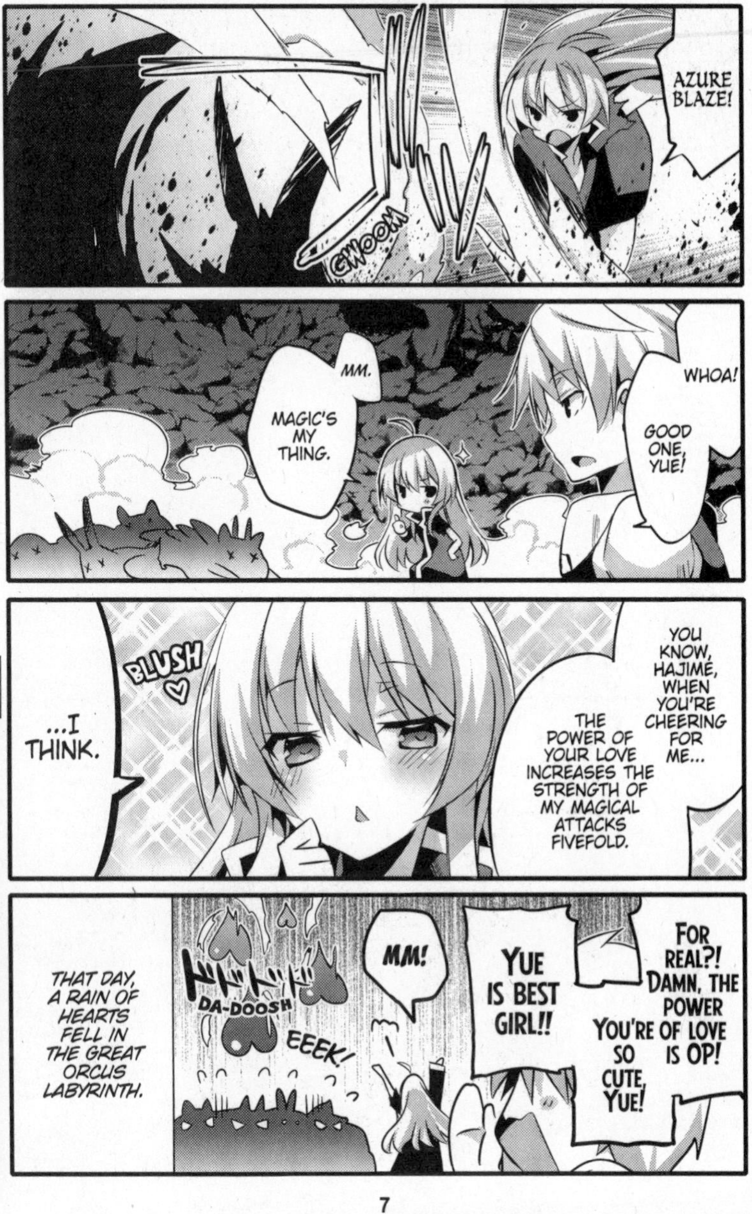
AZURE BLAZE!
GWOOM
WHOA!
GOOD ONE, YUE!
MM.
MAGIC'S MY THING.
YOU KNOW, HAJIME, WHEN YOU'RE CHEERING FOR ME...
THE POWER OF YOUR LOVE INCREASES THE STRENGTH OF MY MAGICAL ATTACKS FIVEFOLD.
BLUSH ♡
...I THINK.
FOR REAL?! DAMN, THE POWER OF LOVE IS OP!
YOU'RE SO CUTE, YUE!
YUE IS BEST GIRL!!
MM!
ドドドドド
DA-DOOSH
EEEK!
THAT DAY, A RAIN OF HEARTS FELL IN THE GREAT ORCUS LABYRINTH.

FORECAST: AZURE SKIES, WITH SPORADIC HEART SHOWERS.

A TERRIFYING VISION

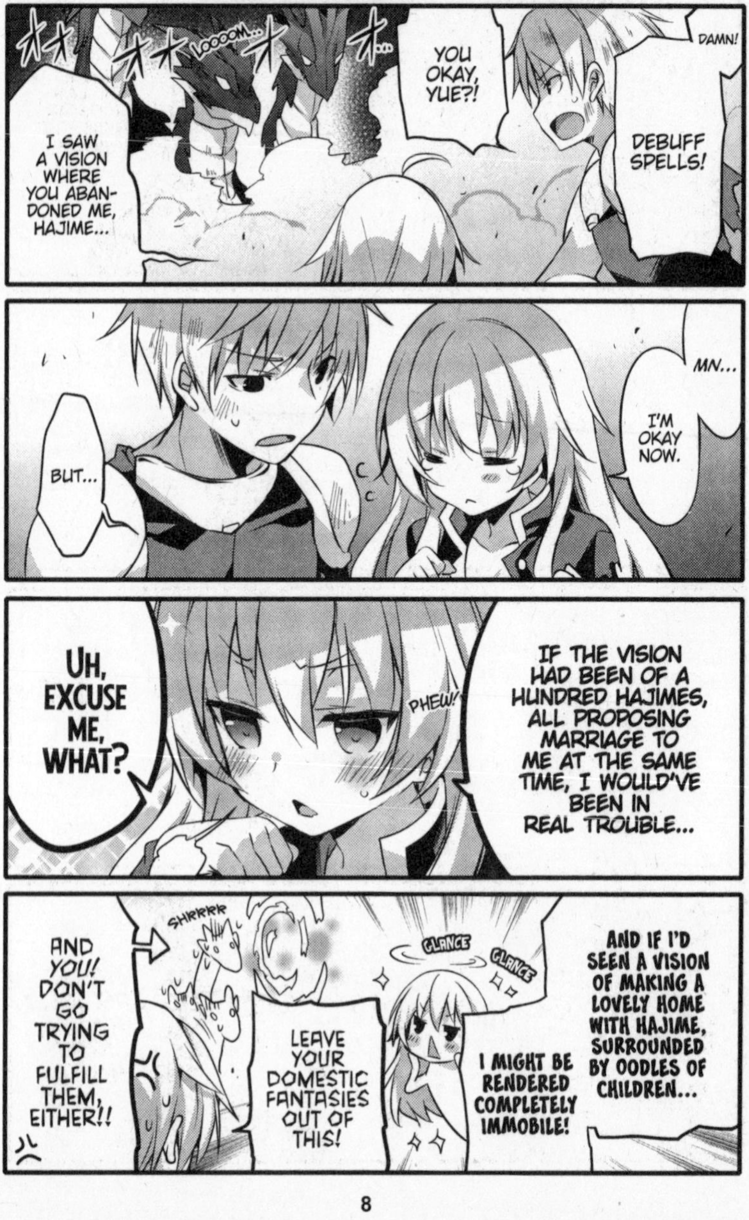
DAMN!
YOU OKAY, YUE?!
DEBUFF SPELLS!
オ...
オ
オオ LOOOOM...
オオ
I SAW A VISION WHERE YOU ABANDONED ME, HAJIME...
MN...
I'M OKAY NOW.
BUT...
IF THE VISION HAD BEEN OF A HUNDRED HAJIMES, ALL PROPOSING MARRIAGE TO ME AT THE SAME TIME, I WOULD'VE BEEN IN REAL TROUBLE...
PHEW!
UH, EXCUSE ME, WHAT?
AND IF I'D SEEN A VISION OF MAKING A LOVELY HOME WITH HAJIME, SURROUNDED BY OODLES OF CHILDREN...
GLANCE
GLANCE
I MIGHT BE RENDERED COMPLETELY IMMOBILE!
LEAVE YOUR DOMESTIC FANTASIES OUT OF THIS!
SHRRRR
AND YOU! DON'T GO TRYING TO FULFILL THEM, EITHER!!

GOOD CUSTOMER SERVICE FROM THAT ONE.

AWESOME, TO SAY THE LEAST

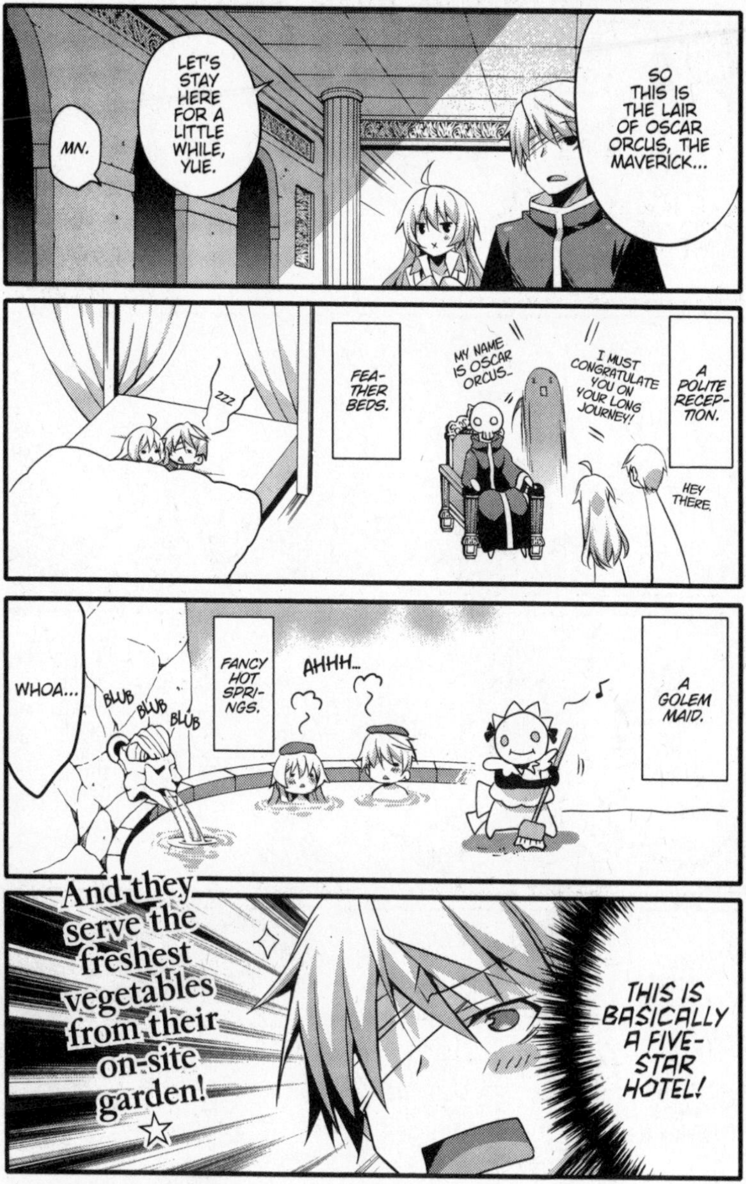

SO THIS IS THE LAIR OF OSCAR ORCUS, THE MAVERICK...
LET'S STAY HERE FOR A LITTLE WHILE, YUE.
MN.
A POLITE RECEPTION.
HEY THERE.
I MUST CONGRATULATE YOU ON YOUR LONG JOURNEY!
MY NAME IS OSCAR ORCUS...
FEATHER BEDS.
ZZZ
A GOLEM MAID.
AHHH...
FANCY HOT SPRINGS.
BLUB
BLUB
BLUB
WHOA...
THIS IS BASICALLY A FIVE-STAR HOTEL!
And they serve the freshest vegetables from their on-site garden! ☆

THIS REALLY SAVED OUR BACON.

ISSUES WITH THE IN-LAWS

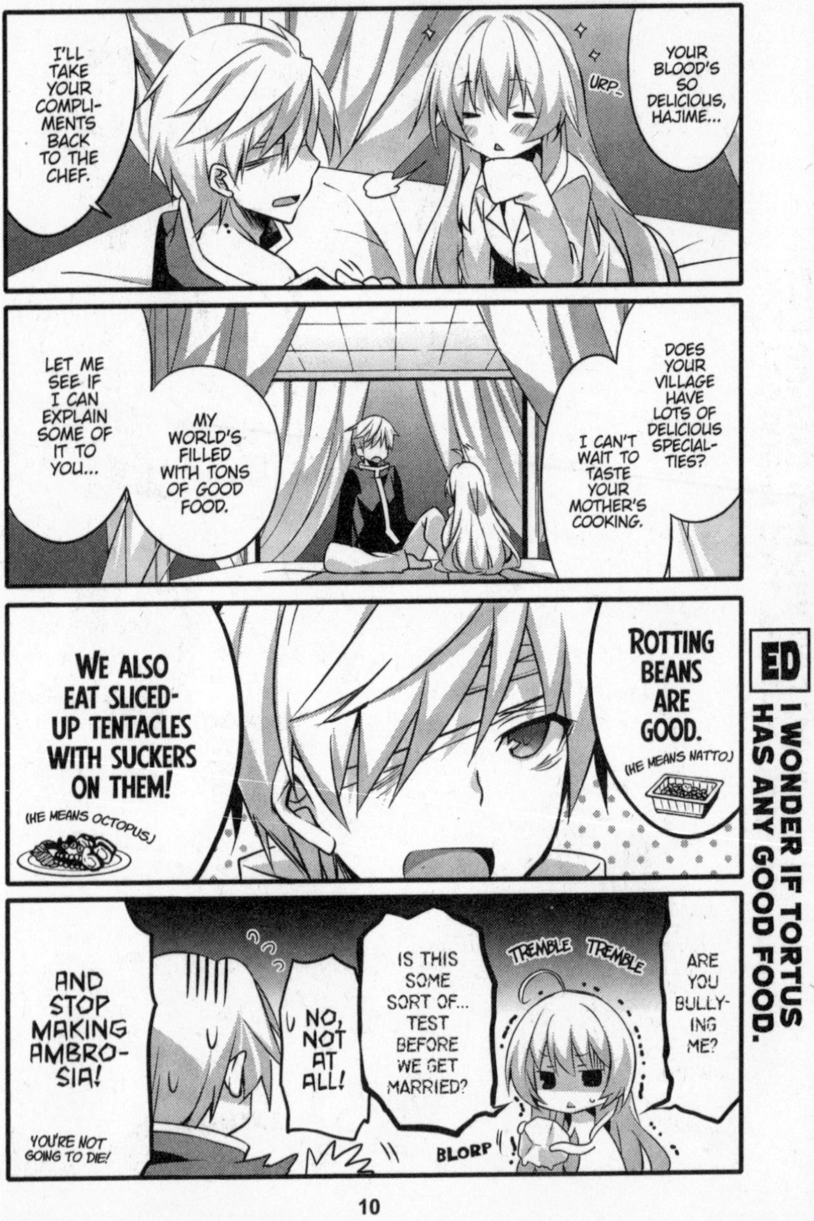
YOUR BLOOD'S SO DELICIOUS, HAJIME...
URP..
I'LL TAKE YOUR COMPLIMENTS BACK TO THE CHEF.
DOES YOUR VILLAGE HAVE LOTS OF DELICIOUS SPECIALTIES?
I CAN'T WAIT TO TASTE YOUR MOTHER'S COOKING.
MY WORLD'S FILLED WITH TONS OF GOOD FOOD.
LET ME SEE IF I CAN EXPLAIN SOME OF IT TO YOU...
ROTTING BEANS ARE GOOD.
(HE MEANS NATTO)
WE ALSO EAT SLICED-UP TENTACLES WITH SUCKERS ON THEM!
(HE MEANS OCTOPUS)
ARE YOU BULLYING ME?
TREMBLE TREMBLE
IS THIS SOME SORT OF... TEST BEFORE WE GET MARRIED?
NO, NOT AT ALL!
AND STOP MAKING AMBROSIA!
BLORP
YOU'RE NOT GOING TO DIE!
ED
I WONDER IF TORTUS HAS ANY GOOD FOOD.

HAJIME'S PREFERENCES

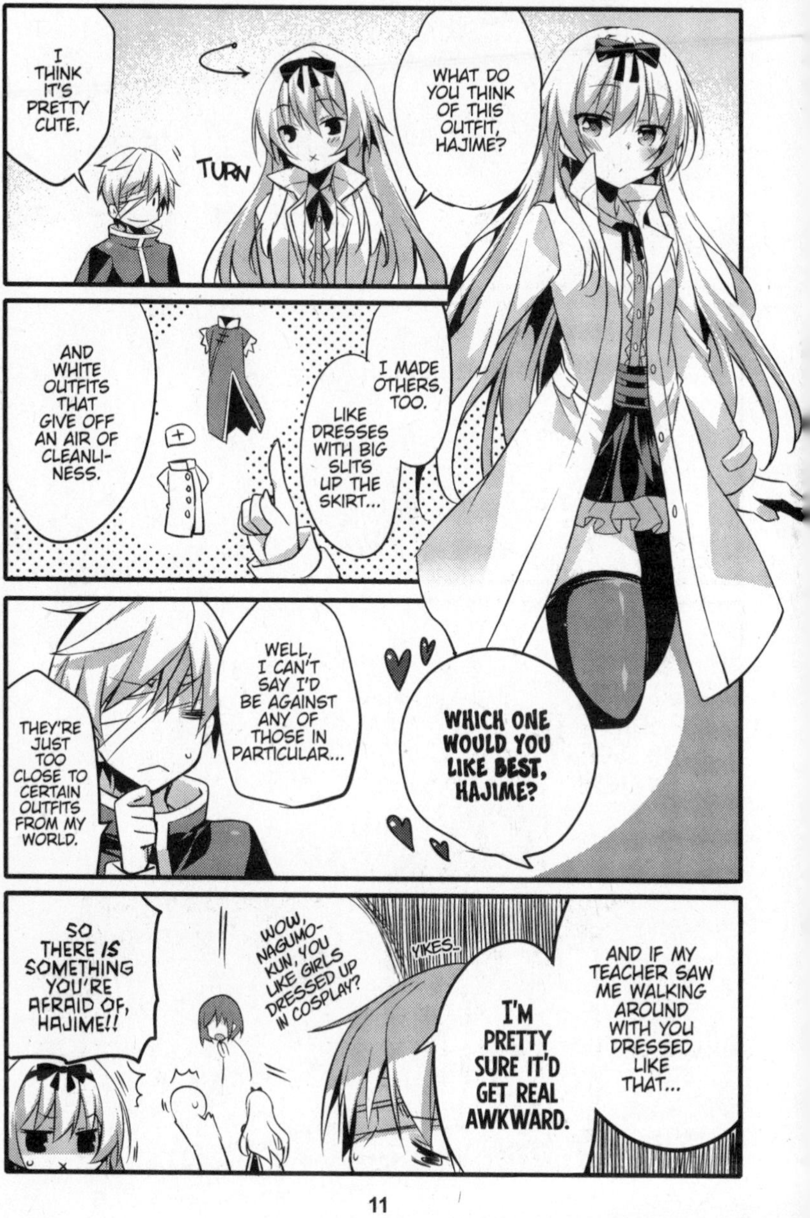
WHAT DO YOU THINK OF THIS OUTFIT, HAJIME?
TURN
I THINK IT'S PRETTY CUTE.
I MADE OTHERS, TOO.
LIKE DRESSES WITH BIG SLITS UP THE SKIRT...
AND WHITE OUTFITS THAT GIVE OFF AN AIR OF CLEANLINESS.
WHICH ONE WOULD YOU LIKE BEST, HAJIME?
WELL, I CAN'T SAY I'D BE AGAINST ANY OF THOSE IN PARTICULAR...
THEY'RE JUST TOO CLOSE TO CERTAIN OUTFITS FROM MY WORLD.
AND IF MY TEACHER SAW ME WALKING AROUND WITH YOU DRESSED LIKE THAT...
I'M PRETTY SURE IT'D GET REAL AWKWARD.
YIKES..
WOW, NAGUMO-KUN, YOU LIKE GIRLS DRESSED UP IN COSPLAY?
SO THERE *IS* SOMETHING YOU'RE AFRAID OF, HAJIME!!

YOU MIGHT CALL THESE OUTFITS VAMPIRE COUTURE.

WHAT A SWORD

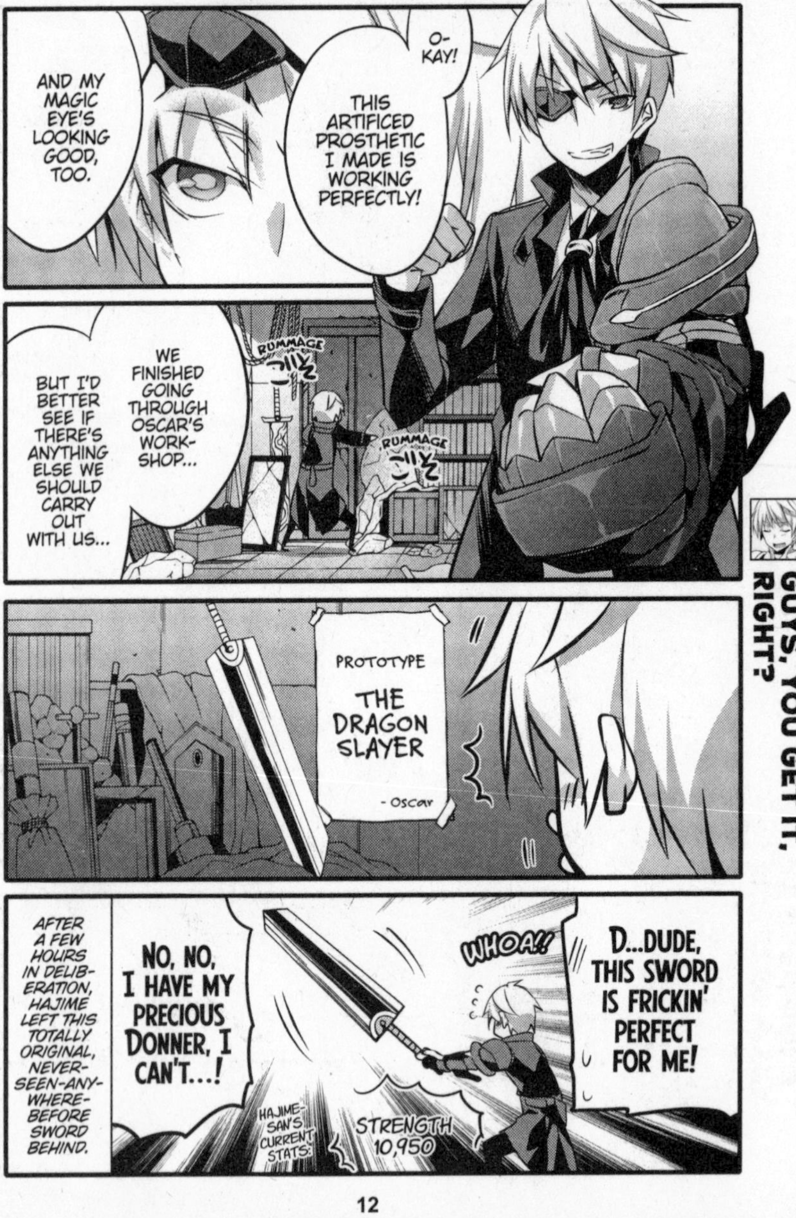
O-KAY!
THIS ARTIFICED PROSTHETIC I MADE IS WORKING PERFECTLY!
AND MY MAGIC EYE'S LOOKING GOOD, TOO.
RUMMAGE
RUMMAGE
WE FINISHED GOING THROUGH OSCAR'S WORK-SHOP...
BUT I'D BETTER SEE IF THERE'S ANYTHING ELSE WE SHOULD CARRY OUT WITH US...
PROTOTYPE
THE DRAGON SLAYER
- Oscar
D...DUDE, THIS SWORD IS FRICKIN' PERFECT FOR ME!
WHOA!!
STRENGTH 10,950
HAJIME-SAN'S CURRENT STATS:
NO, NO, I HAVE MY PRECIOUS DONNER, I CAN'T...!
AFTER A FEW HOURS IN DELIB-ERATION, HAJIME LEFT THIS TOTALLY ORIGINAL, NEVER-SEEN-ANY-WHERE-BEFORE SWORD BEHIND.
GUYS, YOU GET IT, RIGHT?

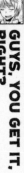

BACK TO REALITY

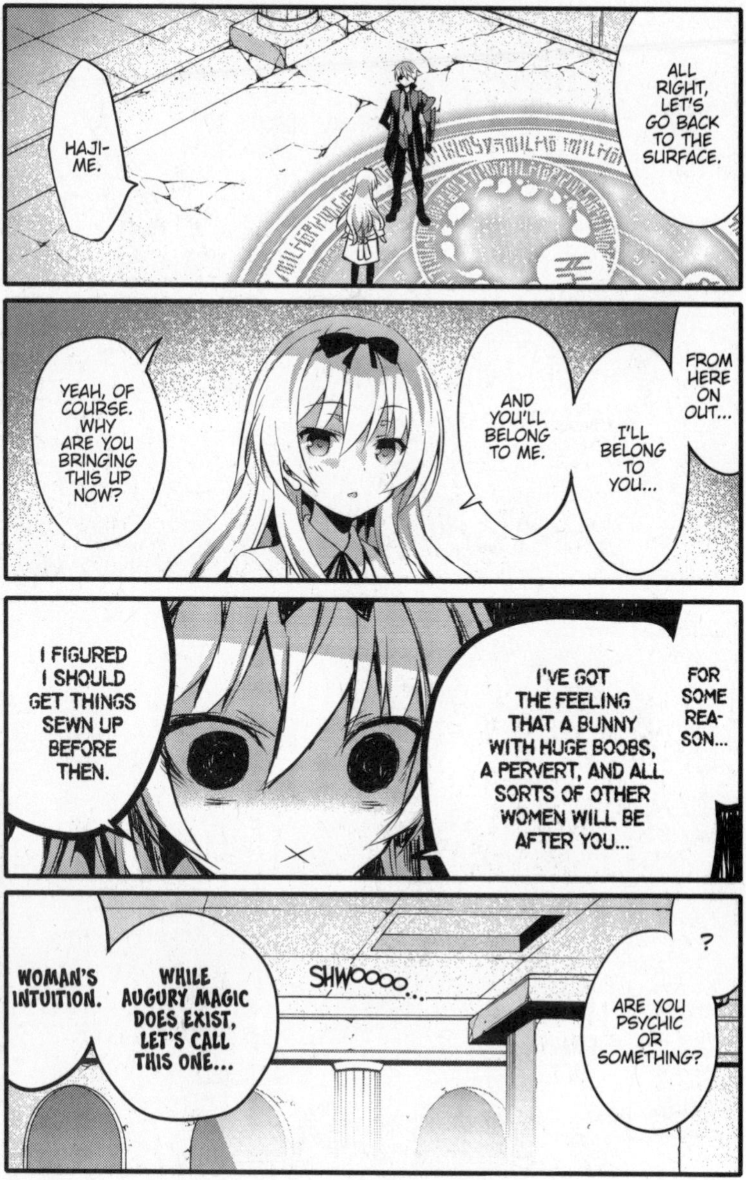
ALL RIGHT, LET'S GO BACK TO THE SURFACE.
HAJI-ME.
FROM HERE ON OUT...
I'LL BELONG TO YOU...
AND YOU'LL BELONG TO ME.
YEAH, OF COURSE. WHY ARE YOU BRINGING THIS UP NOW?
FOR SOME REA-SON...
I'VE GOT THE FEELING THAT A BUNNY WITH HUGE BOOBS, A PERVERT, AND ALL SORTS OF OTHER WOMEN WILL BE AFTER YOU...
I FIGURED I SHOULD GET THINGS SEWN UP BEFORE THEN.
?
ARE YOU PSYCHIC OR SOMETHING?
SHWOOOO...
WHILE AUGURY MAGIC DOES EXIST, LET'S CALL THIS ONE...
WOMAN'S INTUITION.

HER EYES WERE DEAD SERIOUS...

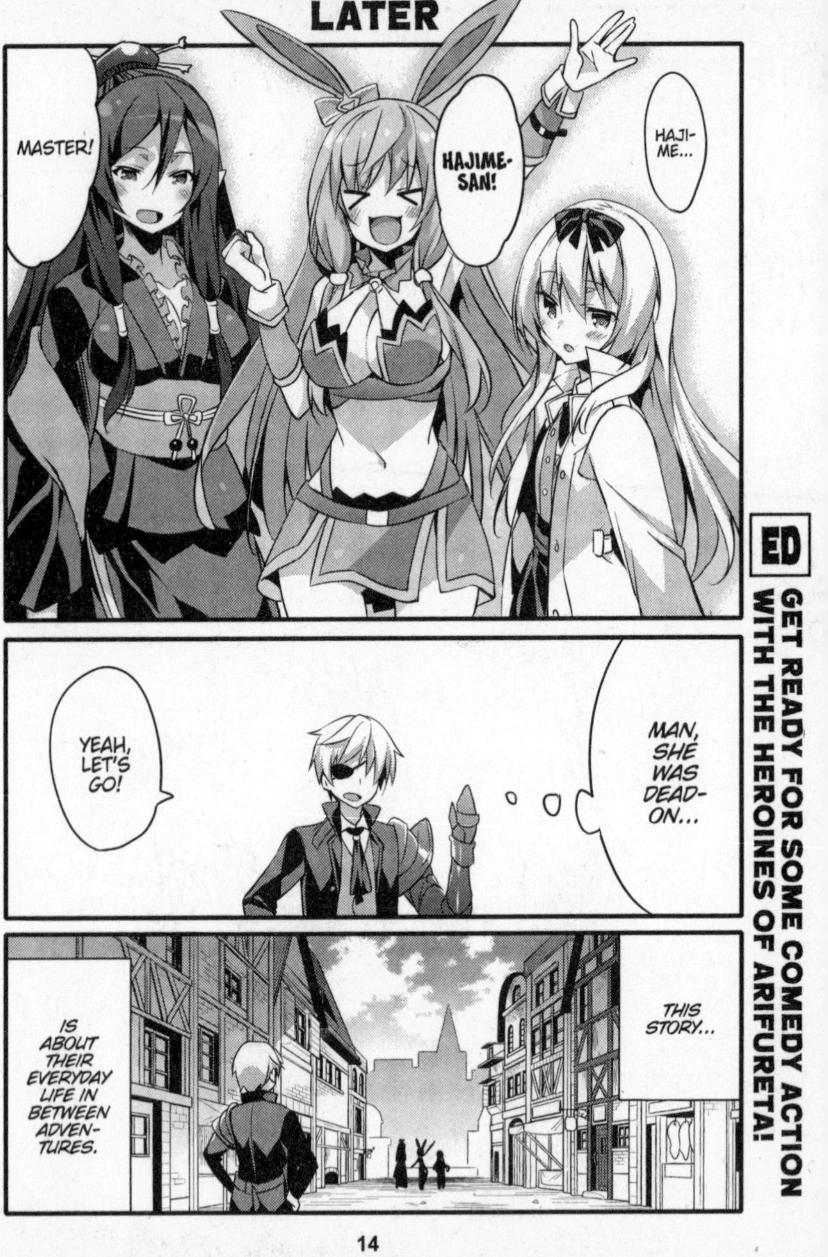
LATER
HAJI-ME...
HAJIME-SAN!
MASTER!
MAN, SHE WAS DEAD-ON...
YEAH, LET'S GO!
THIS STORY...
IS ABOUT THEIR EVERYDAY LIFE IN BETWEEN ADVENTURES.

ED
GET READY FOR SOME COMEDY ACTION WITH THE HEROINES OF ARIFURETA!

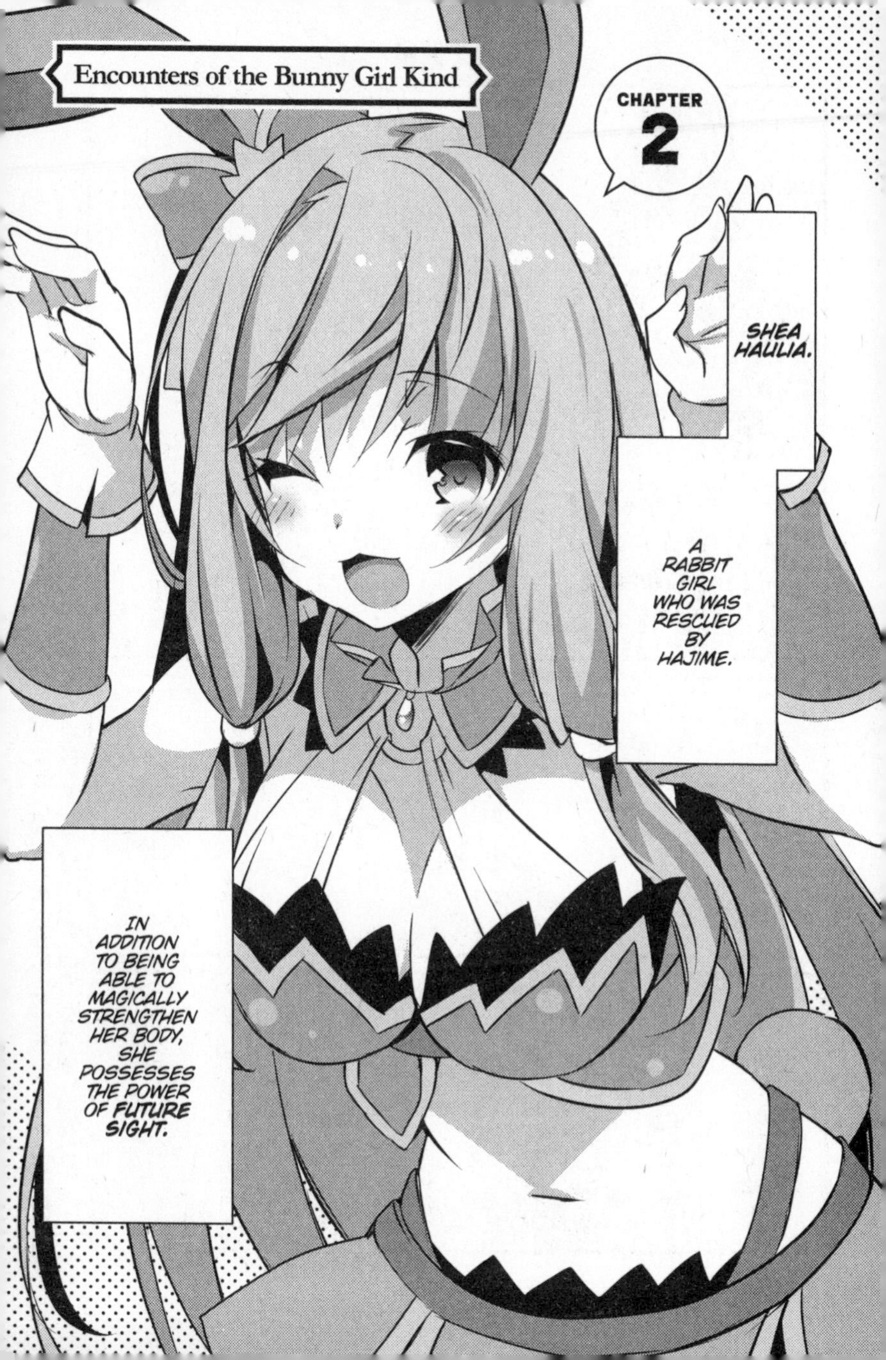
Encounters of the Bunny Girl Kind
CHAPTER 2
SHEA HAULIA.
A RABBIT GIRL WHO WAS RESCUED BY HAJIME.
IN ADDITION TO BEING ABLE TO MAGICALLY STRENGTHEN HER BODY, SHE POSSESSES THE POWER OF FUTURE SIGHT.

REISEN GORGE

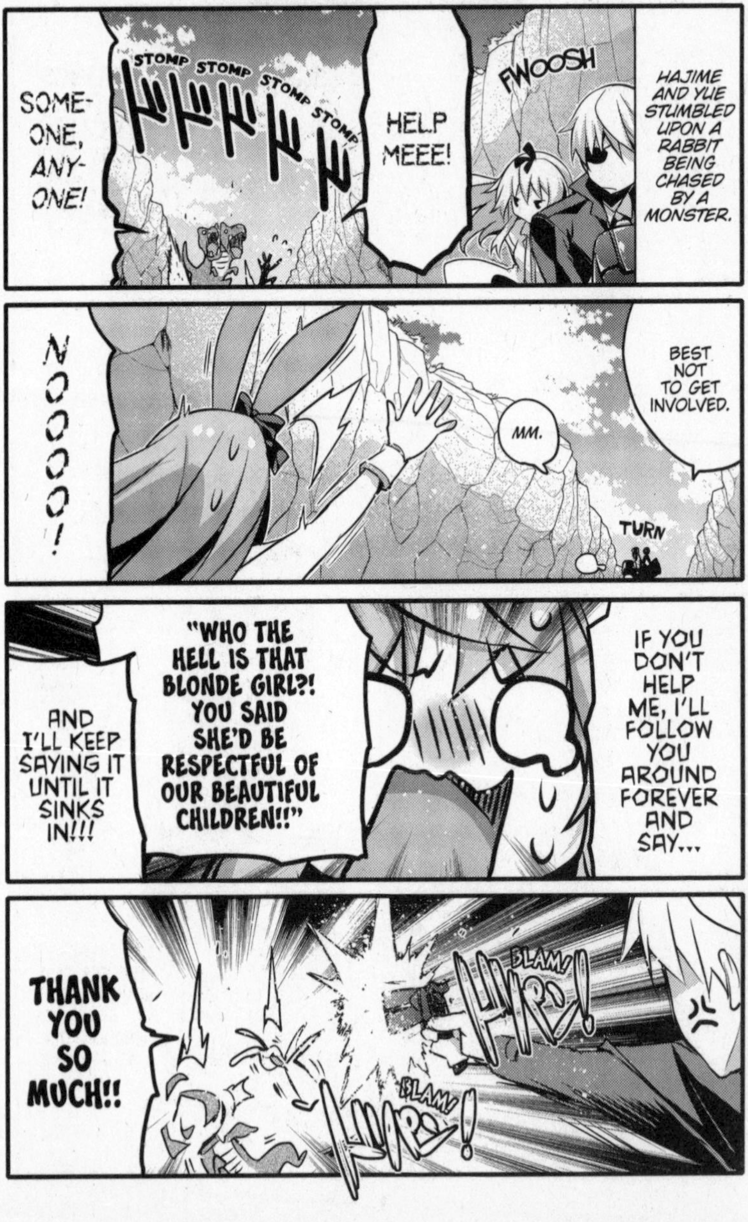

HAJIME AND YUE STUMBLED UPON A RABBIT BEING CHASED BY A MONSTER.
FWOOSH
HELP MEEE!
STOMP STOMP STOMP STOMP
ドドドドド
SOME-ONE, ANY-ONE!
BEST NOT TO GET INVOLVED.
MM.
TURN
NOOOOOO!
IF YOU DON'T HELP ME, I'LL FOLLOW YOU AROUND FOREVER AND SAY...
"WHO THE HELL IS THAT BLONDE GIRL?! YOU SAID SHE'D BE RESPECTFUL OF OUR BEAUTIFUL CHILDREN!!"
AND I'LL KEEP SAYING IT UNTIL IT SINKS IN!!!
BLAM!
BLAM!
THANK YOU SO MUCH!!

I DON'T REMEMBER IT GOING DOWN LIKE THAT.

RESCUED

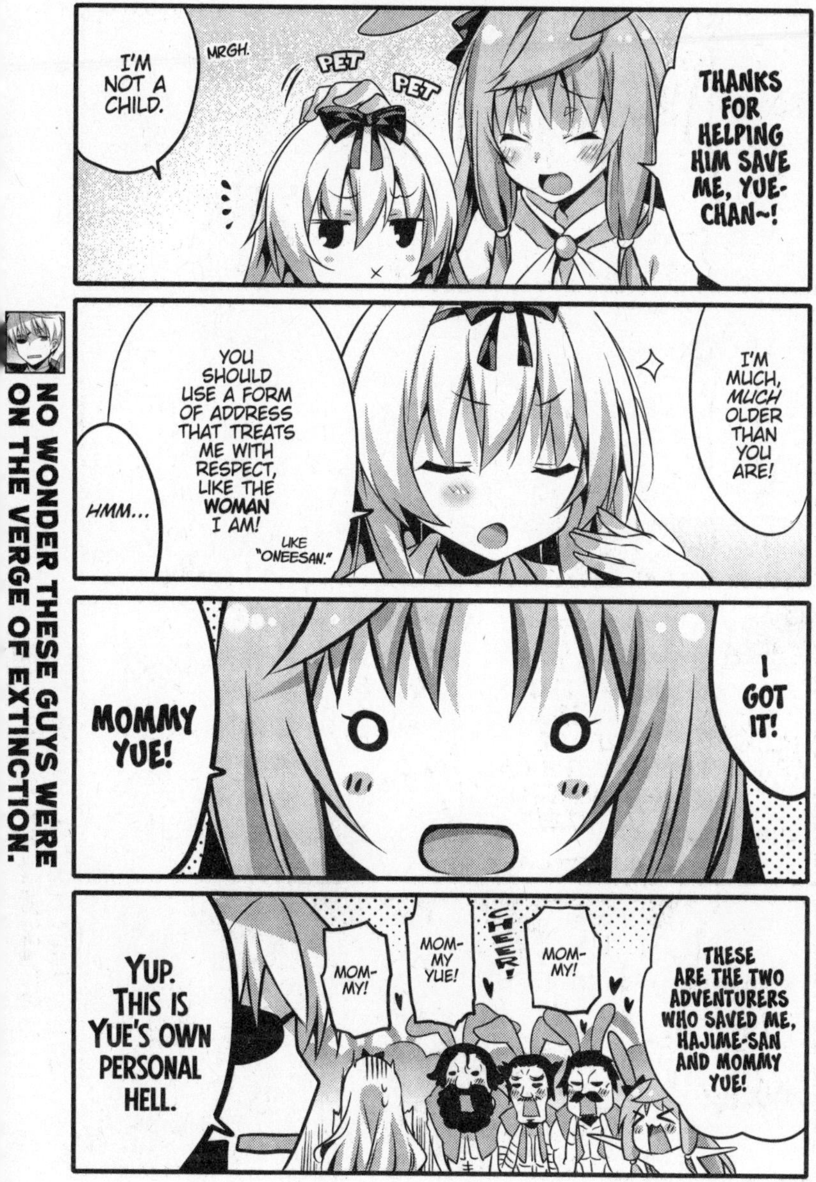
THANKS FOR HELPING HIM SAVE ME, YUE-CHAN~!
PET PET
MRGH.
I'M NOT A CHILD.
I'M MUCH, MUCH OLDER THAN YOU ARE!
YOU SHOULD USE A FORM OF ADDRESS THAT TREATS ME WITH RESPECT, LIKE THE WOMAN I AM!
LIKE "ONEESAN."
HMM...
I GOT IT!
MOMMY YUE!
THESE ARE THE TWO ADVENTURERS WHO SAVED ME, HAJIME-SAN AND MOMMY YUE!
MOM-MY!
CHEER!
MOM-MY YUE!
MOM-MY!
YUP. THIS IS YUE'S OWN PERSONAL HELL.
NO WONDER THESE GUYS WERE ON THE VERGE OF EXTINCTION.

BUTT BULLYING

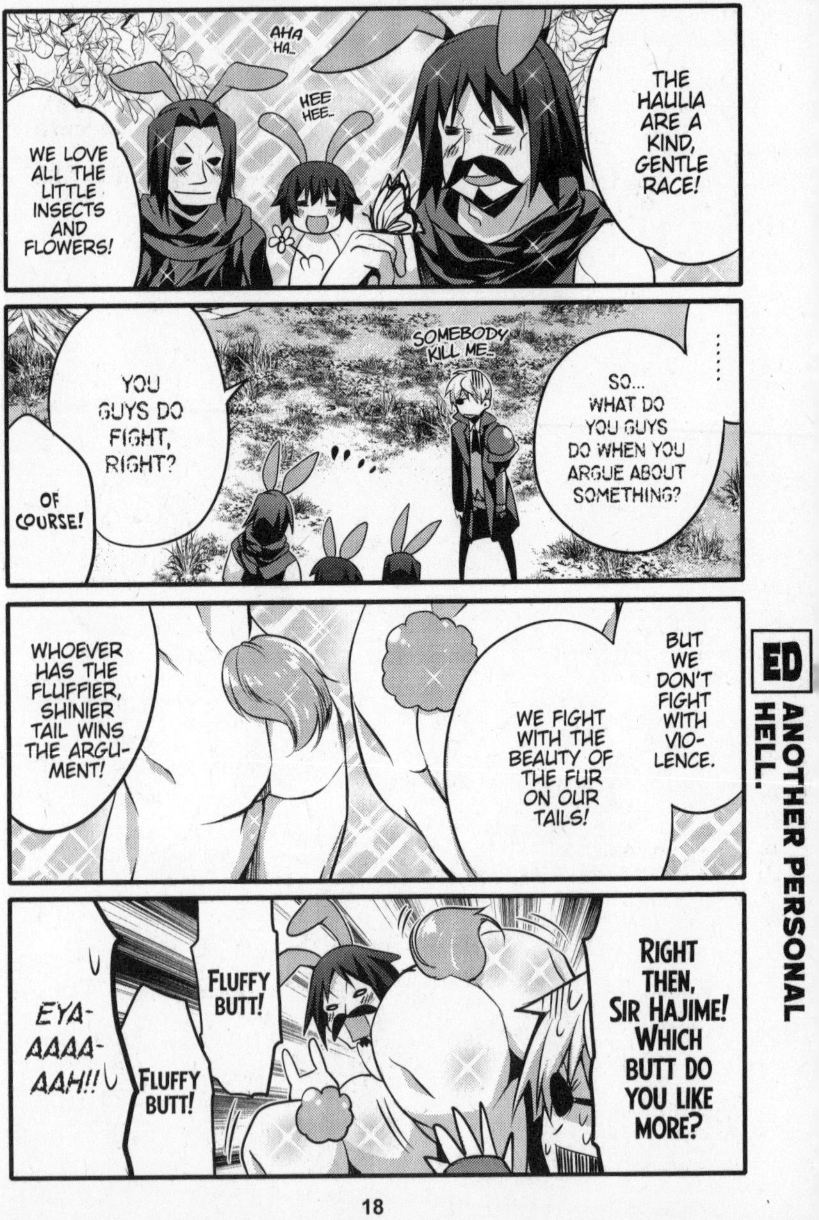
THE HAULIA ARE A KIND, GENTLE RACE!
AHA HA...
HEE HEE...
WE LOVE ALL THE LITTLE INSECTS AND FLOWERS!
......
SO... WHAT DO YOU GUYS DO WHEN YOU ARGUE ABOUT SOMETHING?
SOMEBODY KILL ME...
YOU GUYS DO FIGHT, RIGHT?
OF COURSE!
BUT WE DON'T FIGHT WITH VIO-LENCE.
WE FIGHT WITH THE BEAUTY OF THE FUR ON OUR TAILS!
WHOEVER HAS THE FLUFFIER, SHINIER TAIL WINS THE ARGU-MENT!
RIGHT THEN, SIR HAJIME! WHICH BUTT DO YOU LIKE MORE?
FLUFFY BUTT!
FLUFFY BUTT!
EYA-AAAA-AAH!!

ED ANOTHER PERSONAL HELL.

THEY SEEM HAPPY

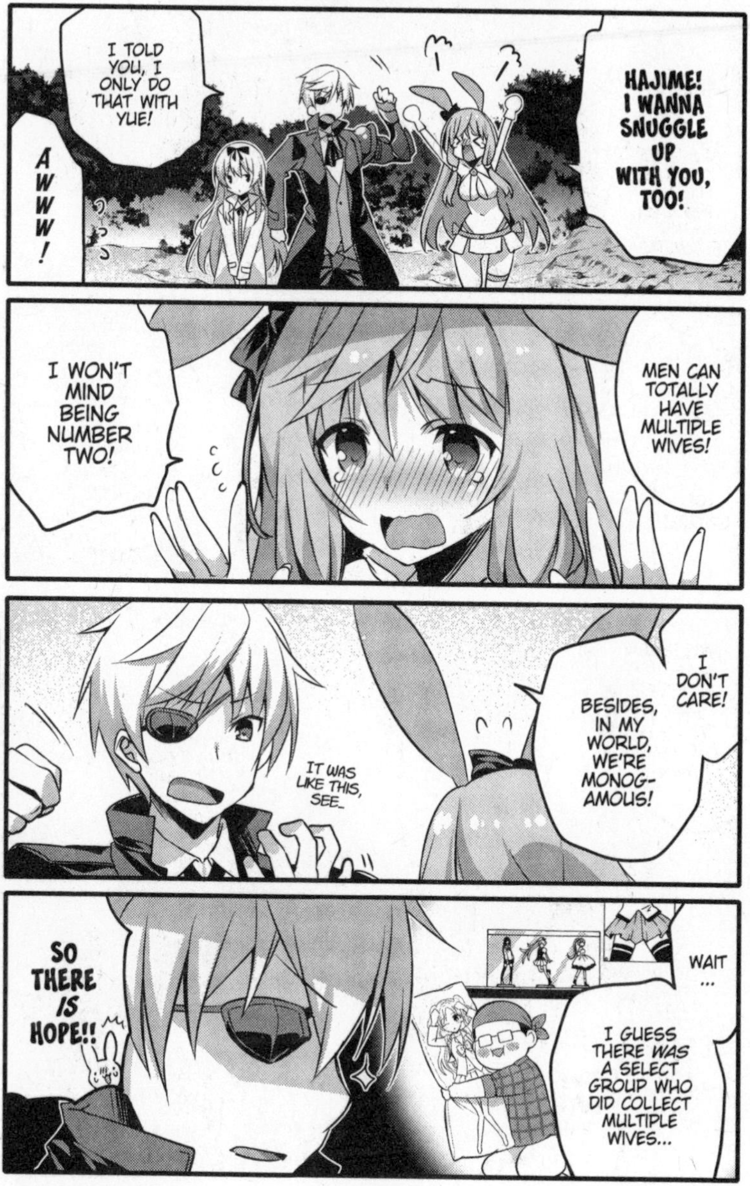
HAJIME! I WANNA SNUGGLE UP WITH YOU, TOO!
I TOLD YOU, I ONLY DO THAT WITH YUE!
AWWW!
MEN CAN TOTALLY HAVE MULTIPLE WIVES!
I WON'T MIND BEING NUMBER TWO!
I DON'T CARE!
BESIDES, IN MY WORLD, WE'RE MONOG-AMOUS!
IT WAS LIKE THIS, SEE...
WAIT ...
I GUESS THERE WAS A SELECT GROUP WHO DID COLLECT MULTIPLE WIVES...
SO THERE IS HOPE!!

ED THEY FOUND A LOOPHOLE!

BUNION

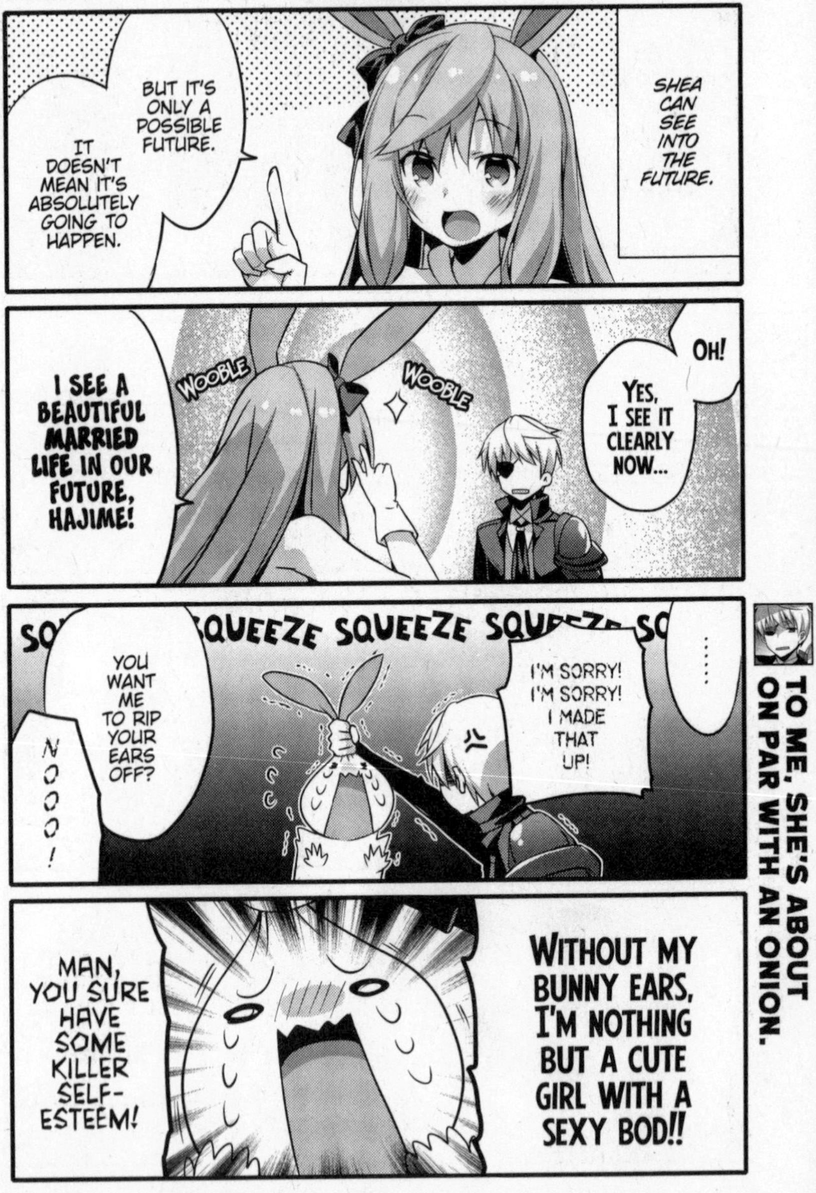
SHEA CAN SEE INTO THE FUTURE.
BUT IT'S ONLY A POSSIBLE FUTURE.
IT DOESN'T MEAN IT'S ABSOLUTELY GOING TO HAPPEN.
OH!
YES, I SEE IT CLEARLY NOW...
WOOBLE
WOOBLE
I SEE A BEAUTIFUL MARRIED LIFE IN OUR FUTURE, HAJIME!
......
I'M SORRY! I'M SORRY! I MADE THAT UP!
SQUEEZE SQUEEZE
YOU WANT ME TO RIP YOUR EARS OFF?
NOOOO!
WITHOUT MY BUNNY EARS, I'M NOTHING BUT A CUTE GIRL WITH A SEXY BOD!!
MAN, YOU SURE HAVE SOME KILLER SELF-ESTEEM!
TO ME, SHE'S ABOUT ON PAR WITH AN ONION.

SHE NEVER SAID "PHYSICALLY"

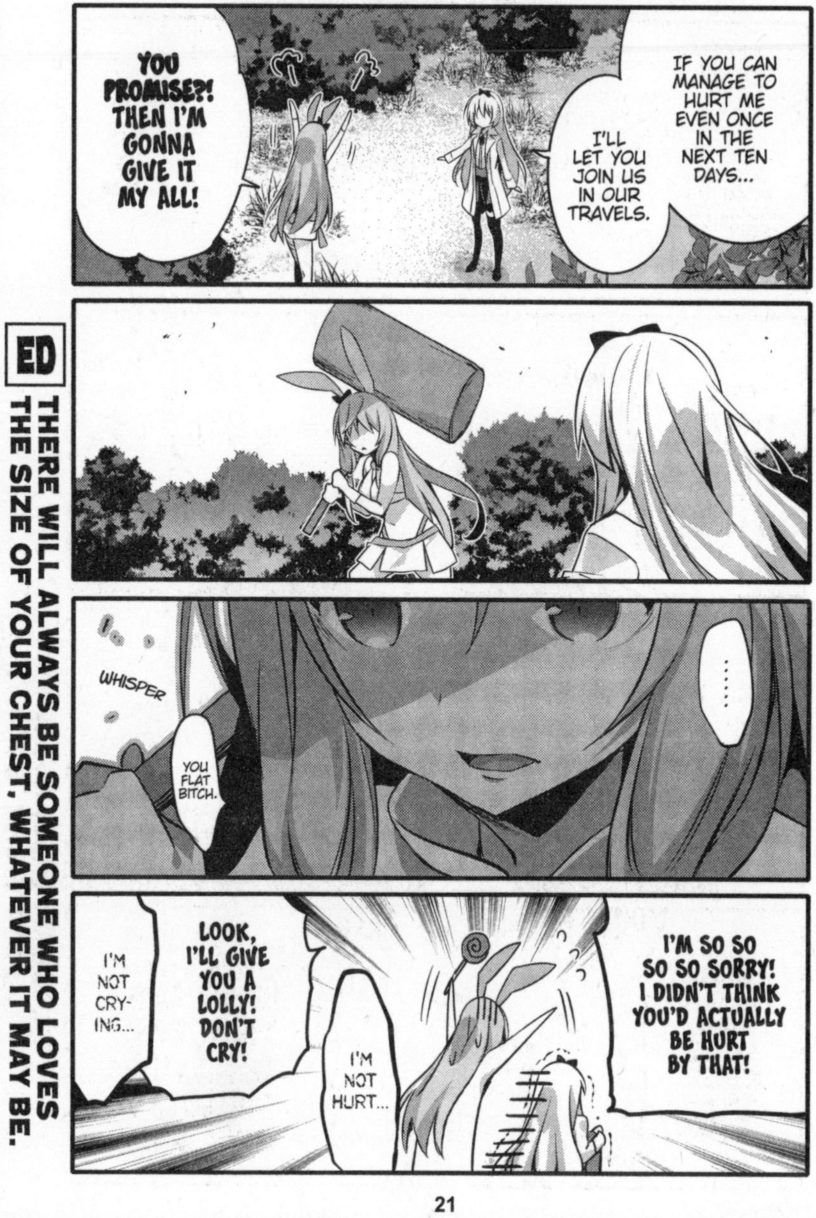

IF YOU CAN MANAGE TO HURT ME EVEN ONCE IN THE NEXT TEN DAYS...
I'LL LET YOU JOIN US IN OUR TRAVELS.
YOU PROMISE?! THEN I'M GONNA GIVE IT MY ALL!
......
WHISPER
YOU FLAT BITCH.
I'M SO SO SO SO SORRY! I DIDN'T THINK YOU'D ACTUALLY BE HURT BY THAT!
I'M NOT HURT...
LOOK, I'LL GIVE YOU A LOLLY! DON'T CRY!
I'M NOT CRYING...

ED THERE WILL ALWAYS BE SOMEONE WHO LOVES THE SIZE OF YOUR CHEST, WHATEVER IT MAY BE.

HER LOVE IS TOO HEAVY

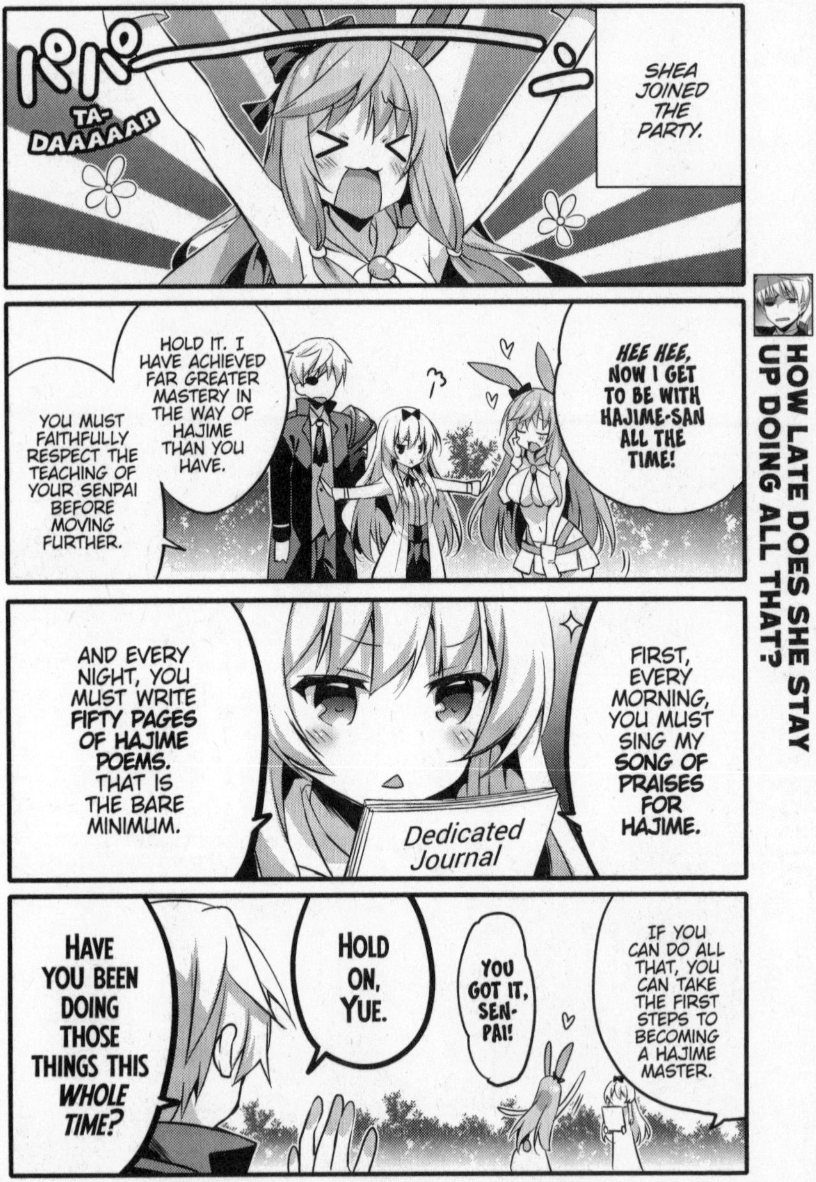
HOW LATE DOES SHE STAY UP DOING ALL THAT?
SHEA JOINED THE PARTY.
TA-DAAAAAAH
HEE HEE, NOW I GET TO BE WITH HAJIME-SAN ALL THE TIME!
HOLD IT. I HAVE ACHIEVED FAR GREATER MASTERY IN THE WAY OF HAJIME THAN YOU HAVE.
YOU MUST FAITHFULLY RESPECT THE TEACHING OF YOUR SENPAI BEFORE MOVING FURTHER.
FIRST, EVERY MORNING, YOU MUST SING MY SONG OF PRAISES FOR HAJIME.
Dedicated Journal
AND EVERY NIGHT, YOU MUST WRITE FIFTY PAGES OF HAJIME POEMS. THAT IS THE BARE MINIMUM.
IF YOU CAN DO ALL THAT, YOU CAN TAKE THE FIRST STEPS TO BECOMING A HAJIME MASTER.
YOU GOT IT, SEN-PAI!
HOLD ON, YUE.
HAVE YOU BEEN DOING THOSE THINGS THIS WHOLE TIME?

SHE LIFTS

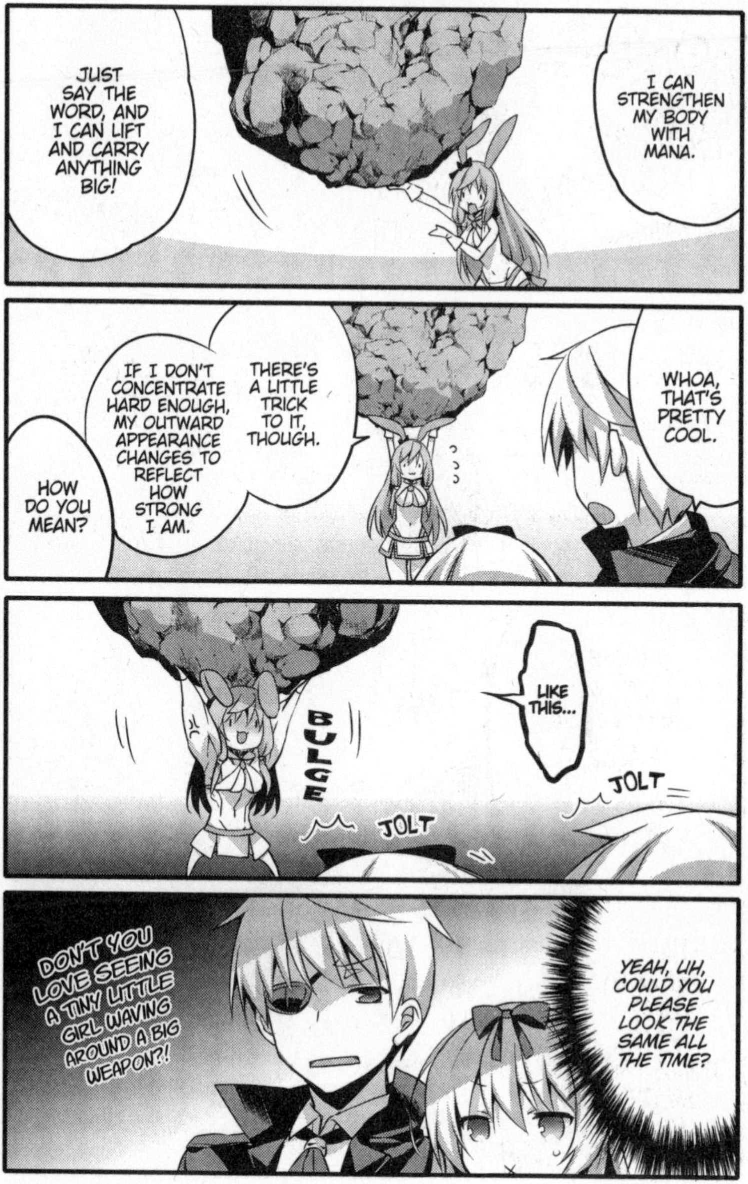

I CAN STRENGTHEN MY BODY WITH MANA.
JUST SAY THE WORD, AND I CAN LIFT AND CARRY ANYTHING BIG!
WHOA, THAT'S PRETTY COOL.
THERE'S A LITTLE TRICK TO IT, THOUGH.
IF I DON'T CONCENTRATE HARD ENOUGH, MY OUTWARD APPEARANCE CHANGES TO REFLECT HOW STRONG I AM.
HOW DO YOU MEAN?
LIKE THIS...
JOLT
BULGE
JOLT
YEAH, UH, COULD YOU PLEASE LOOK THE SAME ALL THE TIME?
DON'T YOU LOVE SEEING A TINY LITTLE GIRL WAVING AROUND A BIG WEAPON?!

ED YOU GOT IT!

THE SUSPENSION BRIDGE EFFECT

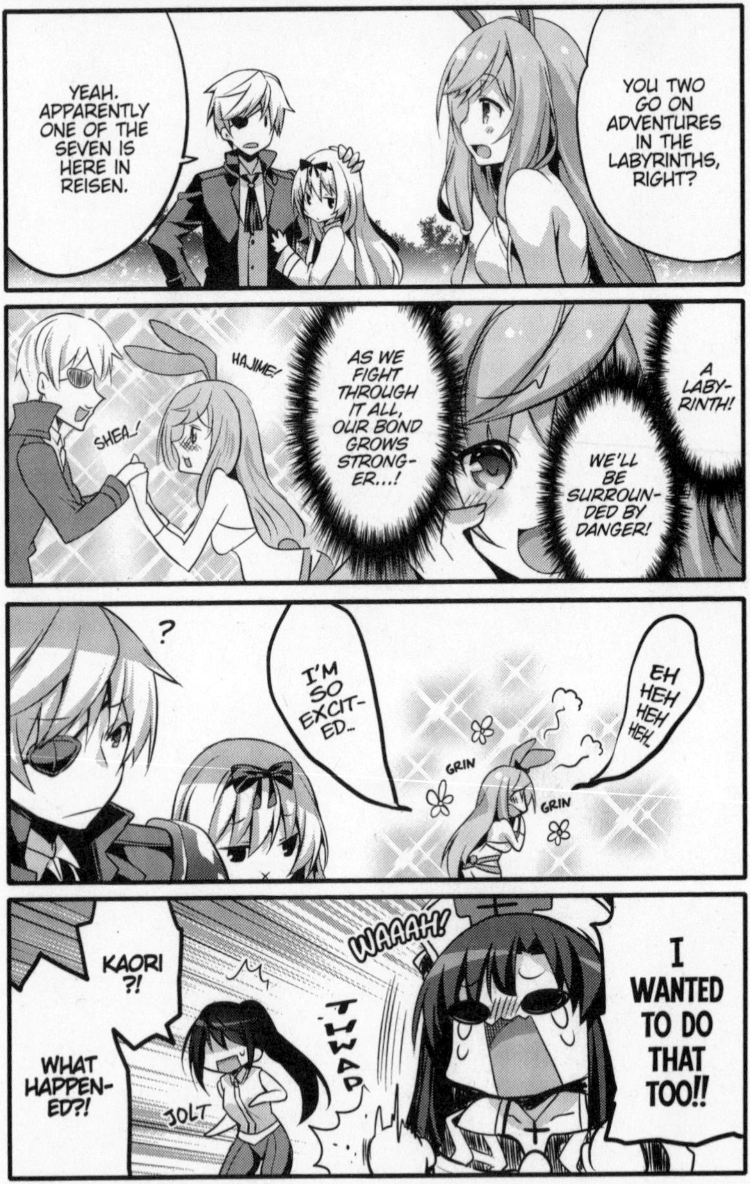
YOU TWO GO ON ADVENTURES IN THE LABYRINTHS, RIGHT?
YEAH. APPARENTLY ONE OF THE SEVEN IS HERE IN REISEN.
A LABY-RINTH!
WE'LL BE SURROUN-DED BY DANGER!
AS WE FIGHT THROUGH IT ALL, OUR BOND GROWS STRONG-ER...!
HAJIME!
SHEA!
EH HEH HEH HEH
GRIN
GRIN
I'M SO EXCIT-ED...
?
I WANTED TO DO THAT TOO!!
WAAAH!
THWAP
KAORI?!
WHAT HAPPEN-ED?!
JOLT

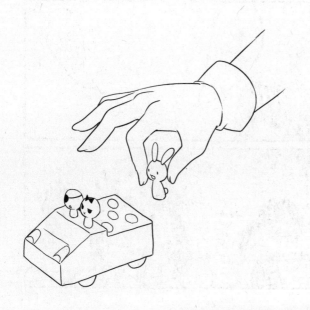

ARIFURETA:

ARIFURETA SHOKUGYOU DE SEKAISAIKYOU

I ♥ Isekai

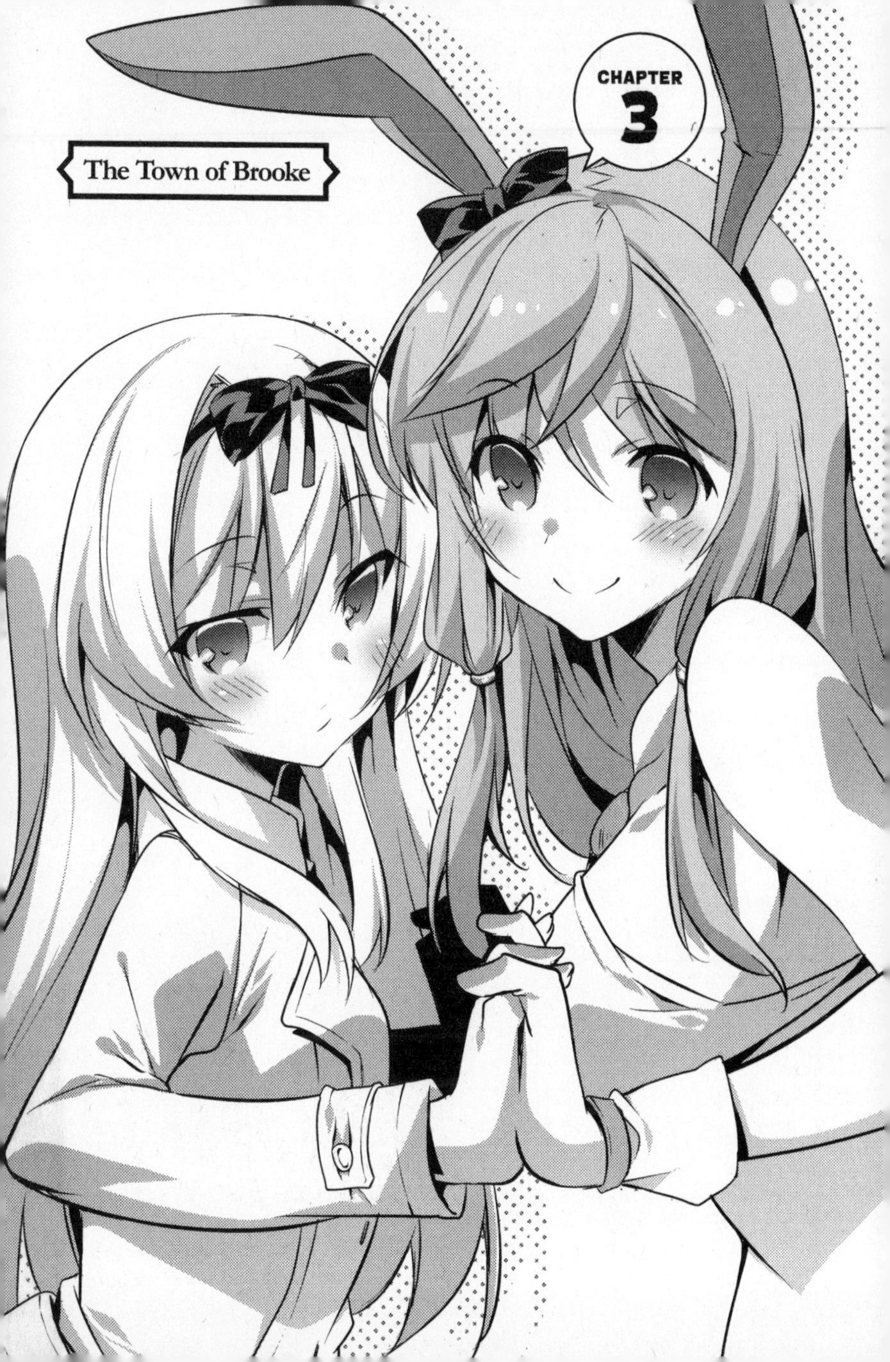
CHAPTER
3
The Town of Brooke

KING OF HEARTS

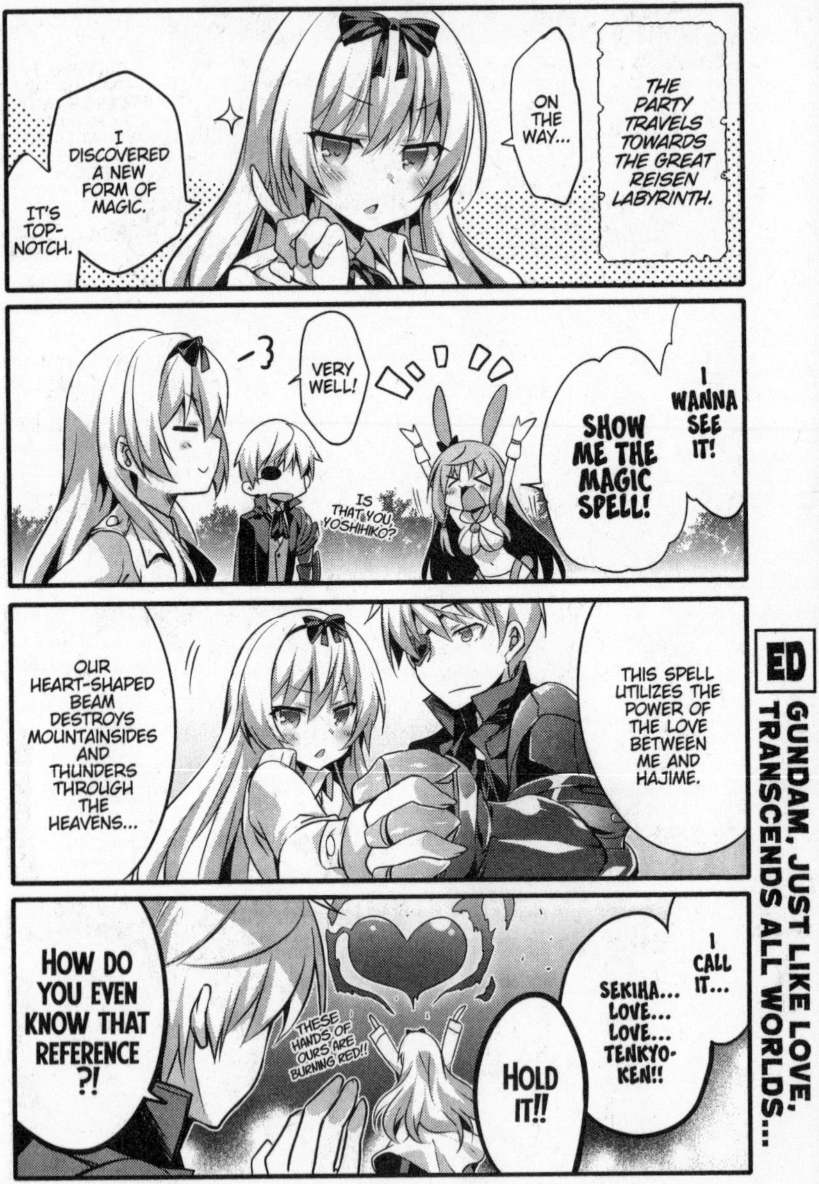

THE PARTY TRAVELS TOWARDS THE GREAT REISEN LABYRINTH.
ON THE WAY...
I DISCOVERED A NEW FORM OF MAGIC.
IT'S TOP-NOTCH.
I WANNA SEE IT!
SHOW ME THE MAGIC SPELL!
IS THAT YOU, YOSHIHIKO?
VERY WELL!
THIS SPELL UTILIZES THE POWER OF THE LOVE BETWEEN ME AND HAJIME.
OUR HEART-SHAPED BEAM DESTROYS MOUNTAINSIDES AND THUNDERS THROUGH THE HEAVENS...
I CALL IT...
SEKIHA... LOVE... LOVE... TENKYO-KEN!!
HOLD IT!!
THESE HANDS OF OURS ARE BURNING RED!!
HOW DO YOU EVEN KNOW THAT REFERENCE?!
ED
GUNDAM, JUST LIKE LOVE, TRANSCENDS ALL WORLDS...

WORD OF ADVICE

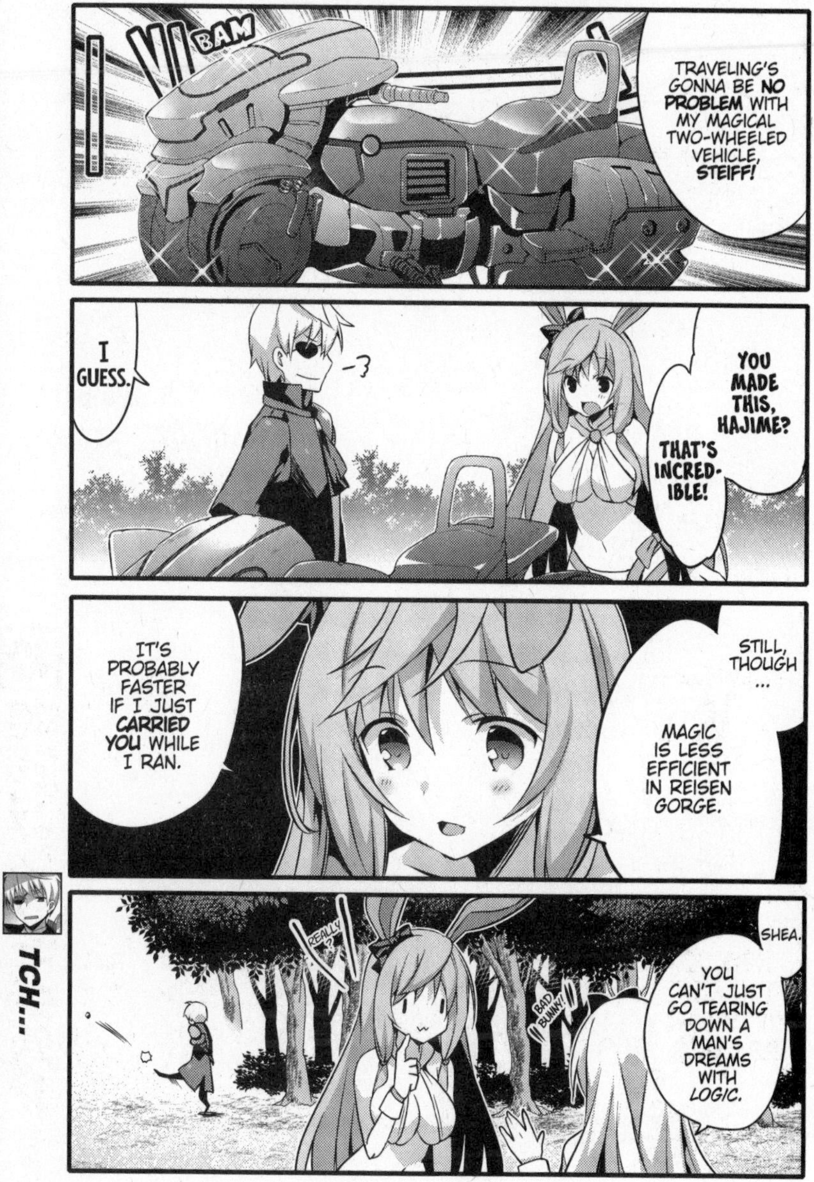

TRAVELING'S GONNA BE **NO PROBLEM** WITH MY MAGICAL TWO-WHEELED VEHICLE, **STEIFF!**
BAM
YOU MADE THIS, HAJIME?
THAT'S INCREDIBLE!
I GUESS.
STILL, THOUGH...
MAGIC IS LESS EFFICIENT IN REISEN GORGE.
IT'S PROBABLY FASTER IF I JUST **CARRIED YOU** WHILE I RAN.
SHEA.
YOU CAN'T JUST GO TEARING DOWN A MAN'S DREAMS WITH *LOGIC.*
BAD BUNNY!
REALLY?
TCH...

A FRIENDLY QUIP

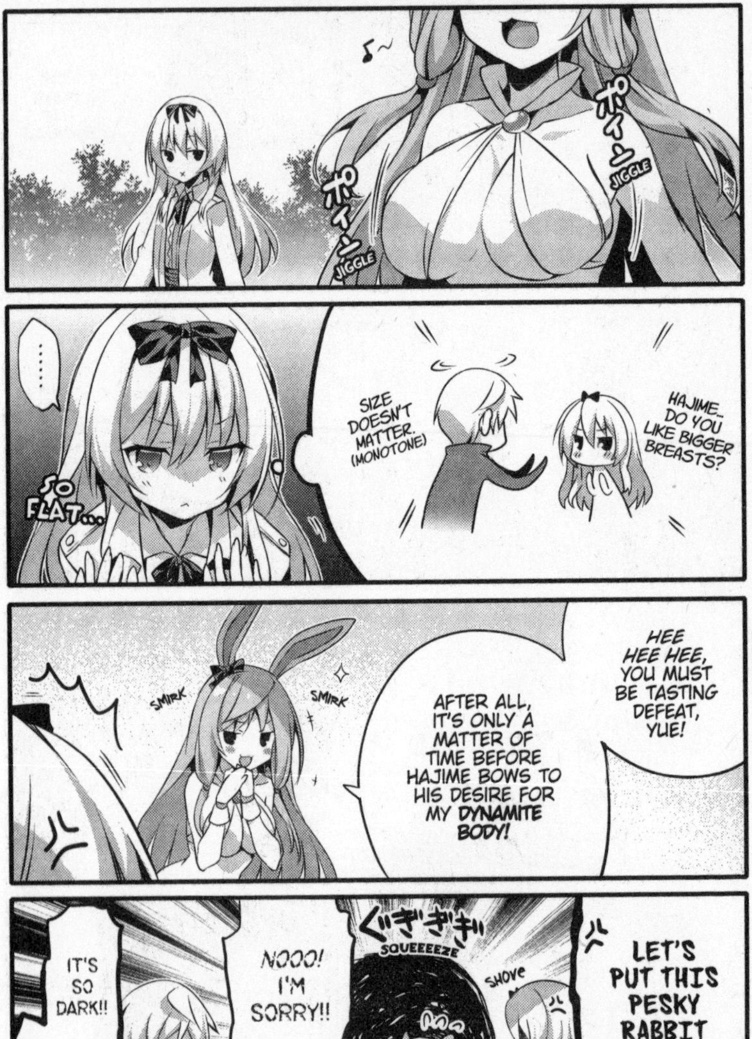

ポイーン
JIGGLE
ポイーン
JIGGLE
HAJIME... DO YOU LIKE BIGGER BREASTS?
SIZE DOESN'T MATTER. (MONOTONE)
......
SO FLAT...
HEE HEE HEE, YOU MUST BE TASTING DEFEAT, YUE!
AFTER ALL, IT'S ONLY A MATTER OF TIME BEFORE HAJIME BOWS TO HIS DESIRE FOR MY **DYNAMITE BODY!**
SMIRK
SMIRK
LET'S PUT THIS PESKY RABBIT IN THE TREASURE TROVE!
SHOVE
SHOVE
ぐぎぎぎ
SQUEEEEEZE
NOOO! I'M SORRY!!
IT'S SO DARK!!
AND *HUGE!!*

ED DON'T DO THIS AT HOME, KIDS!

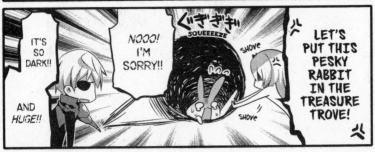

RABBITS ARE POPULAR SLAVES

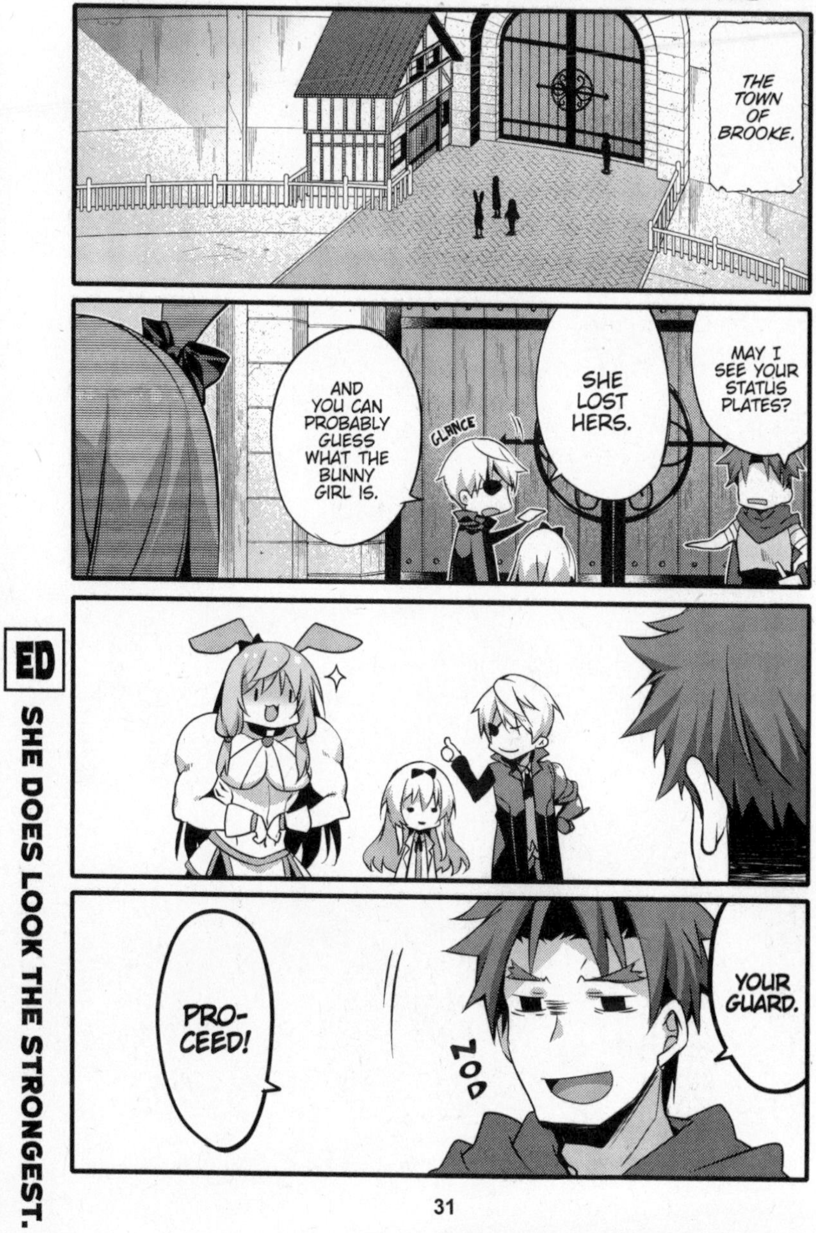
THE TOWN OF BROOKE.
MAY I SEE YOUR STATUS PLATES?
SHE LOST HERS.
GLANCE
AND YOU CAN PROBABLY GUESS WHAT THE BUNNY GIRL IS.
YOUR GUARD.
ZOOD
PRO-CEED!

ED

SHE DOES LOOK THE STRONGEST.

A HANDY DEVICE

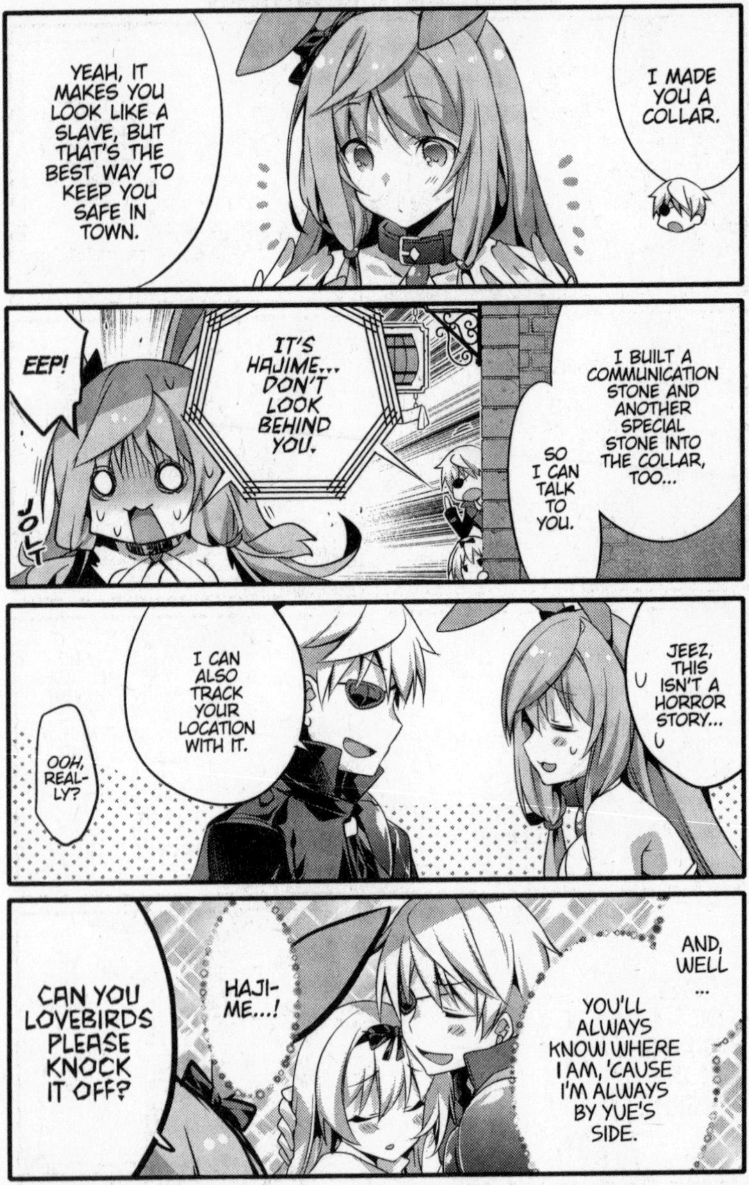
I MADE YOU A COLLAR.
YEAH, IT MAKES YOU LOOK LIKE A SLAVE, BUT THAT'S THE BEST WAY TO KEEP YOU SAFE IN TOWN.
I BUILT A COMMUNICATION STONE AND ANOTHER SPECIAL STONE INTO THE COLLAR, TOO...
SO I CAN TALK TO YOU.
IT'S HAJIME... DON'T LOOK BEHIND YOU.
EEP!
JOLT
JEEZ, THIS ISN'T A HORROR STORY...
I CAN ALSO TRACK YOUR LOCATION WITH IT.
OOH, REAL-LY?
AND, WELL ...
YOU'LL ALWAYS KNOW WHERE I AM, 'CAUSE I'M ALWAYS BY YUE'S SIDE.
HAJI-ME...!
CAN YOU LOVEBIRDS PLEASE KNOCK IT OFF?

CATHERINE'S MAP

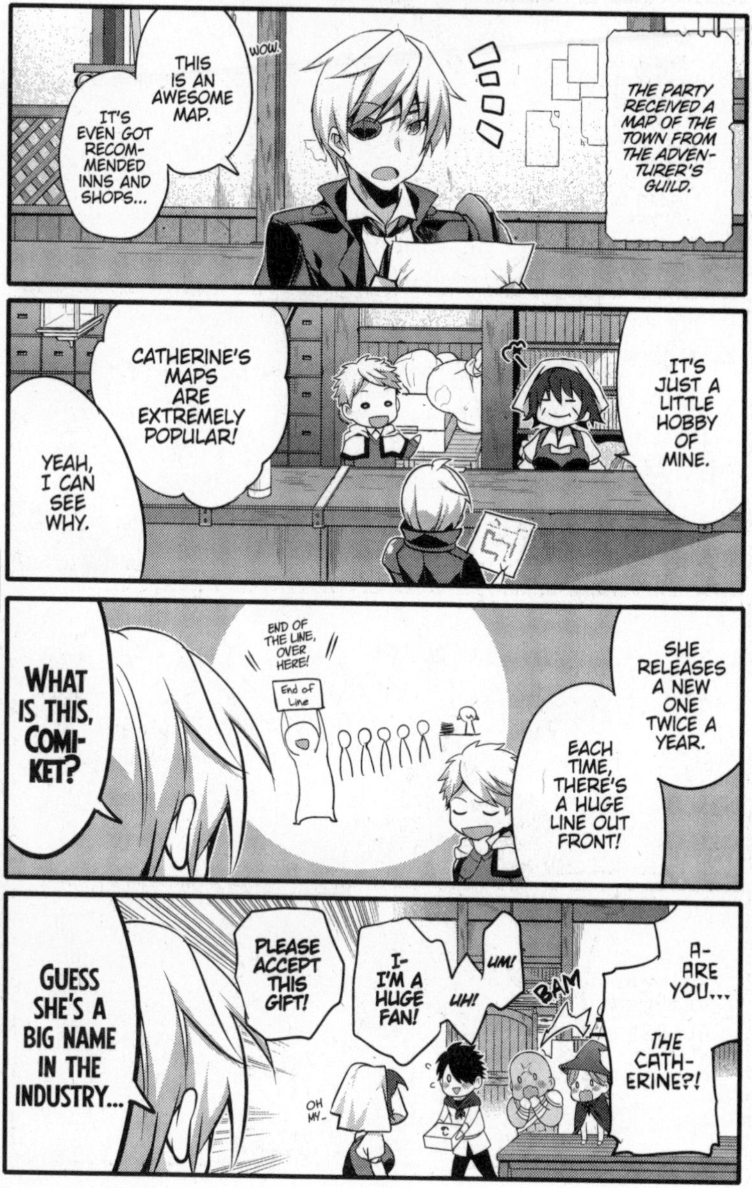

THE PARTY RECEIVED A MAP OF THE TOWN FROM THE ADVENTURER'S GUILD.
WOW.
THIS IS AN AWESOME MAP.
IT'S EVEN GOT RECOMMENDED INNS AND SHOPS...
IT'S JUST A LITTLE HOBBY OF MINE.
CATHERINE'S MAPS ARE EXTREMELY POPULAR!
YEAH, I CAN SEE WHY.
SHE RELEASES A NEW ONE TWICE A YEAR.
EACH TIME, THERE'S A HUGE LINE OUT FRONT!
END OF THE LINE, OVER HERE!
End of Line
WHAT IS THIS, COMIKET?
A-ARE YOU...
THE CATHERINE?!
BAM
UM!
UH!
I-I'M A HUGE FAN!
PLEASE ACCEPT THIS GIFT!
OH MY...
GUESS SHE'S A BIG NAME IN THE INDUSTRY...

ED I HEAR THIS SUMMER'S COMIKET IS GONNA BE ON THE 10TH.

EXTREMELY LEWD

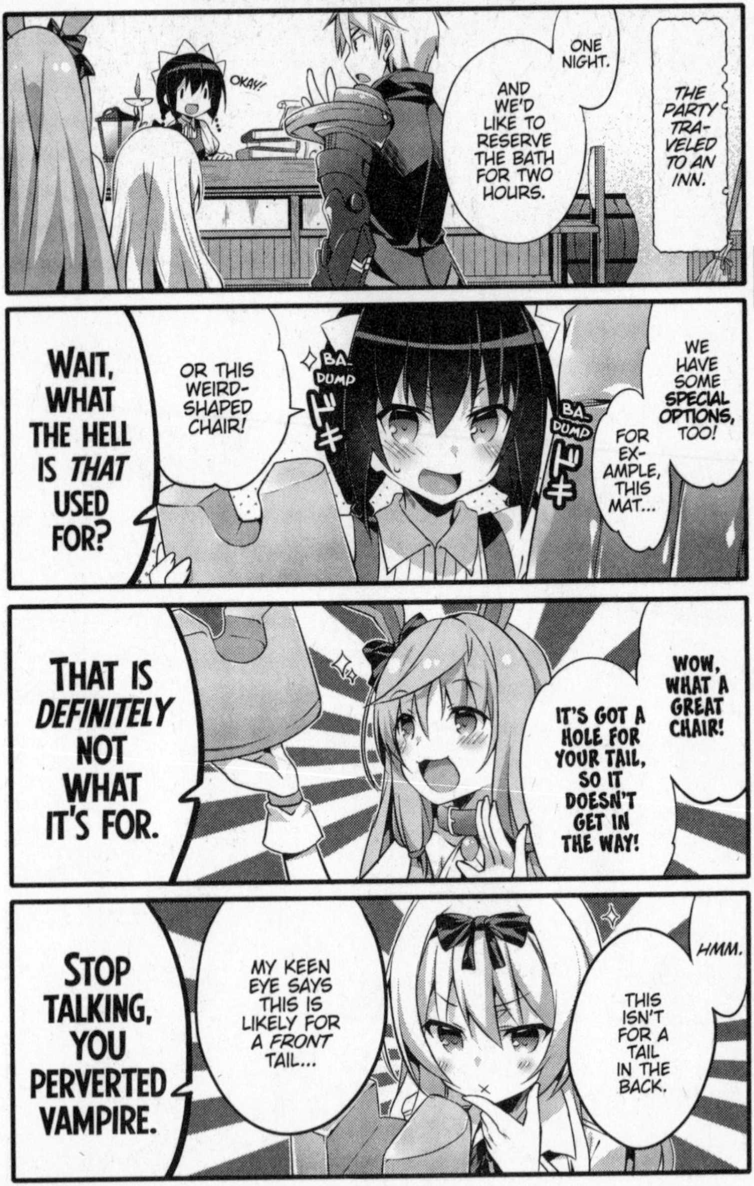
THE PARTY TRAVELED TO AN INN.
ONE NIGHT.
AND WE'D LIKE TO RESERVE THE BATH FOR TWO HOURS.
OKAY!
WE HAVE SOME SPECIAL OPTIONS, TOO!
FOR EXAMPLE, THIS MAT...
BA-DUMP
BA-DUMP
OR THIS WEIRD-SHAPED CHAIR!
WAIT, WHAT THE HELL IS *THAT* USED FOR?
WOW, WHAT A GREAT CHAIR!
IT'S GOT A HOLE FOR YOUR TAIL, SO IT DOESN'T GET IN THE WAY!
THAT IS *DEFINITELY* NOT WHAT IT'S FOR.
HMM.
THIS ISN'T FOR A TAIL IN THE BACK.
MY KEEN EYE SAYS THIS IS LIKELY FOR A *FRONT* TAIL...
STOP TALKING, YOU PERVERTED VAMPIRE.

WHY IS IT THE GIRLS WHO ARE MAKING DIRTY JOKES?

I HOPE YOU ENJOYED YOURSELF LAST NIGHT

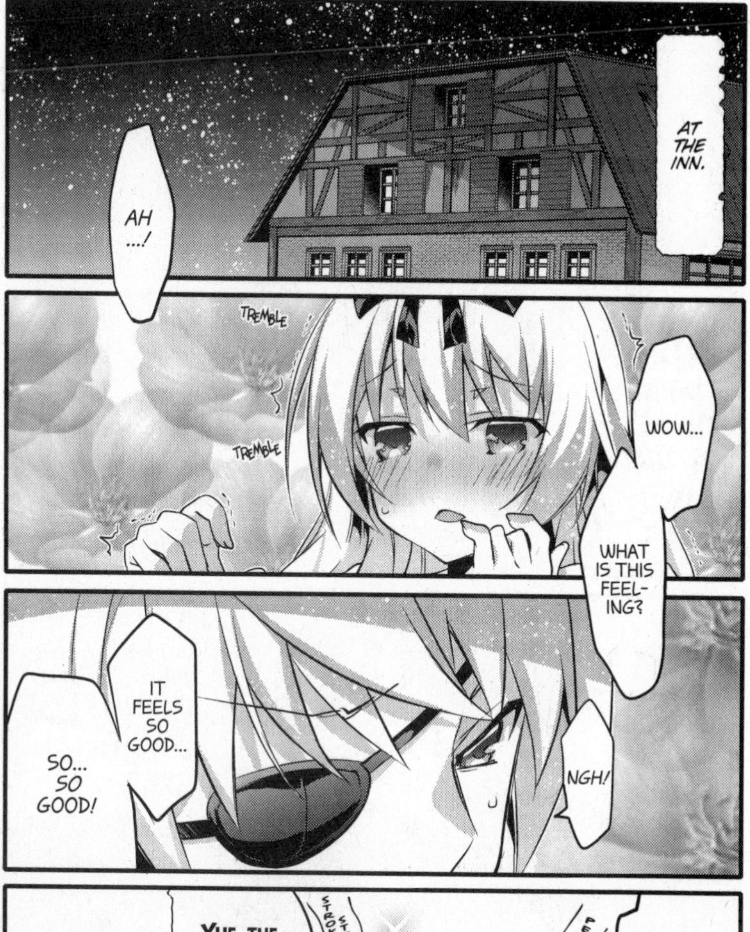
AT THE INN.
AH ...!
WOW...
WHAT IS THIS FEEL-ING?
TREMBLE
TREMBLE
NGH!
IT FEELS SO GOOD...
SO... SO GOOD!
YOUR FRESH-OUT-OF-THE-BATH EARS...
FEEL AMAZ-ING...
PET PET PET PET
STROKE STROKE STROKE
YUE, THE WALLS HERE ARE THIN! LOWER YOUR VOICE!
THE OTHER GUESTS GAVE THEM DIRTY LOOKS WHEN THEY CHECKED OUT.

ED WE GOTTA SELL SOME FLUFFY-EAR MERCH!

HIS MAGIC EYE

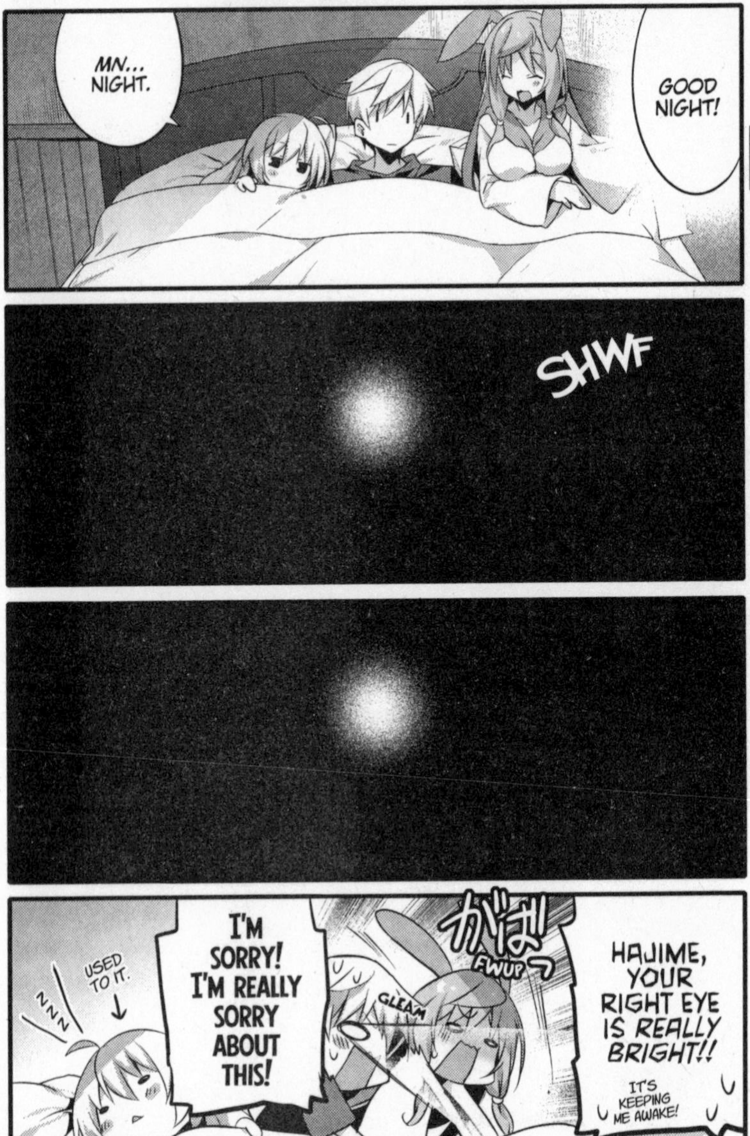
GOOD NIGHT!
MN... NIGHT.
SHWF
HAJIME, YOUR RIGHT EYE IS REALLY BRIGHT!!
IT'S KEEPING ME AWAKE!
がば!!
FWUP
GLEAM
I'M SORRY! I'M REALLY SORRY ABOUT THIS!
USED TO IT.
NNN

ED I LIKE TO HAVE A LITTLE LIGHT ON BY MY BED, SO THIS WOULDN'T BOTHER ME.

Blackout
fabric.

ARIFURETA:

ARIFURETA SHOKUGYOU DE SEKAISAIKYOU

I ♥ Isekai

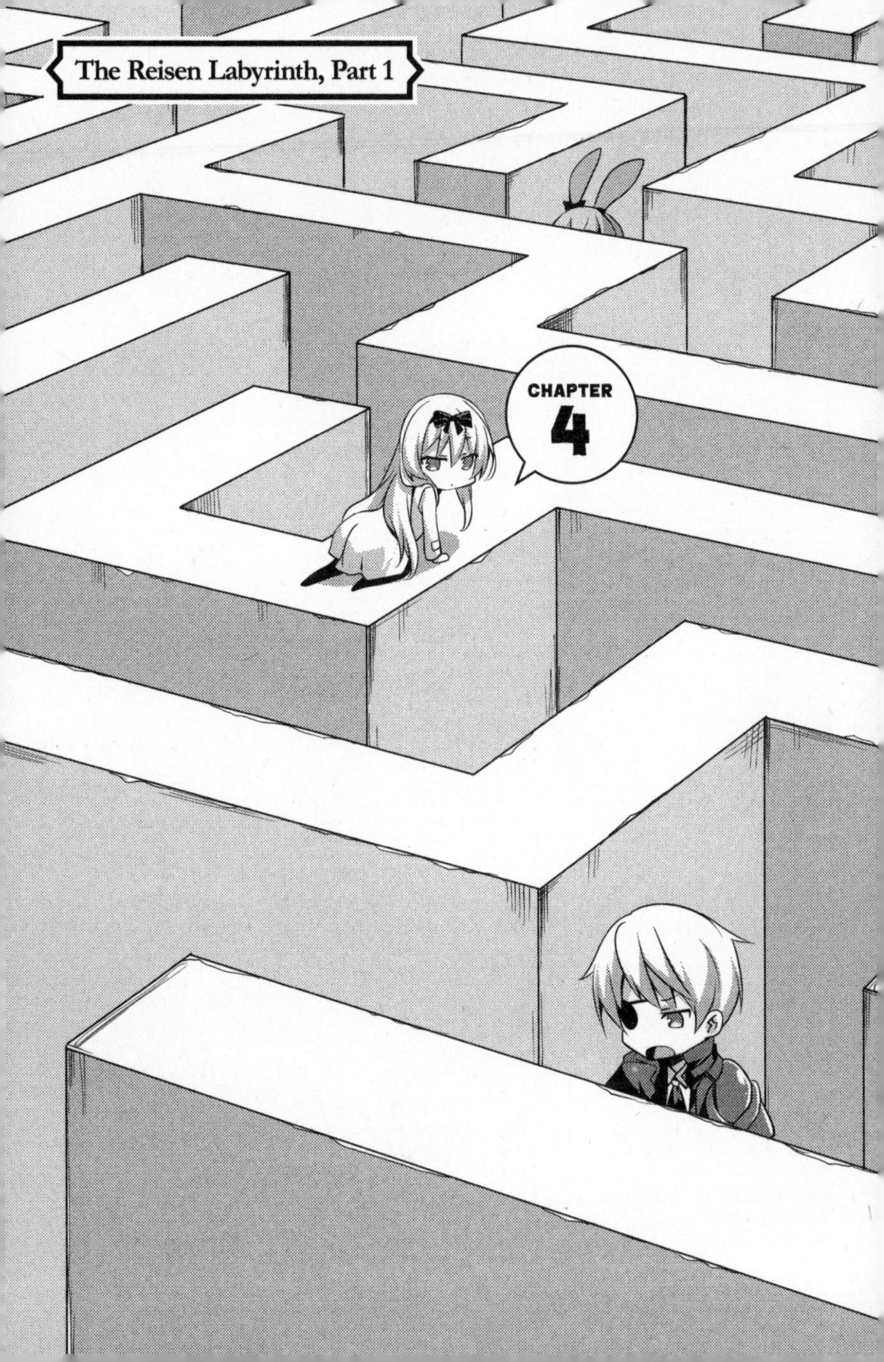
The Reisen Labyrinth, Part 1
CHAPTER 4

ULTIMATE RABBIT

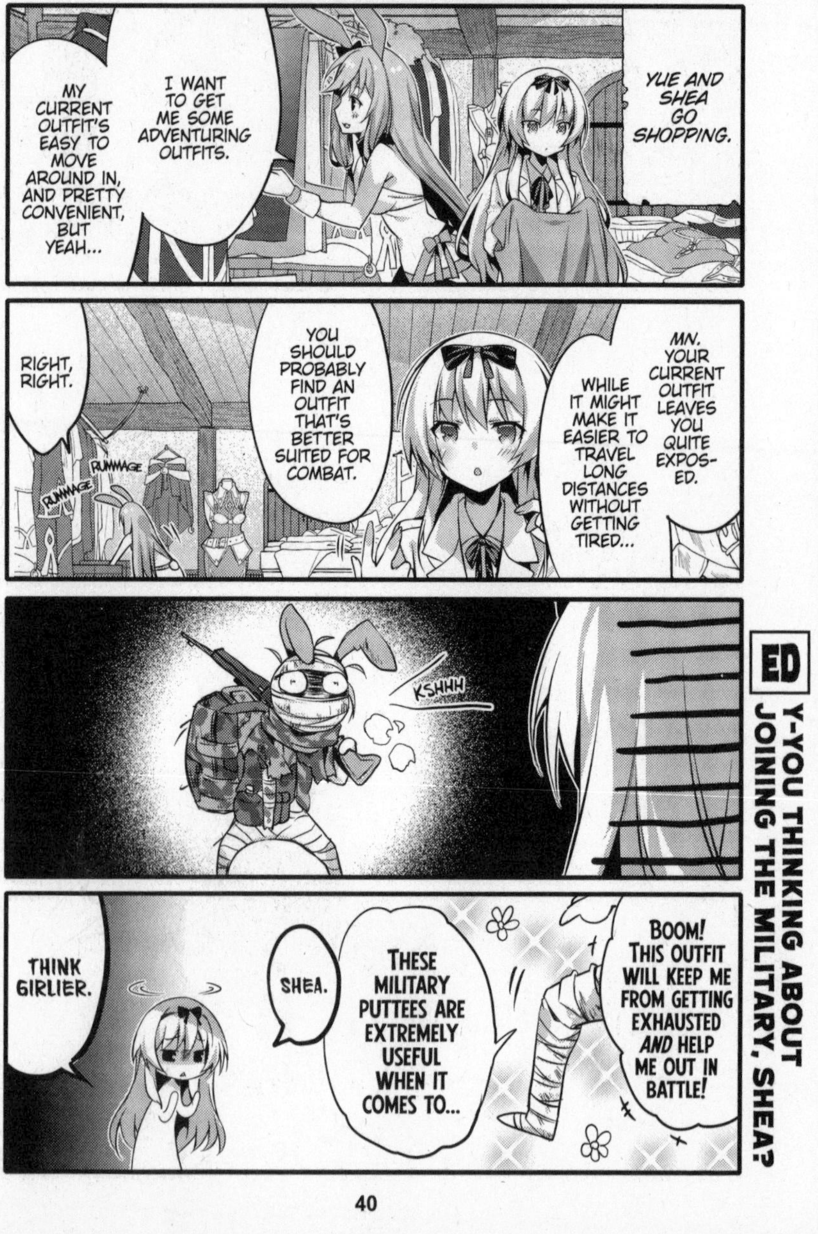

YUE AND SHEA GO SHOPPING.
I WANT TO GET ME SOME ADVENTURING OUTFITS.
MY CURRENT OUTFIT'S EASY TO MOVE AROUND IN, AND PRETTY CONVENIENT, BUT YEAH...
MN. YOUR CURRENT OUTFIT LEAVES YOU QUITE EXPOS-ED.
WHILE IT MIGHT MAKE IT EASIER TO TRAVEL LONG DISTANCES WITHOUT GETTING TIRED...
YOU SHOULD PROBABLY FIND AN OUTFIT THAT'S BETTER SUITED FOR COMBAT.
RIGHT, RIGHT.
RUMMAGE
RUMMAGE
KSHHH
BOOM! THIS OUTFIT WILL KEEP ME FROM GETTING EXHAUSTED *AND* HELP ME OUT IN BATTLE!
THESE MILITARY PUTTEES ARE EXTREMELY USEFUL WHEN IT COMES TO...
SHEA.
THINK GIRLIER.
ED
Y-YOU THINKING ABOUT JOINING THE MILITARY, SHEA?

WHAT THE GIRLS LIKE

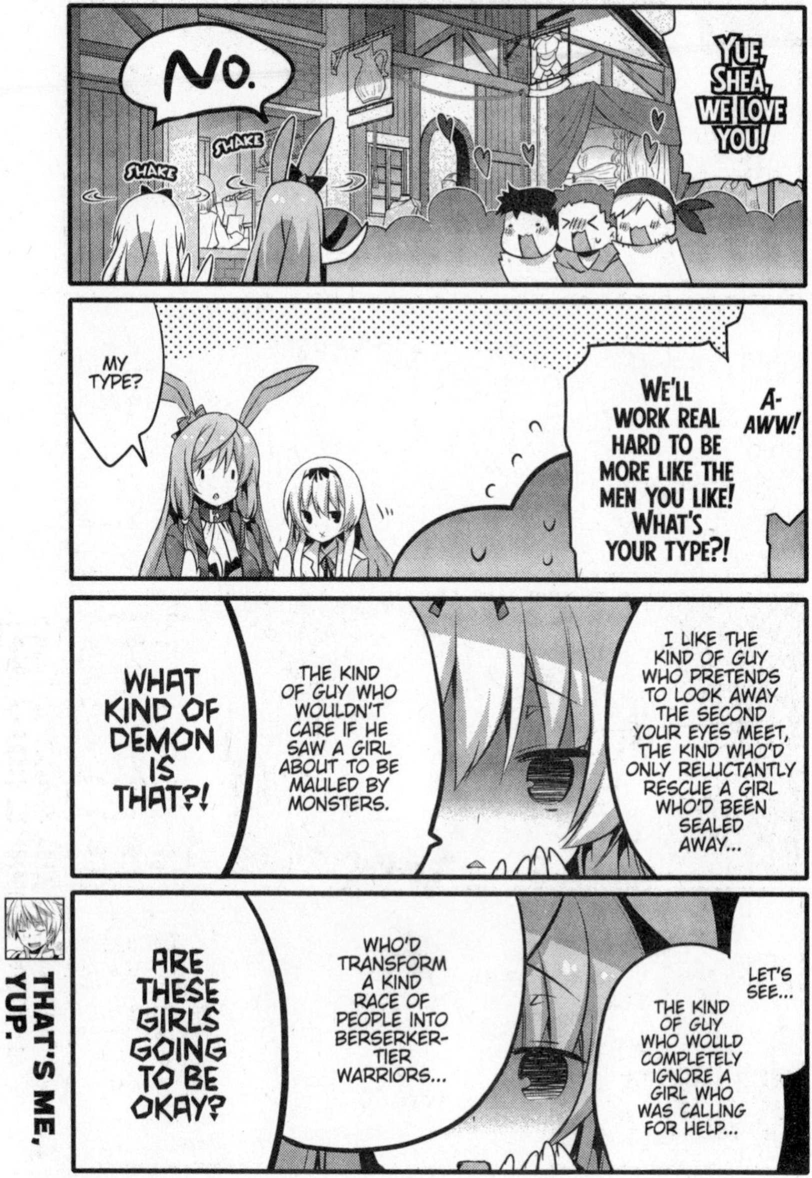
YUE, SHEA, WE LOVE YOU!
SHAKE
SHAKE
No.
A-AWW!
WE'LL WORK REAL HARD TO BE MORE LIKE THE MEN YOU LIKE! WHAT'S YOUR TYPE?!
MY TYPE?
I LIKE THE KIND OF GUY WHO PRETENDS TO LOOK AWAY THE SECOND YOUR EYES MEET, THE KIND WHO'D ONLY RELUCTANTLY RESCUE A GIRL WHO'D BEEN SEALED AWAY...
THE KIND OF GUY WHO WOULDN'T CARE IF HE SAW A GIRL ABOUT TO BE MAULED BY MONSTERS.
WHAT KIND OF DEMON IS THAT?!
LET'S SEE...
THE KIND OF GUY WHO WOULD COMPLETELY IGNORE A GIRL WHO WAS CALLING FOR HELP...
WHO'D TRANSFORM A KIND RACE OF PEOPLE INTO BERSERKER-TIER WARRIORS...
ARE THESE GIRLS GOING TO BE OKAY?
THAT'S ME, YUP.

HAJIME'S PRIZED CREATION

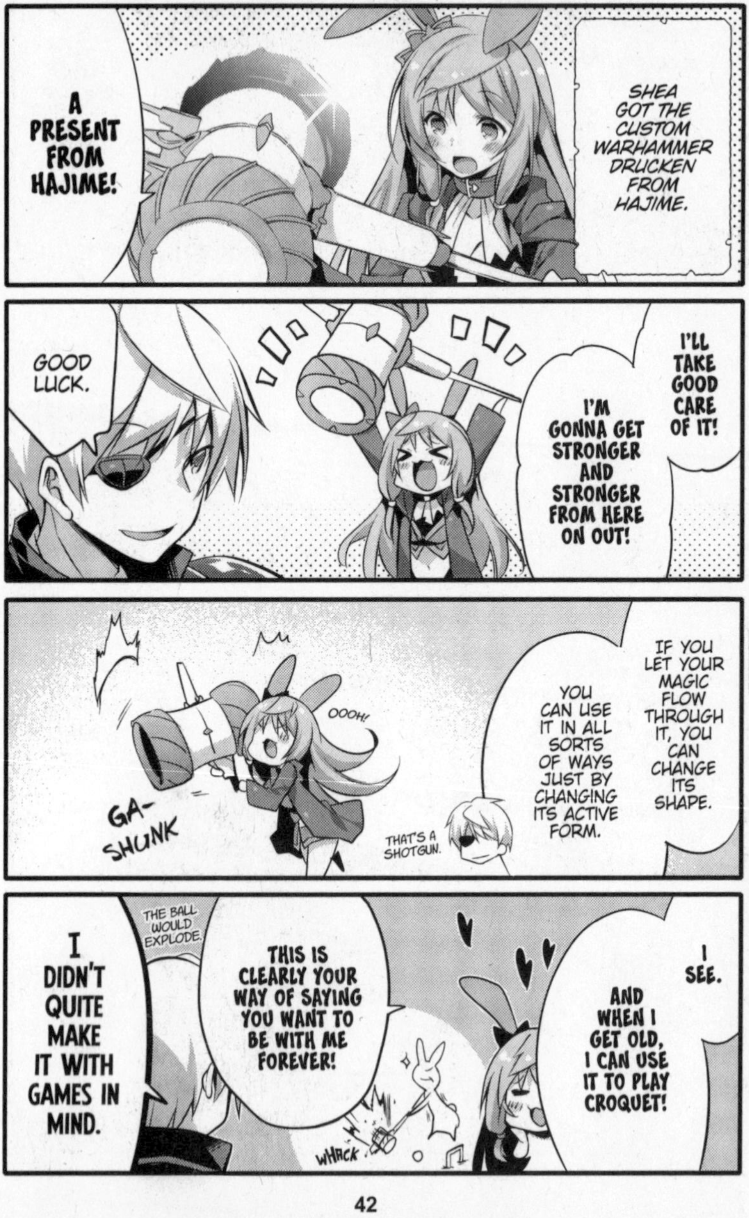
SHEA GOT THE CUSTOM WARHAMMER DRUCKEN FROM HAJIME.
A PRESENT FROM HAJIME!
I'LL TAKE GOOD CARE OF IT!
I'M GONNA GET STRONGER AND STRONGER FROM HERE ON OUT!
GOOD LUCK.
IF YOU LET YOUR MAGIC FLOW THROUGH IT, YOU CAN CHANGE ITS SHAPE.
YOU CAN USE IT IN ALL SORTS OF WAYS JUST BY CHANGING ITS ACTIVE FORM.
OOOH!
THAT'S A SHOTGUN.
GA-SHUNK
I SEE.
AND WHEN I GET OLD, I CAN USE IT TO PLAY CROQUET!
WHACK
THIS IS CLEARLY YOUR WAY OF SAYING YOU WANT TO BE WITH ME FOREVER!
THE BALL WOULD EXPLODE.
I DIDN'T QUITE MAKE IT WITH GAMES IN MIND.

ED IT ALSO HAS AN ABILITY CALLED "SPARK."

LET'S JUST GET SOME TAKEOUT

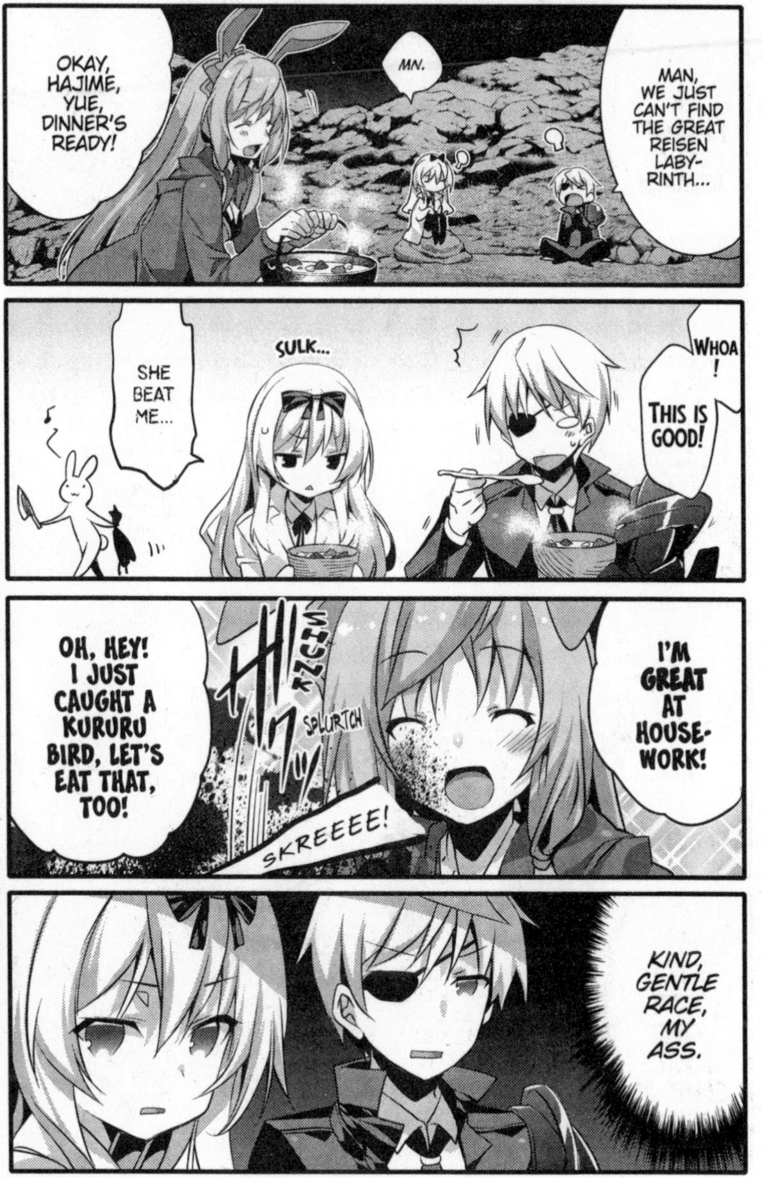
MAN, WE JUST CAN'T FIND THE GREAT REISEN LABYRINTH...
MN.
OKAY, HAJIME, YUE, DINNER'S READY!
WHOA!
THIS IS GOOD!
SULK...
SHE BEAT ME...
I'M GREAT AT HOUSE-WORK!
SHUNK
SPLURTCH
OH, HEY! I JUST CAUGHT A KURURU BIRD, LET'S EAT THAT, TOO!
SKREEEEE!
KIND, GENTLE RACE, MY ASS.

THAT HORRIBLE SQUEAL IS GONNA HAUNT MY DREAMS!

WHAT YEAR IS IT?

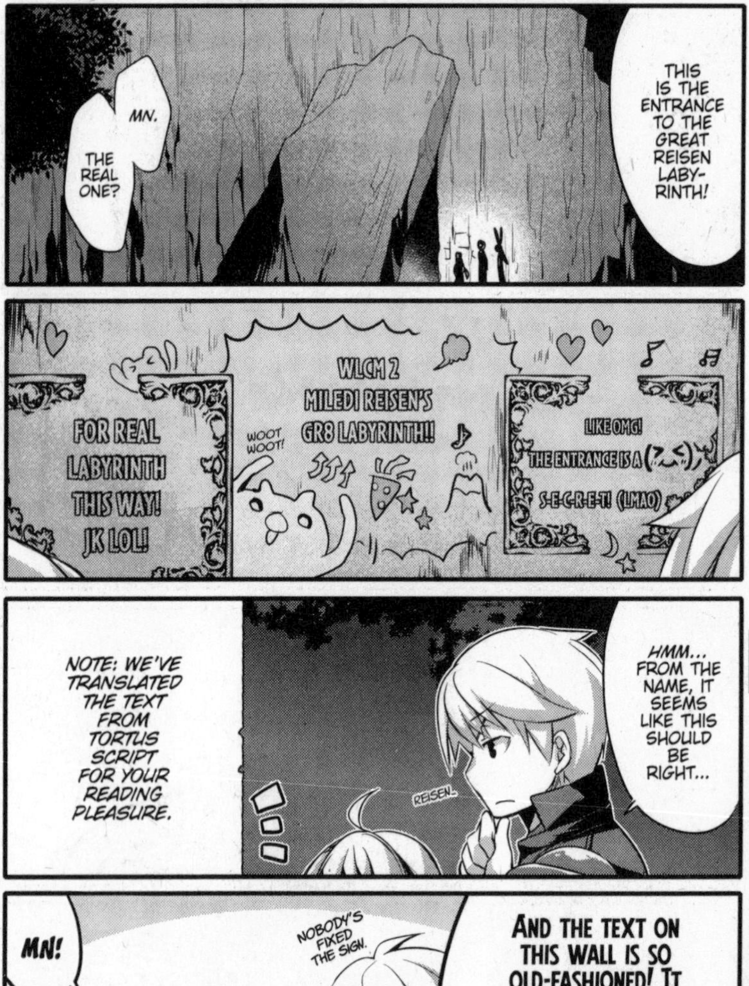
THIS IS THE ENTRANCE TO THE GREAT REISEN LABY-RINTH!
MN.
THE REAL ONE?
LIKE OMG! THE ENTRANCE IS A S-E-C-R-E-T! (LMAO)
WLCM 2 MILEDI REISEN'S GR8 LABYRINTH!!
WOOT WOOT!
FOR REAL LABYRINTH THIS WAY! JK LOL!
HMM... FROM THE NAME, IT SEEMS LIKE THIS SHOULD BE RIGHT...
REISEN...
NOTE: WE'VE TRANSLATED THE TEXT FROM TORTUS SCRIPT FOR YOUR READING PLEASURE.
AND THE TEXT ON THIS WALL IS SO OLD-FASHIONED! IT MUST BE A SIGN THAT NO ADVENTURERS HAVE COME HERE IN A WHILE. THAT MEANS IT MUST BE THE REAL LABYRINTH!
NOBODY'S FIXED THE SIGN.
MN!
NOD

ED I WISH I COULD BE BLISSFULLY YOUNG FOREVER.

A BEAUTIFUL MAZE

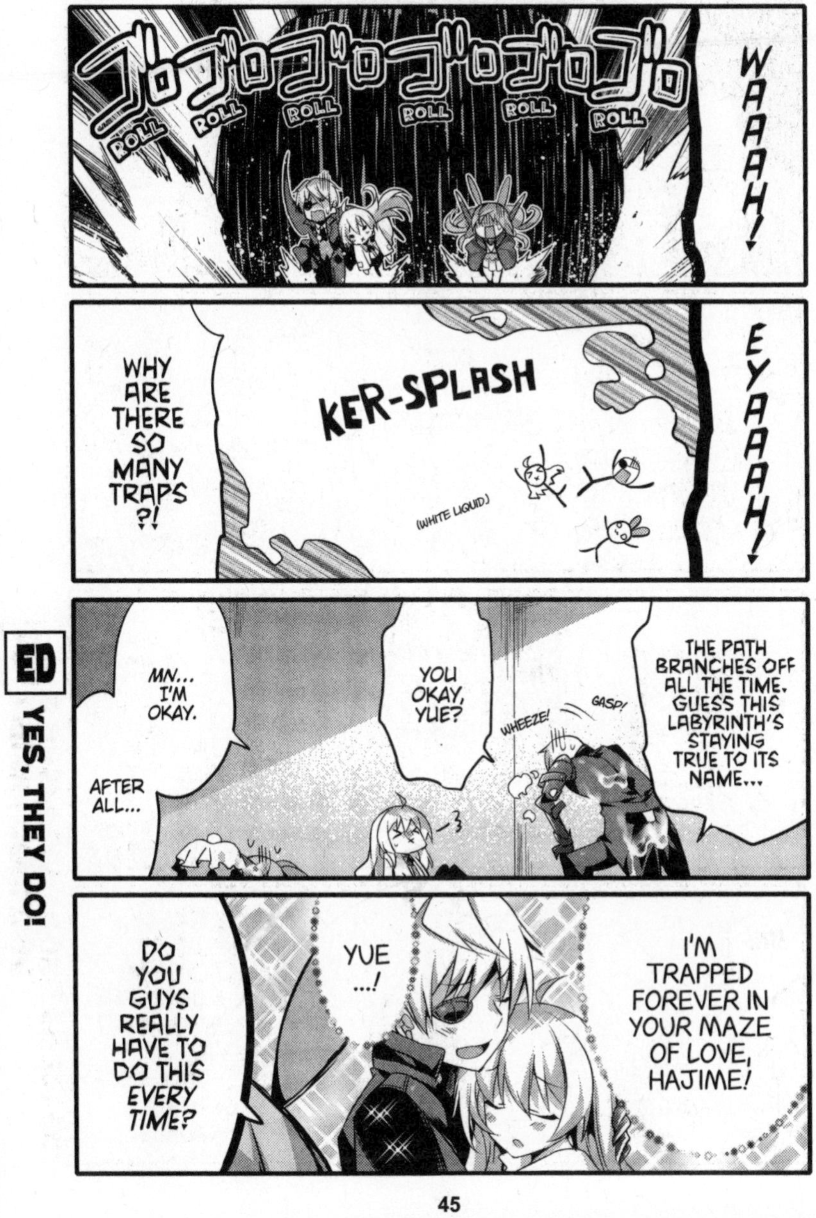

WAAAH!
ゴロゴロゴロゴロゴロゴロ
ROLL ROLL ROLL ROLL ROLL ROLL
EYAAAAH!
KER-SPLASH
(WHITE LIQUID)
WHY ARE THERE SO MANY TRAPS?!
THE PATH BRANCHES OFF ALL THE TIME. GUESS THIS LABYRINTH'S STAYING TRUE TO ITS NAME...
GASP!
WHEEZE!
YOU OKAY, YUE?
MN... I'M OKAY.
AFTER ALL...
I'M TRAPPED FOREVER IN YOUR MAZE OF LOVE, HAJIME!
YUE ...!
DO YOU GUYS REALLY HAVE TO DO THIS EVERY TIME?

ED YES, THEY DO!

1 LUTA = APPROX. 1 YEN

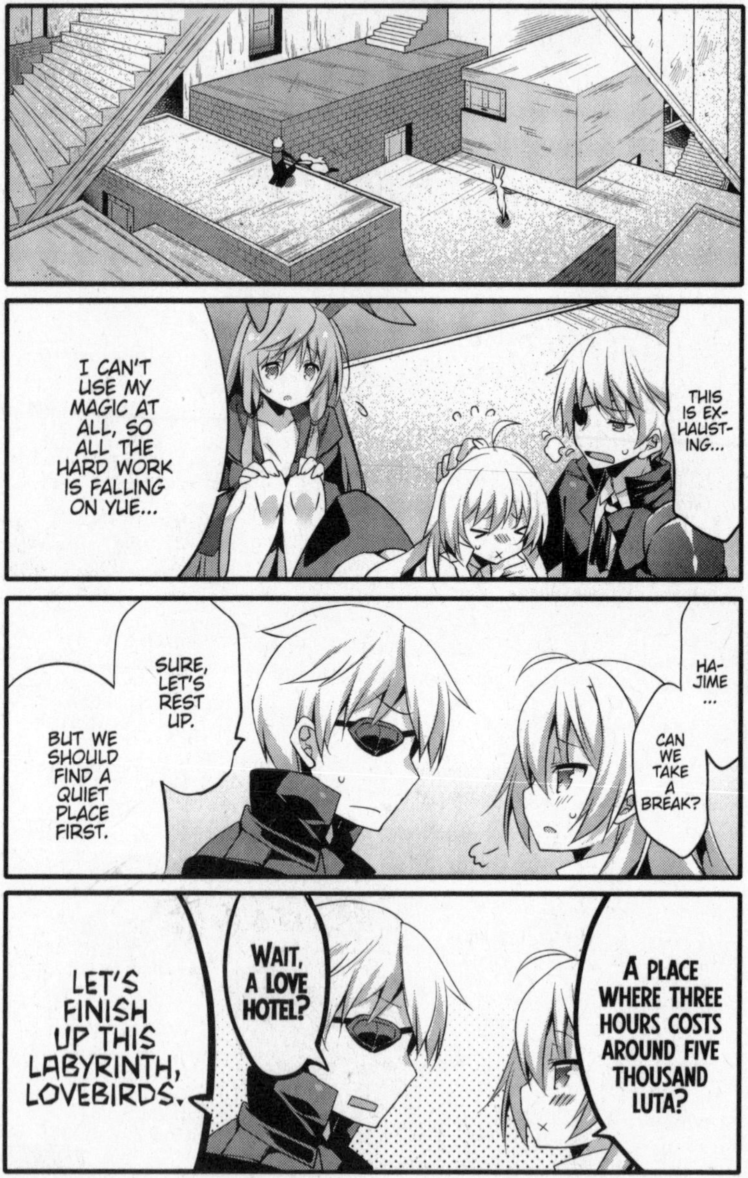

THIS IS EX-HAUST-ING...
I CAN'T USE MY MAGIC AT ALL, SO ALL THE HARD WORK IS FALLING ON YUE...
HA-JIME...
CAN WE TAKE A BREAK?
SURE, LET'S REST UP.
BUT WE SHOULD FIND A QUIET PLACE FIRST.
A PLACE WHERE THREE HOURS COSTS AROUND FIVE THOUSAND LUTA?
WAIT, A LOVE HOTEL?
LET'S FINISH UP THIS LABYRINTH, LOVEBIRDS.

ED KEEP SAYING IT, SHEA!

THEY STARTED GETTING CARELESS ON DAY FOUR

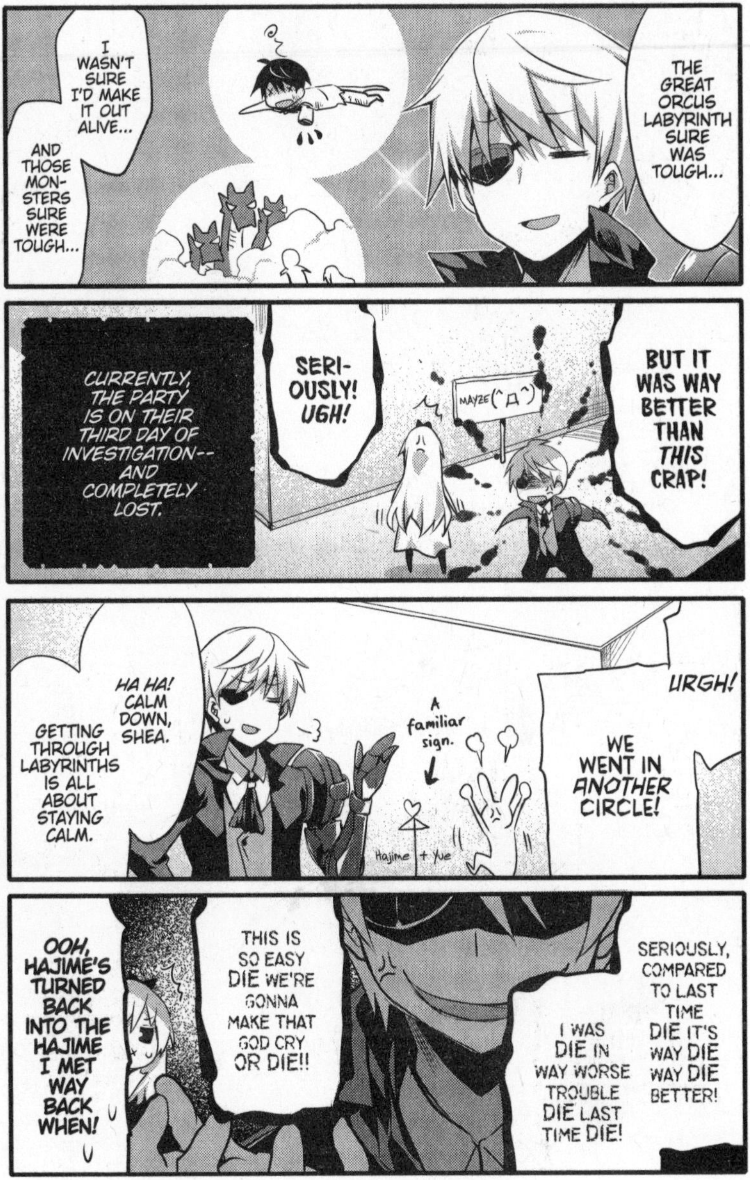
THE GREAT ORCUS LABYRINTH SURE WAS TOUGH...
I WASN'T SURE I'D MAKE IT OUT ALIVE...
AND THOSE MONSTERS SURE WERE TOUGH...
BUT IT WAS WAY BETTER THAN THIS CRAP!
MAYZE(^Д^)
SERIOUSLY! UGH!
CURRENTLY, THE PARTY IS ON THEIR THIRD DAY OF INVESTIGATION--AND COMPLETELY LOST.
URGH!
WE WENT IN ANOTHER CIRCLE!
A familiar sign.
Hajime + Yue
HA HA! CALM DOWN, SHEA.
GETTING THROUGH LABYRINTHS IS ALL ABOUT STAYING CALM.
SERIOUSLY, COMPARED TO LAST TIME DIE IT'S WAY DIE WAY DIE BETTER!
I WAS DIE IN WAY WORSE TROUBLE DIE LAST TIME DIE!
THIS IS SO EASY DIE WE'RE GONNA MAKE THAT GOD CRY OR DIE!!
OOH, HAJIME'S TURNED BACK INTO THE HAJIME I MET WAY BACK WHEN!

ED

TO SEE MORE OF SERIOUS HAJIME, CHECK OUT THE MANGA ADAPTATION OF THE LIGHT NOVEL!

MEANWHILE, THE HEROES WERE...

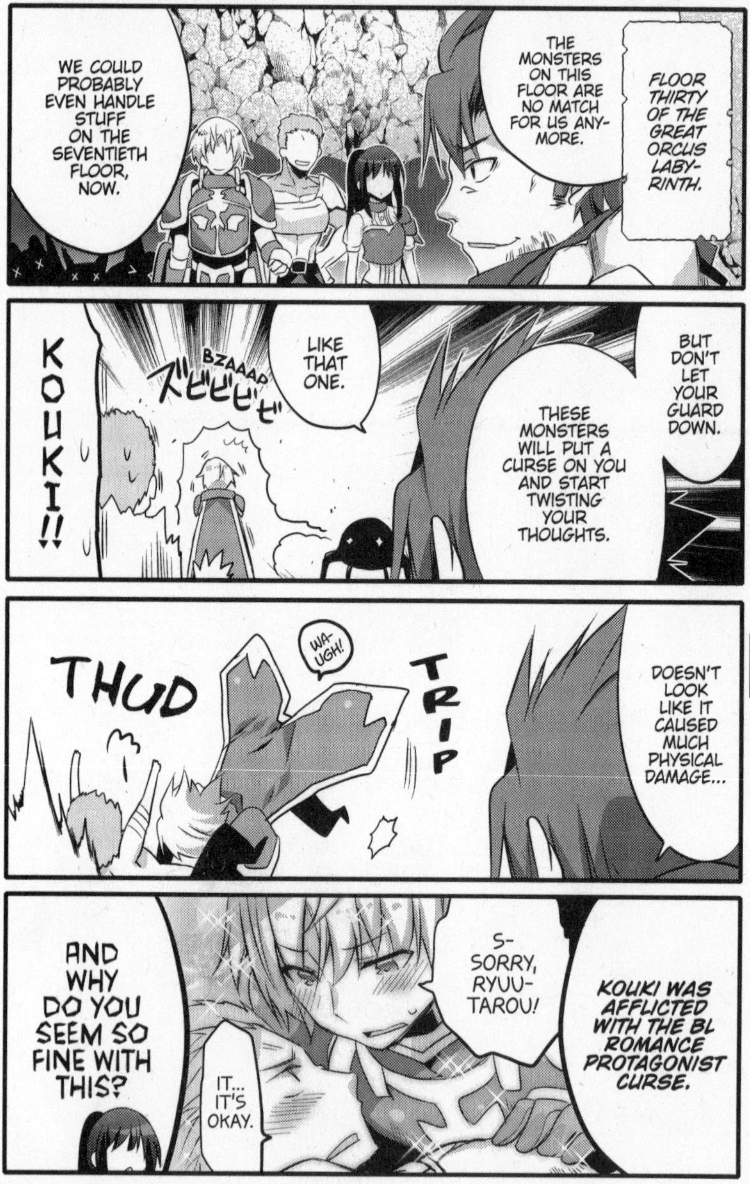

FLOOR THIRTY OF THE GREAT ORCUS LABYRINTH.
THE MONSTERS ON THIS FLOOR ARE NO MATCH FOR US ANYMORE.
WE COULD PROBABLY EVEN HANDLE STUFF ON THE SEVENTIETH FLOOR, NOW.
BUT DON'T LET YOUR GUARD DOWN.
THESE MONSTERS WILL PUT A CURSE ON YOU AND START TWISTING YOUR THOUGHTS.
LIKE THAT ONE.
BZAAAP
KOUKI!!
DOESN'T LOOK LIKE IT CAUSED MUCH PHYSICAL DAMAGE...
TRIP
WA-UGH!
THUD
KOUKI WAS AFFLICTED WITH THE BL ROMANCE PROTAGONIST CURSE.
S-SORRY, RYUUTAROU!
IT... IT'S OKAY.
AND WHY DO YOU SEEM SO FINE WITH THIS?

ED
NO FUJOSHI HERE.

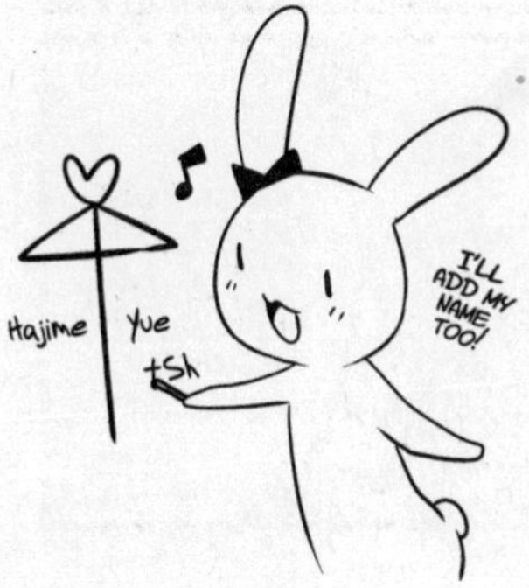
Hajime
Yue
+Sh
I'LL ADD MY NAME TOO!

ARIFURETA:

ARIFURETA SHOKUGYOU DE SEKAISAIKYOU

I ♥ Isekai

The Reisen Labyrinth, Part 2

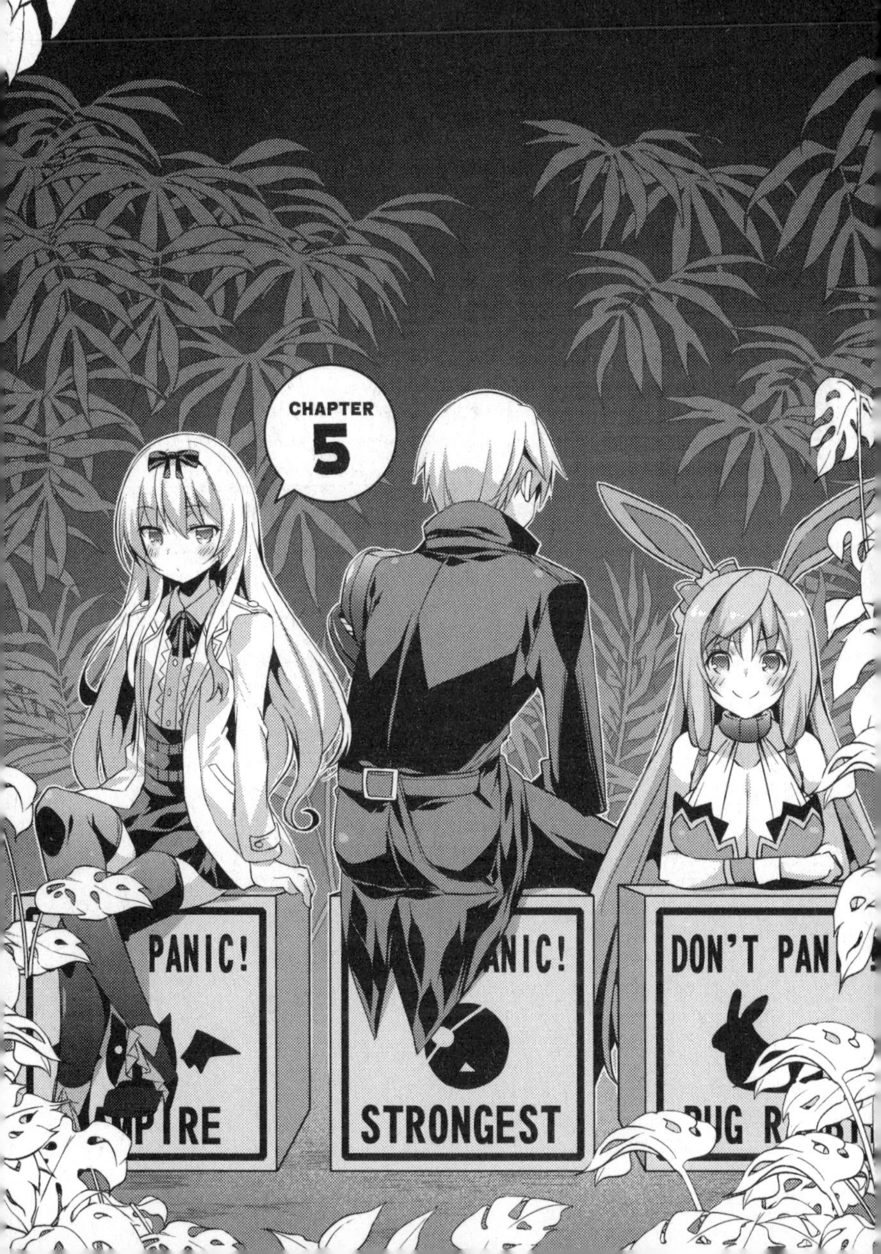
CHAPTER 5
PANIC!
STRONGEST
DON'T

LABYRINTH MARKETING

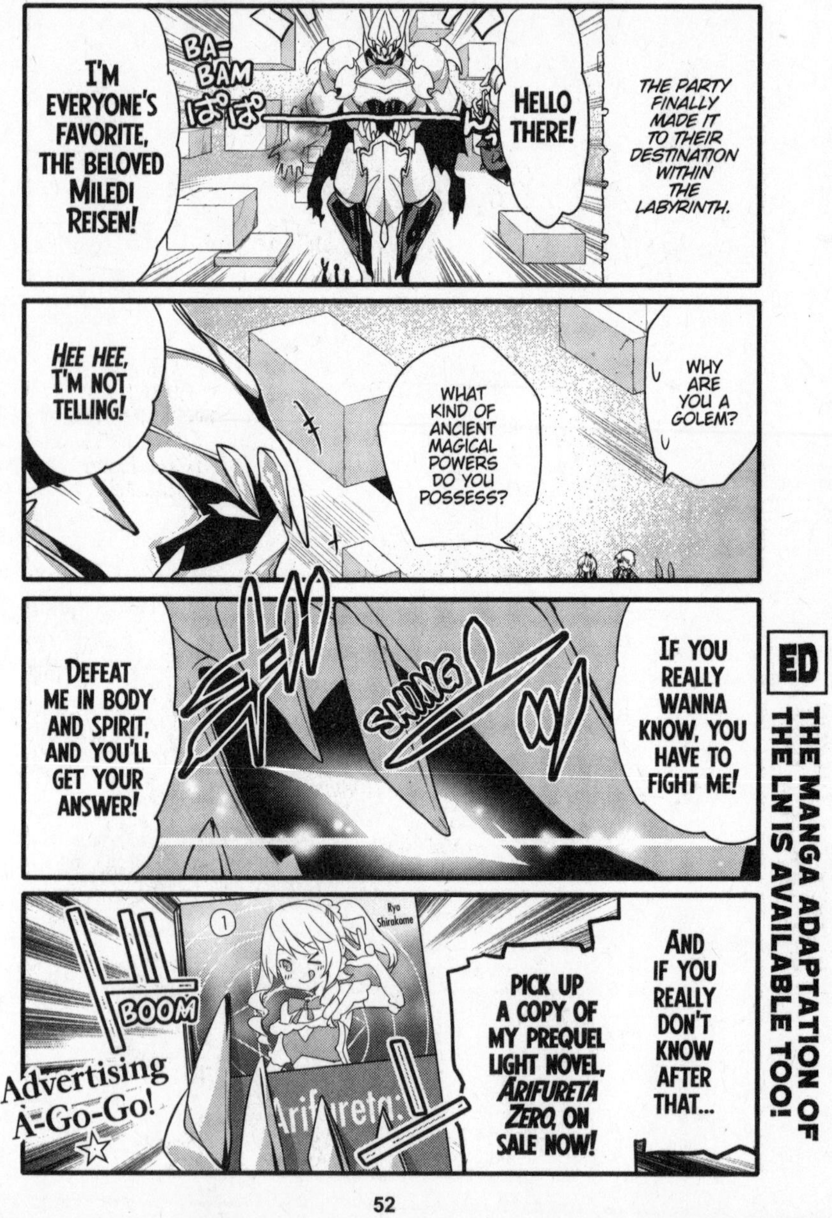

THE PARTY FINALLY MADE IT TO THEIR DESTINATION WITHIN THE LABYRINTH.
HELLO THERE!
BA-BAM
ぱぱ
I'M EVERYONE'S FAVORITE, THE BELOVED MILEDI REISEN!
WHY ARE YOU A GOLEM?
WHAT KIND OF ANCIENT MAGICAL POWERS DO YOU POSSESS?
HEE HEE, I'M NOT TELLING!
IF YOU REALLY WANNA KNOW, YOU HAVE TO FIGHT ME!
SHING
DEFEAT ME IN BODY AND SPIRIT, AND YOU'LL GET YOUR ANSWER!
AND IF YOU REALLY DON'T KNOW AFTER THAT...
PICK UP A COPY OF MY PREQUEL LIGHT NOVEL, *ARIFURETA ZERO*, ON SALE NOW!
1
Ryo Shirakome
Arifureta:
BOOM
Advertising A-Go-Go! ☆

ED

THE MANGA ADAPTATION OF THE LN IS AVAILABLE TOO!

PENT-UP RAGE

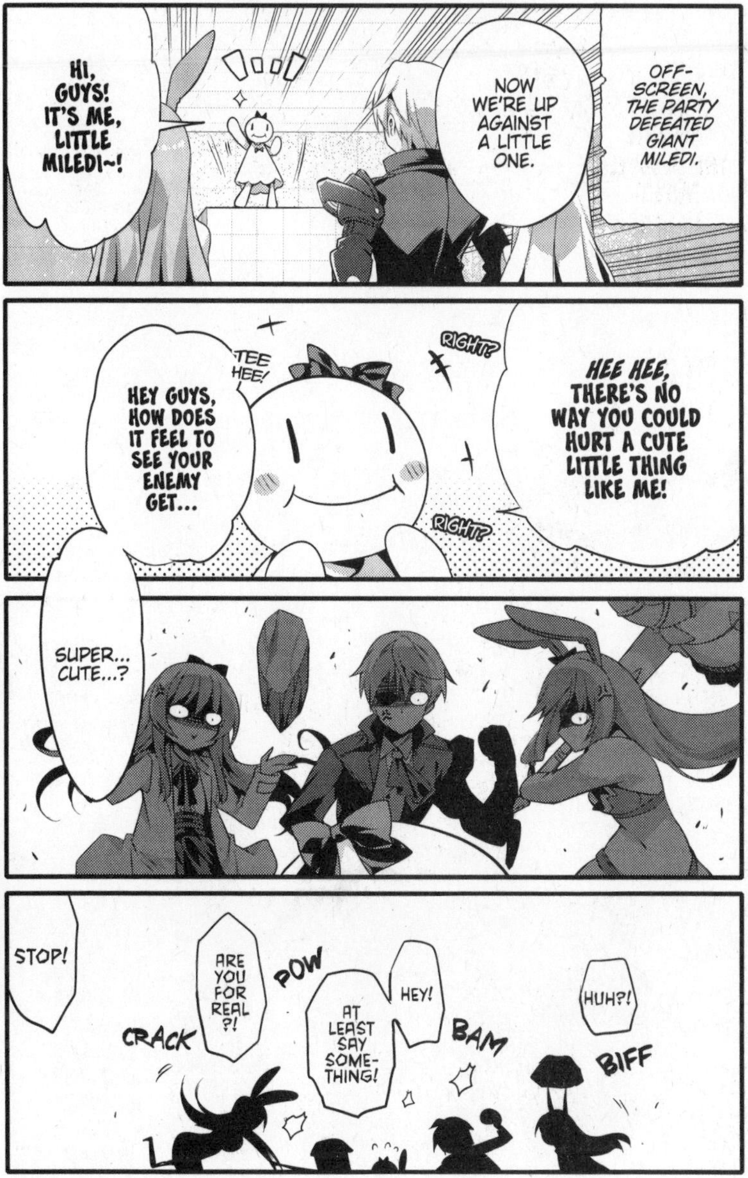
OFF-SCREEN, THE PARTY DEFEATED GIANT MILEDI.
NOW WE'RE UP AGAINST A LITTLE ONE.
HI, GUYS! IT'S ME, LITTLE MILEDI~!
RIGHT?
HEE HEE, THERE'S NO WAY YOU COULD HURT A CUTE LITTLE THING LIKE ME!
RIGHT?
TEE HEE!
HEY GUYS, HOW DOES IT FEEL TO SEE YOUR ENEMY GET...
SUPER... CUTE...?
HUH?!
BIFF
HEY!
BAM
AT LEAST SAY SOMETHING!
POW
ARE YOU FOR REAL?!
CRACK
STOP!

ED DON'T TAUNT YOUR ENEMY TOO MUCH.

AN UNSCRATCHABLE ITCH

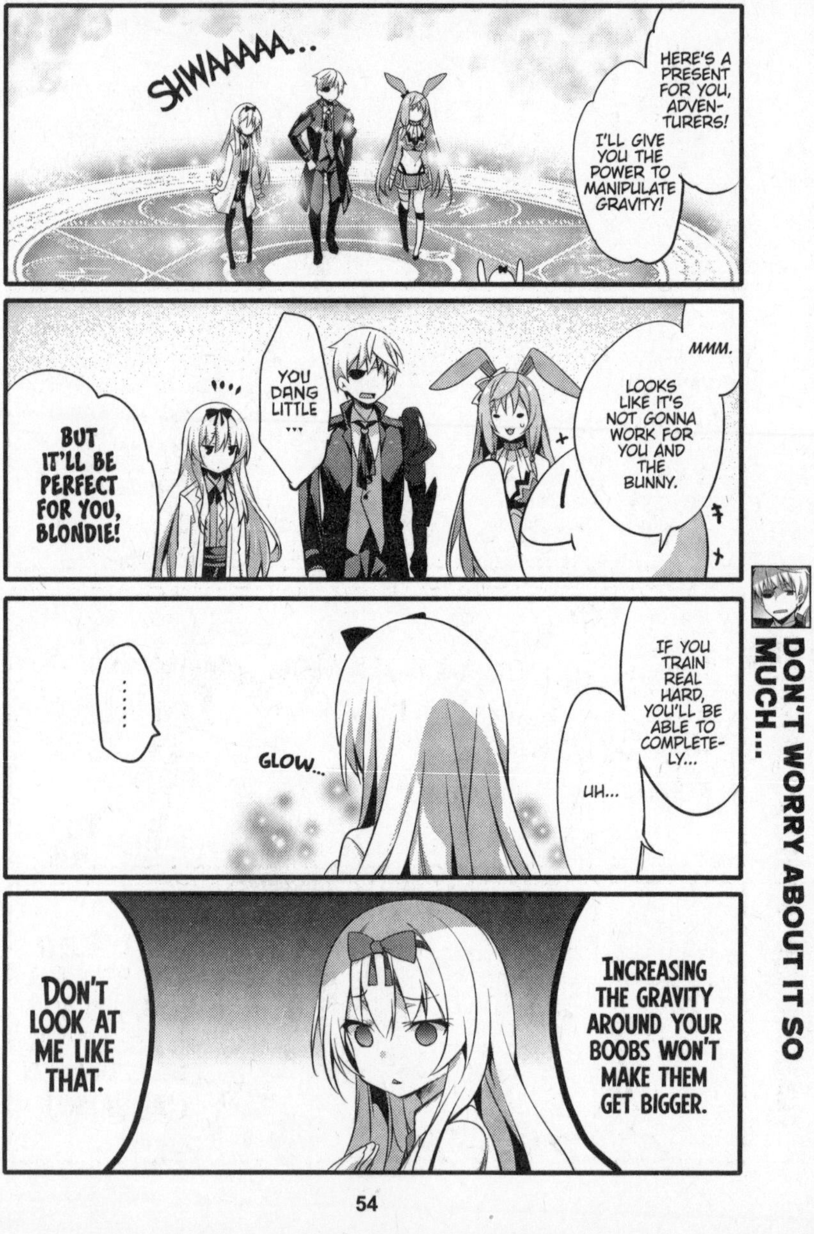
HERE'S A PRESENT FOR YOU, ADVEN-TURERS!
I'LL GIVE YOU THE POWER TO MANIPULATE GRAVITY!
SHWAAAAA...
MMM.
LOOKS LIKE IT'S NOT GONNA WORK FOR YOU AND THE BUNNY.
YOU DANG LITTLE...
BUT IT'LL BE PERFECT FOR YOU, BLONDIE!
IF YOU TRAIN REAL HARD, YOU'LL BE ABLE TO COMPLETE-LY...
UH...
......
GLOW...
INCREASING THE GRAVITY AROUND YOUR BOOBS WON'T MAKE THEM GET BIGGER.
DON'T LOOK AT ME LIKE THAT.
DON'T WORRY ABOUT IT SO MUCH...

SHAKEDOWN

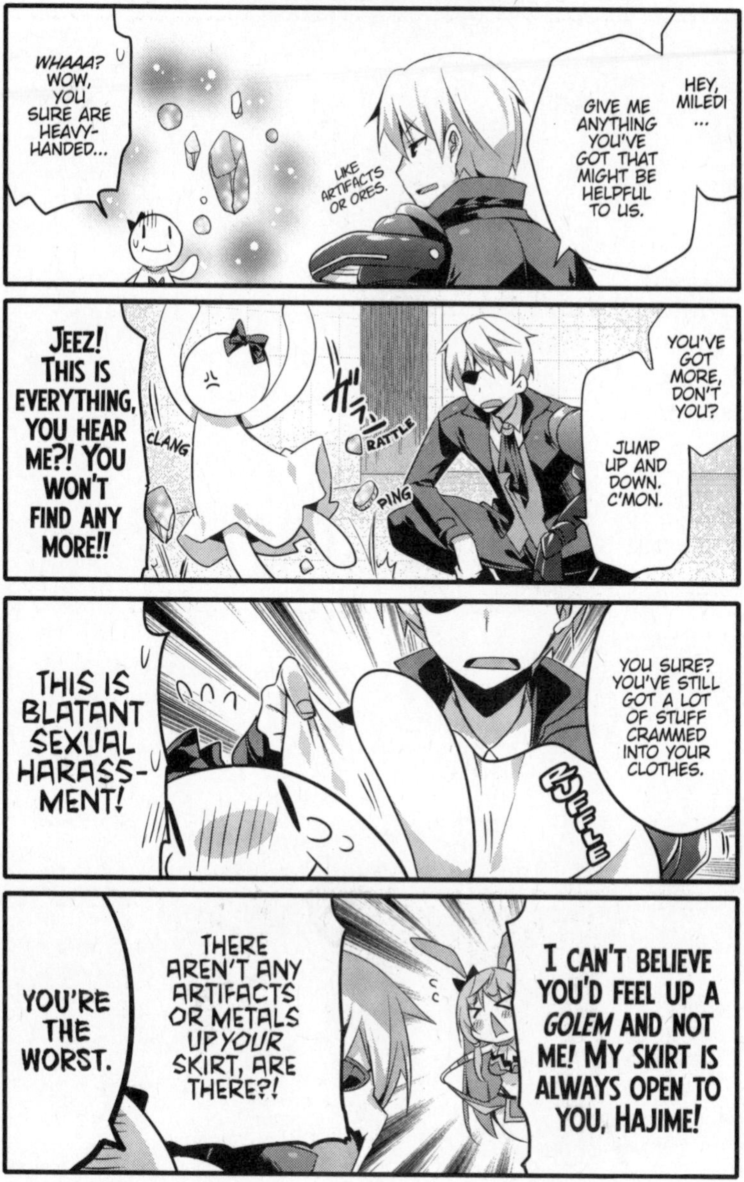

HEY, MILEDI ...
GIVE ME ANYTHING YOU'VE GOT THAT MIGHT BE HELPFUL TO US.
LIKE ARTIFACTS OR ORES.
WHAAA? WOW, YOU SURE ARE HEAVY-HANDED...
YOU'VE GOT MORE, DON'T YOU?
JUMP UP AND DOWN. C'MON.
RATTLE
PING
CLANG
JEEZ! THIS IS EVERYTHING, YOU HEAR ME?! YOU WON'T FIND ANY MORE!!
YOU SURE? YOU'VE STILL GOT A LOT OF STUFF CRAMMED INTO YOUR CLOTHES.
THIS IS BLATANT SEXUAL HARASS-MENT!
I CAN'T BELIEVE YOU'D FEEL UP A *GOLEM* AND NOT ME! MY SKIRT IS ALWAYS OPEN TO YOU, HAJIME!
THERE AREN'T ANY ARTIFACTS OR METALS UP *YOUR* SKIRT, ARE THERE?!
YOU'RE THE WORST.

ED

FORGET GIRLS, GET MONEY!

TIME FOR HER FIRST KISS

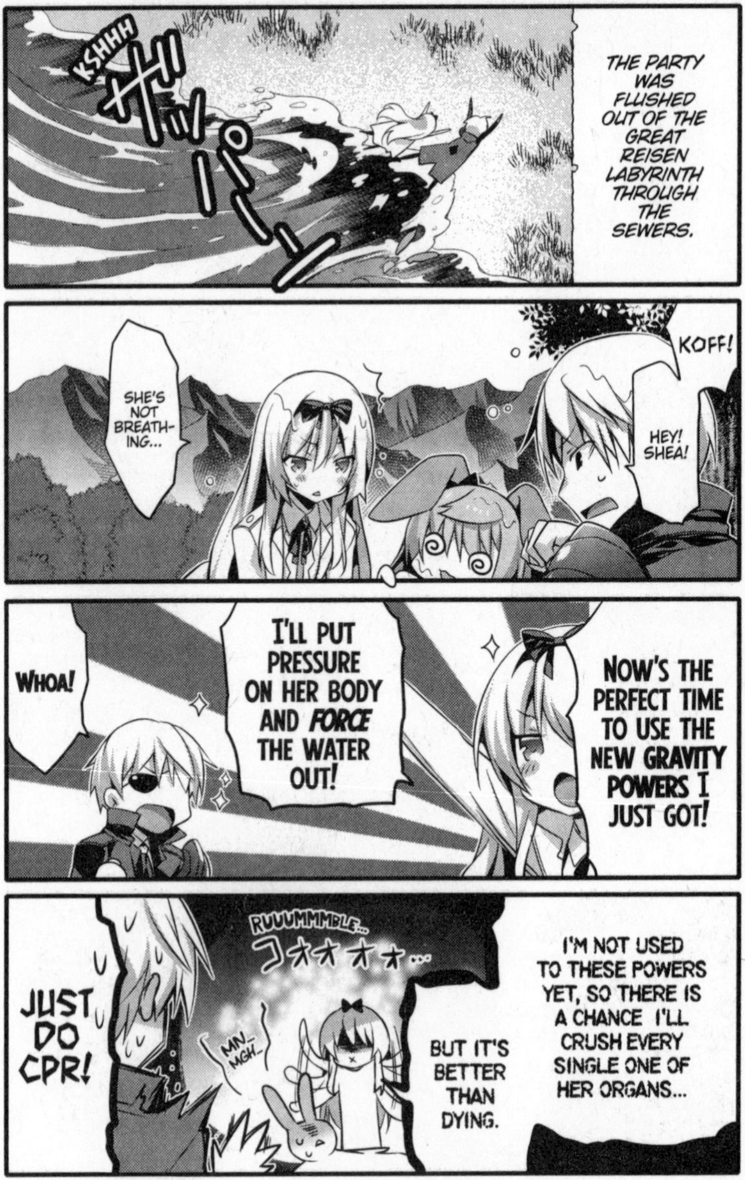
THE PARTY WAS FLUSHED OUT OF THE GREAT REISEN LABYRINTH THROUGH THE SEWERS.
KSHHH
KOFF!
HEY! SHEA!
SHE'S NOT BREATHING...
NOW'S THE PERFECT TIME TO USE THE NEW GRAVITY POWERS I JUST GOT!
I'LL PUT PRESSURE ON HER BODY AND *FORCE* THE WATER OUT!
WHOA!
I'M NOT USED TO THESE POWERS YET, SO THERE IS A CHANCE I'LL CRUSH EVERY SINGLE ONE OF HER ORGANS...
BUT IT'S BETTER THAN DYING.
RUUUMMMBLE...
コオオオオ…
MN... MGH...
JUST DO CPR!

ED THERE'S GOTTA BE AN EASIER WAY!

TWO MAN

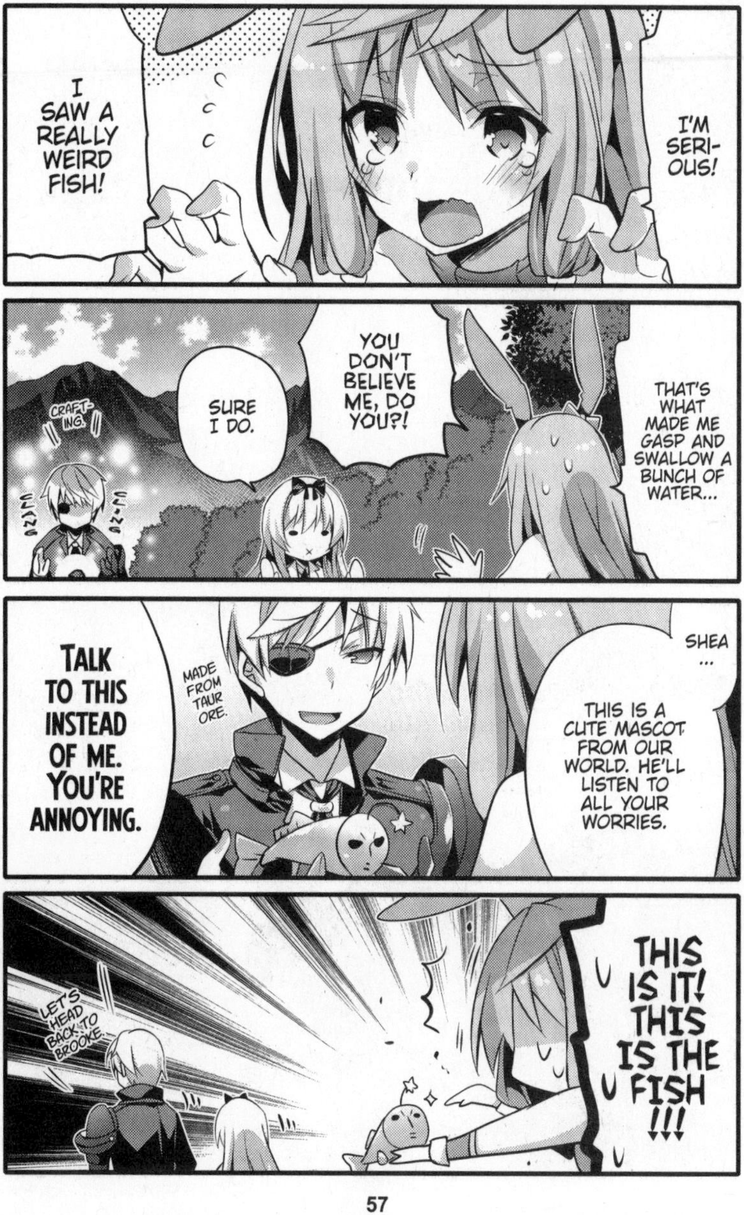
I'M SERI-OUS!
I SAW A REALLY WEIRD FISH!
THAT'S WHAT MADE ME GASP AND SWALLOW A BUNCH OF WATER...
YOU DON'T BELIEVE ME, DO YOU?!
SURE I DO.
CRAFT-ING.
CLING
CLING
SHEA...
THIS IS A CUTE MASCOT FROM OUR WORLD. HE'LL LISTEN TO ALL YOUR WORRIES.
MADE FROM TAUR ORE.
TALK TO THIS INSTEAD OF ME. YOU'RE ANNOYING.
THIS IS IT! THIS IS THE FISH!!!
LET'S HEAD BACK TO BROOKE.

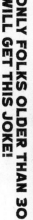

ED ONLY FOLKS OLDER THAN 30 WILL GET THIS JOKE!

DREAM CAST

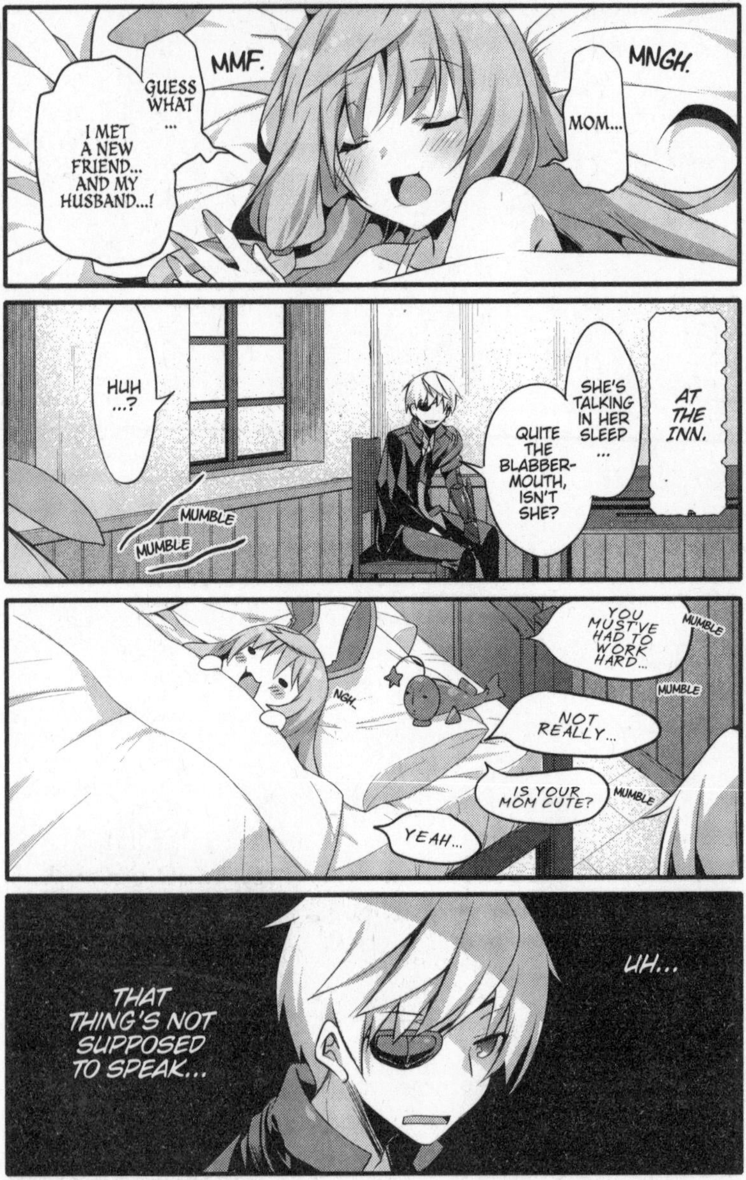
MNGH.
MOM...
MMF.
GUESS WHAT... I MET A NEW FRIEND... AND MY HUSBAND...!
AT THE INN.
SHE'S TALKING IN HER SLEEP...
QUITE THE BLABBERMOUTH, ISN'T SHE?
HUH...?
MUMBLE
MUMBLE
MUMBLE
YOU MUST'VE HAD TO WORK HARD...
MUMBLE
NOT REALLY...
MUMBLE
IS YOUR MOM CUTE?
NGH.
YEAH...
UH...
THAT THING'S NOT SUPPOSED TO SPEAK...

ED THIS REALLY BRINGS ME BACK.

DENIED

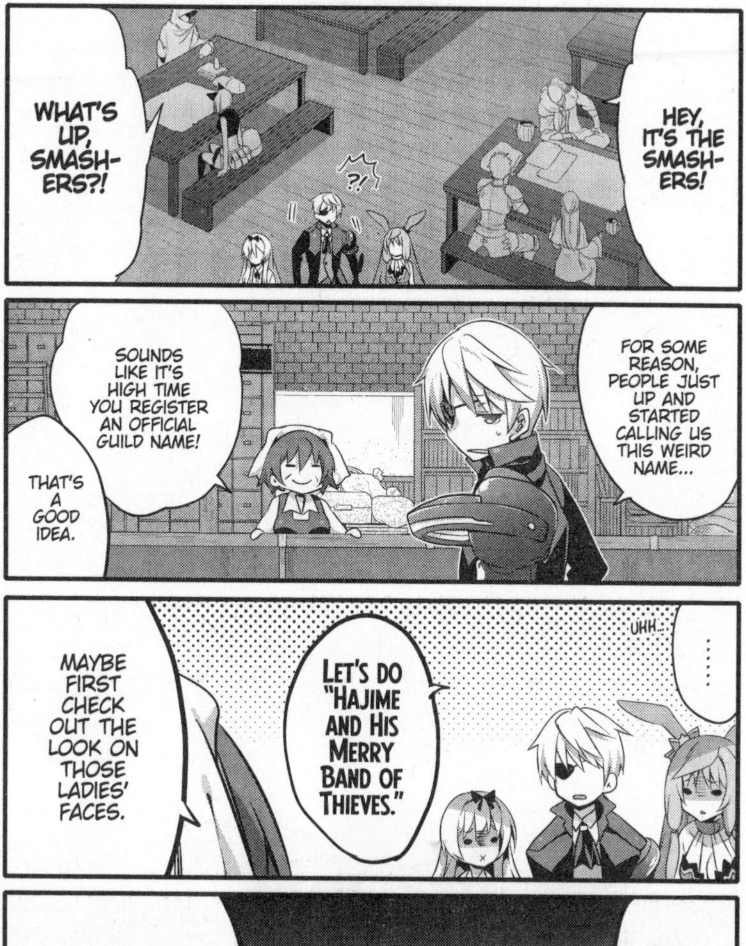
HEY, IT'S THE SMASH-ERS!
?!
WHAT'S UP, SMASH-ERS?!
FOR SOME REASON, PEOPLE JUST UP AND STARTED CALLING US THIS WEIRD NAME...
SOUNDS LIKE IT'S HIGH TIME YOU REGISTER AN OFFICIAL GUILD NAME!
THAT'S A GOOD IDEA.
......
UHH...
LET'S DO "HAJIME AND HIS MERRY BAND OF THIEVES."
MAYBE FIRST CHECK OUT THE LOOK ON THOSE LADIES' FACES.
FINE, JUST MARK IT BLANK.
YOU'RE NOT EVEN TRYING TO *HIDE* HOW ANNOYED YOU ARE!

A WIDE RANGE

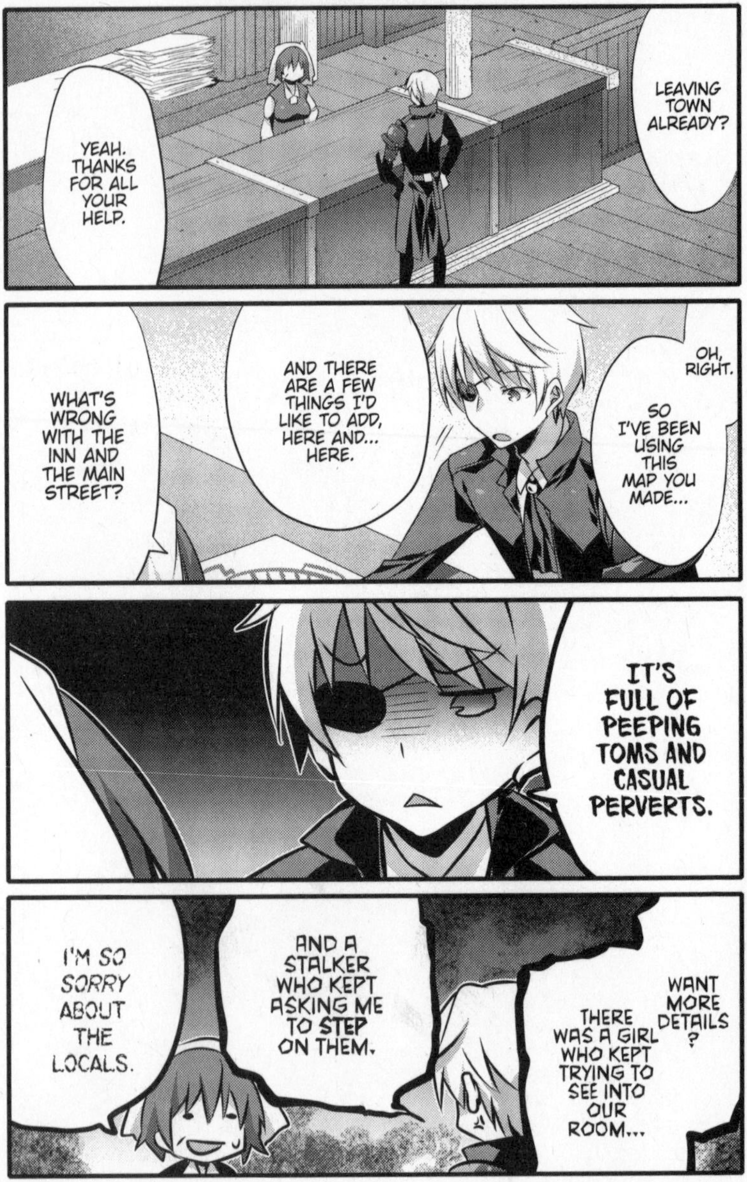

LEAVING TOWN ALREADY?
YEAH. THANKS FOR ALL YOUR HELP.
OH, RIGHT.
SO I'VE BEEN USING THIS MAP YOU MADE...
AND THERE ARE A FEW THINGS I'D LIKE TO ADD, HERE AND... HERE.
WHAT'S WRONG WITH THE INN AND THE MAIN STREET?
IT'S FULL OF PEEPING TOMS AND CASUAL PERVERTS.
WANT MORE DETAILS?
THERE WAS A GIRL WHO KEPT TRYING TO SEE INTO OUR ROOM...
AND A STALKER WHO KEPT ASKING ME TO **STEP** ON THEM.
I'M *SO SORRY* ABOUT THE LOCALS.

ED HOW NICE OF HAJIME TO NOT MURDER THEM ALL!

AN OMEGA MARK THAT
HAS NO REAL MEANING:

The Smashers:
Yue: Thigh Smasher
Hajime: Duel Smasher
(according to the townspeople)

ARIFURETA:

ARIFURETA SHOKUGYOU DE SEKAISAIKYOU

I ♥ Isekai

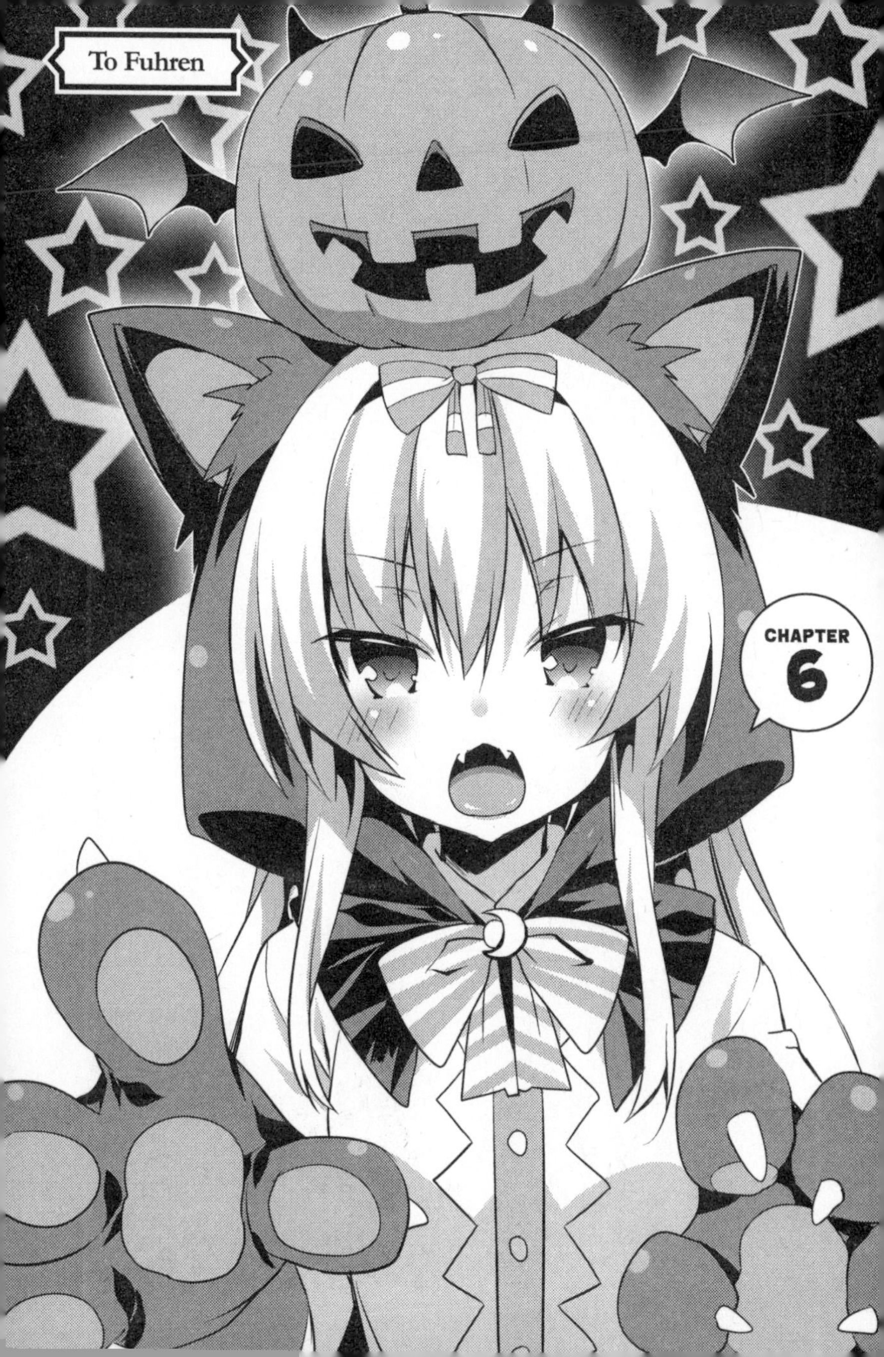
To Fuhren
CHAPTER
6

LET ME FINISH

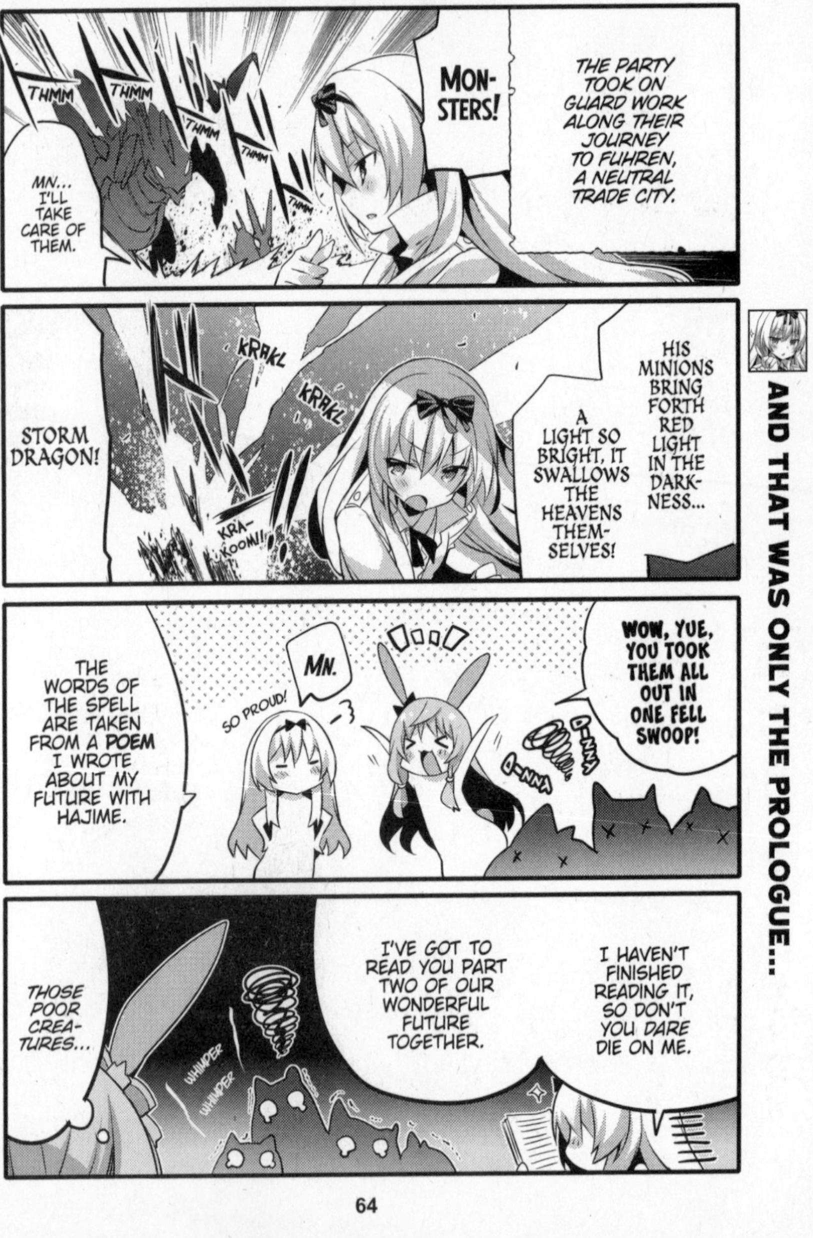
THE PARTY TOOK ON GUARD WORK ALONG THEIR JOURNEY TO FUHREN, A NEUTRAL TRADE CITY.
MON-STERS!
THMM
THMM
THMM
THMM
THMM
MN... I'LL TAKE CARE OF THEM.
HIS MINIONS BRING FORTH RED LIGHT IN THE DARKNESS...
A LIGHT SO BRIGHT, IT SWALLOWS THE HEAVENS THEMSELVES!
KRAKL
KRAKL
KRA-KOOM!!
STORM DRAGON!
WOW, YUE, YOU TOOK THEM ALL OUT IN ONE FELL SWOOP!
D-NNA
D-NNA
MN.
SO PROUD!
THE WORDS OF THE SPELL ARE TAKEN FROM A POEM I WROTE ABOUT MY FUTURE WITH HAJIME.
I HAVEN'T FINISHED READING IT, SO DON'T YOU DARE DIE ON ME.
I'VE GOT TO READ YOU PART TWO OF OUR WONDERFUL FUTURE TOGETHER.
WHIMPER
WHIMPER
THOSE POOR CREATURES...
AND THAT WAS ONLY THE PROLOGUE...

HE DOESN'T ACCEPT RETURNS

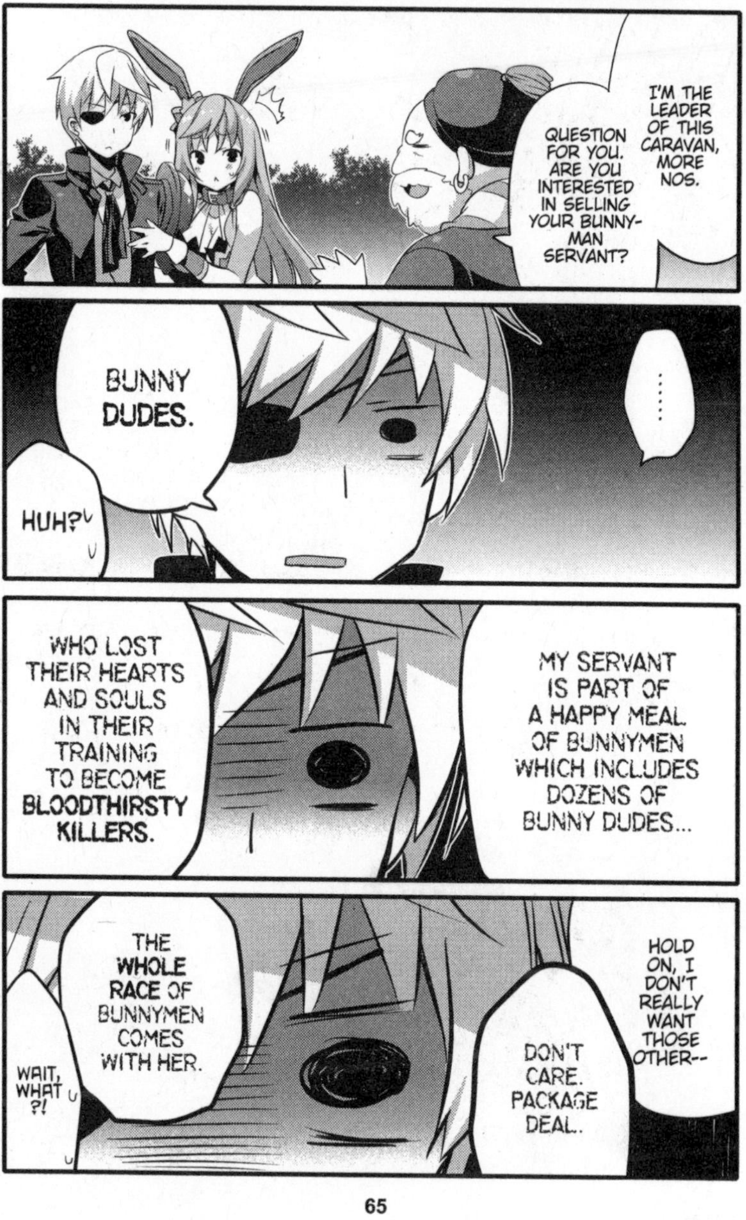
I'M THE LEADER OF THIS CARAVAN, MORE NOS.
QUESTION FOR YOU. ARE YOU INTERESTED IN SELLING YOUR BUNNY-MAN SERVANT?
......
BUNNY DUDES.
HUH?
MY SERVANT IS PART OF A HAPPY MEAL OF BUNNYMEN WHICH INCLUDES DOZENS OF BUNNY DUDES...
WHO LOST THEIR HEARTS AND SOULS IN THEIR TRAINING TO BECOME BLOODTHIRSTY KILLERS.
HOLD ON, I DON'T REALLY WANT THOSE OTHER--
DON'T CARE. PACKAGE DEAL.
THE WHOLE RACE OF BUNNYMEN COMES WITH HER.
WAIT, WHAT?!

BATTLE NECESSITIES

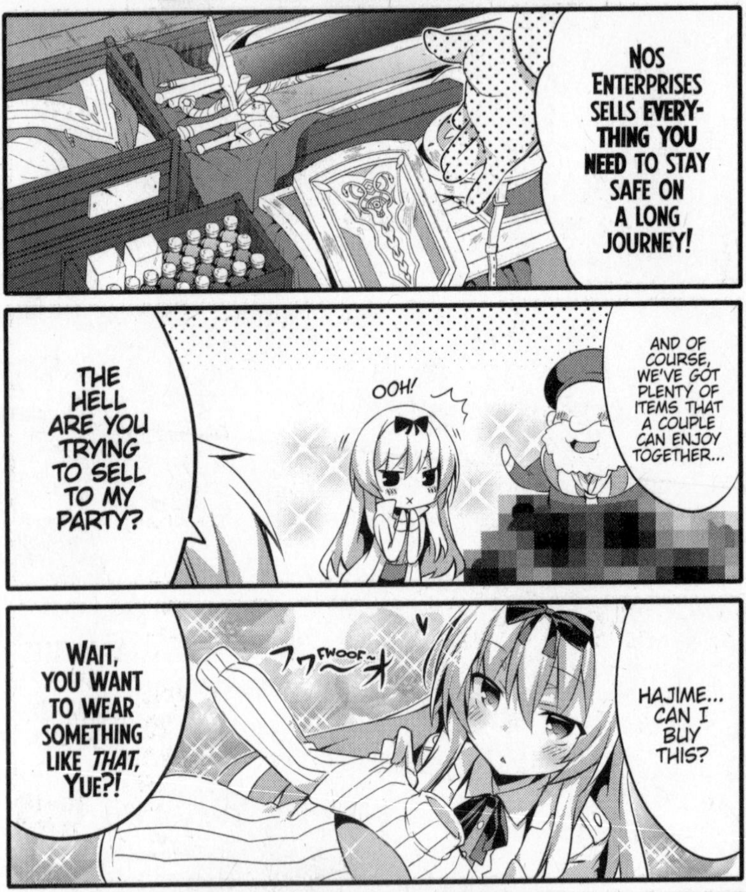
NOS ENTERPRISES SELLS EVERY-THING YOU NEED TO STAY SAFE ON A LONG JOURNEY!
AND OF COURSE, WE'VE GOT PLENTY OF ITEMS THAT A COUPLE CAN ENJOY TOGETHER...
OOH!
THE HELL ARE YOU TRYING TO SELL TO MY PARTY?
HAJIME... CAN I BUY THIS?
フワ〜オ FWOOF~
WAIT, YOU WANT TO WEAR SOMETHING LIKE *THAT*, YUE?!
HYAAA!
Y-Y-Y-Y-YUE, I HAD NO IDEA YOU HAD SUCH LITTLE SHAME!
WOW! OMIGOSH!
IT SHOWS LESS SKIN THAN *YOUR* USUAL OUTFIT. I THINK WE KNOW WHO'S *REALLY* SHAMELESS AROUND HERE.

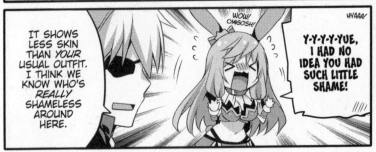

ED DON'T SEE A PROBLEM WITH WEARING LESS CLOTHES.

IT'S JUST LIKE MY DOUJINSHI!

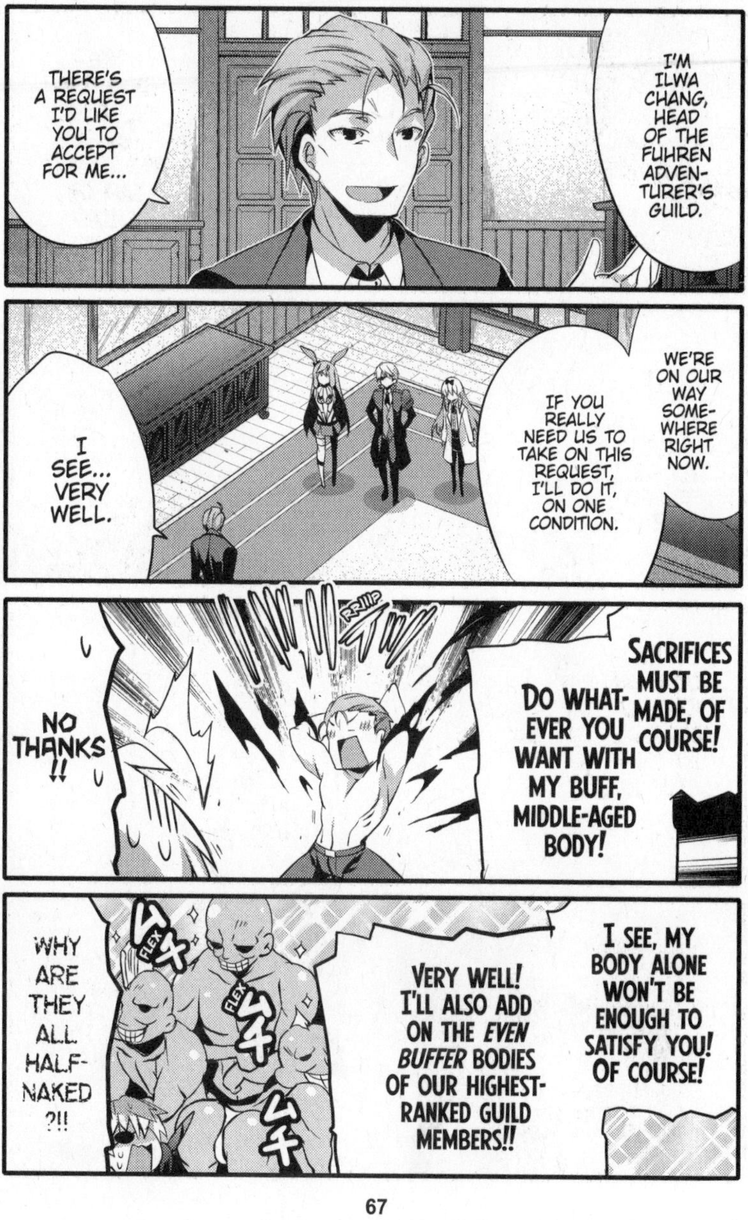
I'M ILWA CHANG, HEAD OF THE FUHREN ADVENTURER'S GUILD.
THERE'S A REQUEST I'D LIKE YOU TO ACCEPT FOR ME...
WE'RE ON OUR WAY SOMEWHERE RIGHT NOW.
IF YOU REALLY NEED US TO TAKE ON THIS REQUEST, I'LL DO IT, ON ONE CONDITION.
I SEE... VERY WELL.
RRIIP
SACRIFICES MUST BE MADE, OF COURSE!
DO WHATEVER YOU WANT WITH MY BUFF, MIDDLE-AGED BODY!
NO THANKS!!
I SEE, MY BODY ALONE WON'T BE ENOUGH TO SATISFY YOU! OF COURSE!
VERY WELL! I'LL ALSO ADD ON THE *EVEN BUFFER* BODIES OF OUR HIGHEST-RANKED GUILD MEMBERS!!
FLEX
FLEX
WHY ARE THEY ALL HALF-NAKED?!!

AND WHY DO THEY ALL LOOK SO HAPPY?!

CLEARING THE PATH

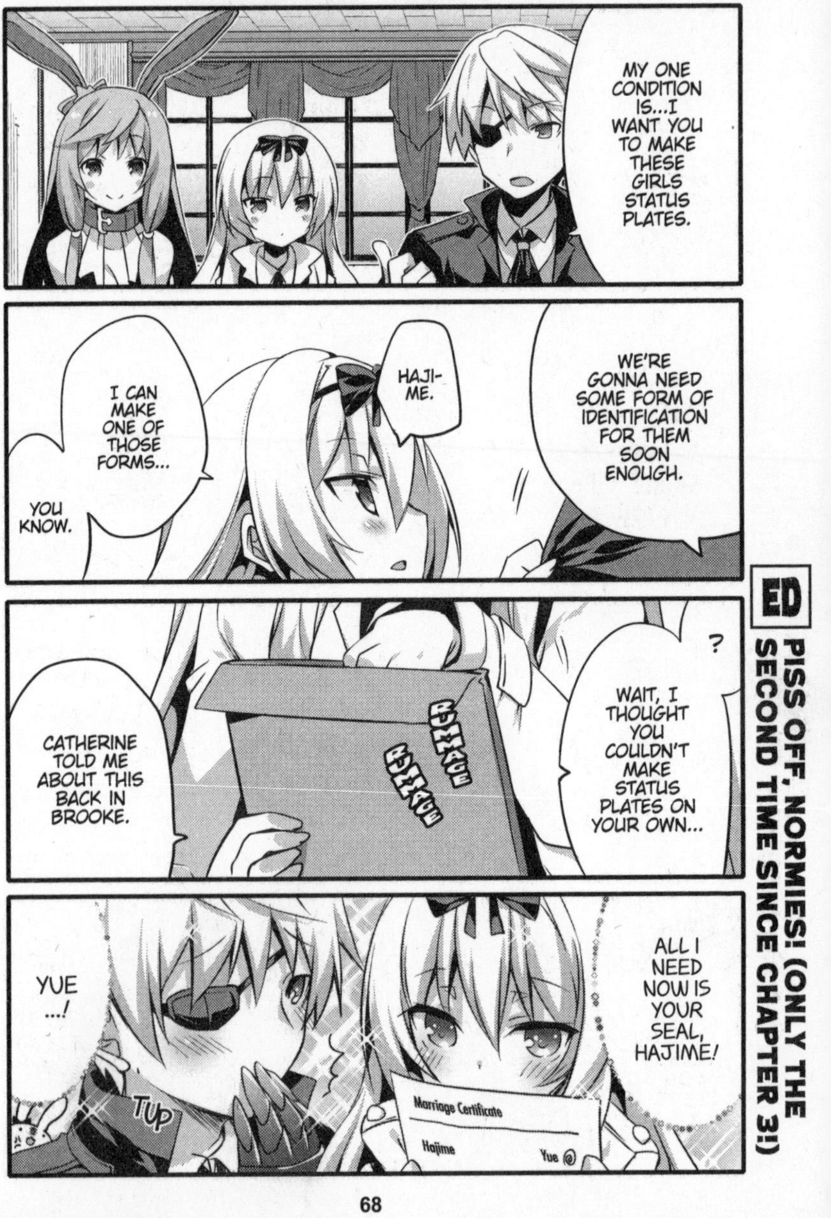
MY ONE CONDITION IS...I WANT YOU TO MAKE THESE GIRLS STATUS PLATES.
WE'RE GONNA NEED SOME FORM OF IDENTIFICATION FOR THEM SOON ENOUGH.
HAJI-ME.
I CAN MAKE ONE OF THOSE FORMS...
YOU KNOW.
?
WAIT, I THOUGHT YOU COULDN'T MAKE STATUS PLATES ON YOUR OWN...
RUMMAGE
RUMMAGE
CATHERINE TOLD ME ABOUT THIS BACK IN BROOKE.
ALL I NEED NOW IS YOUR SEAL, HAJIME!
Marriage Certificate
Hajime
Yue
YUE ...!
TUP

ED PISS OFF, NORMIES! (ONLY THE SECOND TIME SINCE CHAPTER 3!)

BASICALLY A PRO

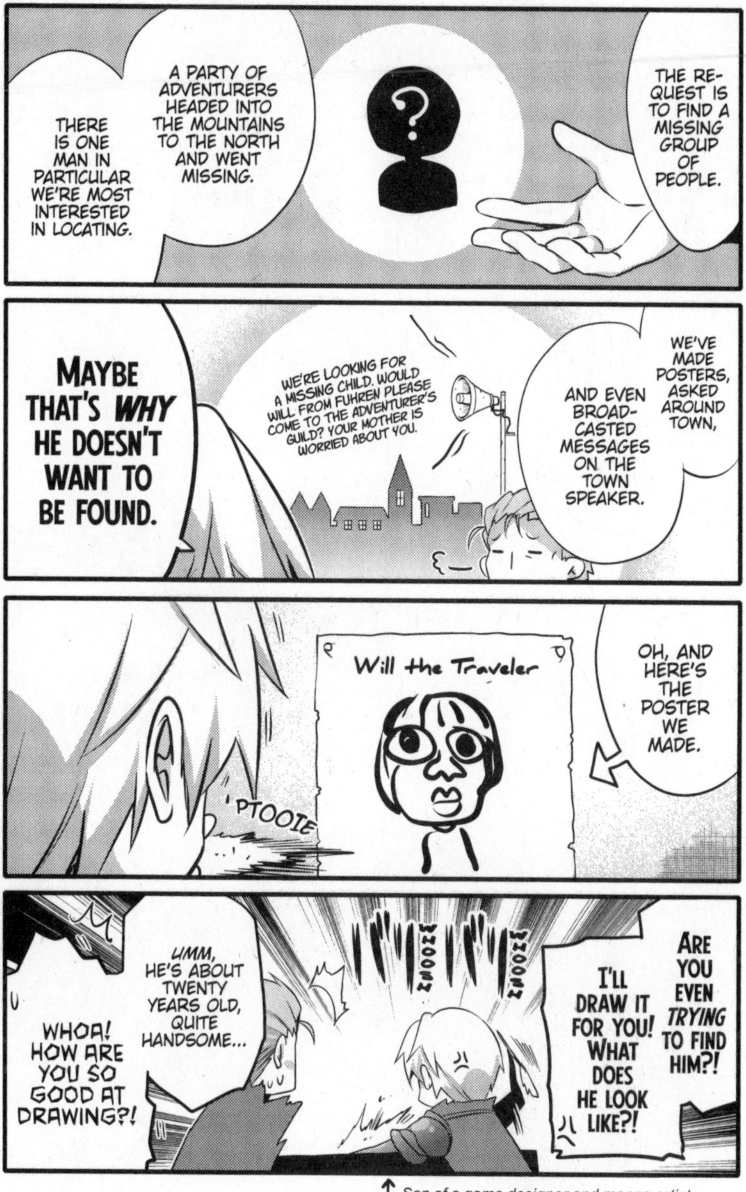
THE REQUEST IS TO FIND A MISSING GROUP OF PEOPLE.
A PARTY OF ADVENTURERS HEADED INTO THE MOUNTAINS TO THE NORTH AND WENT MISSING.
THERE IS ONE MAN IN PARTICULAR WE'RE MOST INTERESTED IN LOCATING.
WE'VE MADE POSTERS, ASKED AROUND TOWN,
AND EVEN BROADCASTED MESSAGES ON THE TOWN SPEAKER.
WE'RE LOOKING FOR A MISSING CHILD. WOULD WILL FROM FUHREN PLEASE COME TO THE ADVENTURER'S GUILD? YOUR MOTHER IS WORRIED ABOUT YOU.
MAYBE THAT'S *WHY* HE DOESN'T WANT TO BE FOUND.
OH, AND HERE'S THE POSTER WE MADE.
Will the Traveler
PTOOIE
ARE YOU EVEN *TRYING* TO FIND HIM?!
I'LL DRAW IT FOR YOU! WHAT DOES HE LOOK LIKE?!
WHOOSH
WHOOSH
UMM, HE'S ABOUT TWENTY YEARS OLD, QUITE HANDSOME...
WHOA! HOW ARE YOU SO GOOD AT DRAWING?!

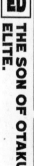

ED THE SON OF OTAKU ELITE.

↑ *Son of a game designer and manga artist.*

IT'S LIKE GOING ON A PICNIC

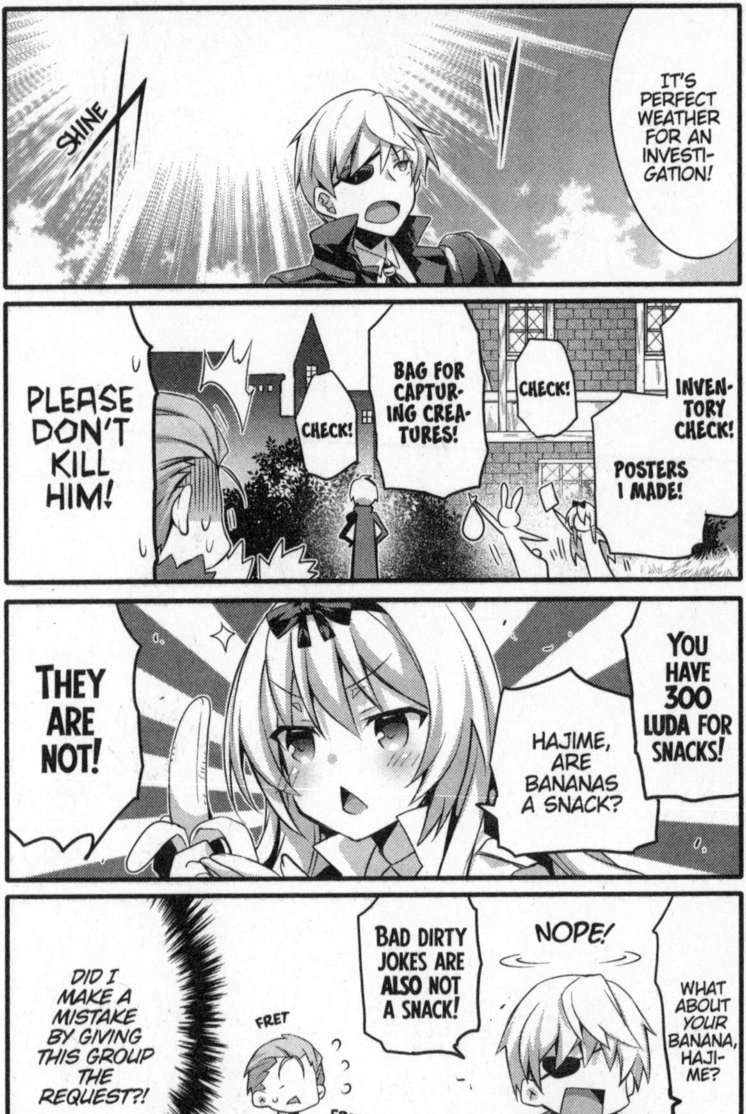
IT'S PERFECT WEATHER FOR AN INVESTI-GATION!
SHINE
INVEN-TORY CHECK!
POSTERS I MADE!
CHECK!
BAG FOR CAPTUR-ING CREA-TURES!
CHECK!
PLEASE DON'T KILL HIM!
YOU HAVE 300 LUDA FOR SNACKS!
HAJIME, ARE BANANAS A SNACK?
THEY ARE NOT!
WHAT ABOUT YOUR BANANA, HAJI-ME?
NOPE!
BAD DIRTY JOKES ARE ALSO NOT A SNACK!
FRET
FRET
FRET
DID I MAKE A MISTAKE BY GIVING THIS GROUP THE REQUEST?!

ED THESE DIRTY JOKES SURE ARE PILING UP.

IT'S ABOUT FOUR TIMES LARGER THAN LAKE BIWA

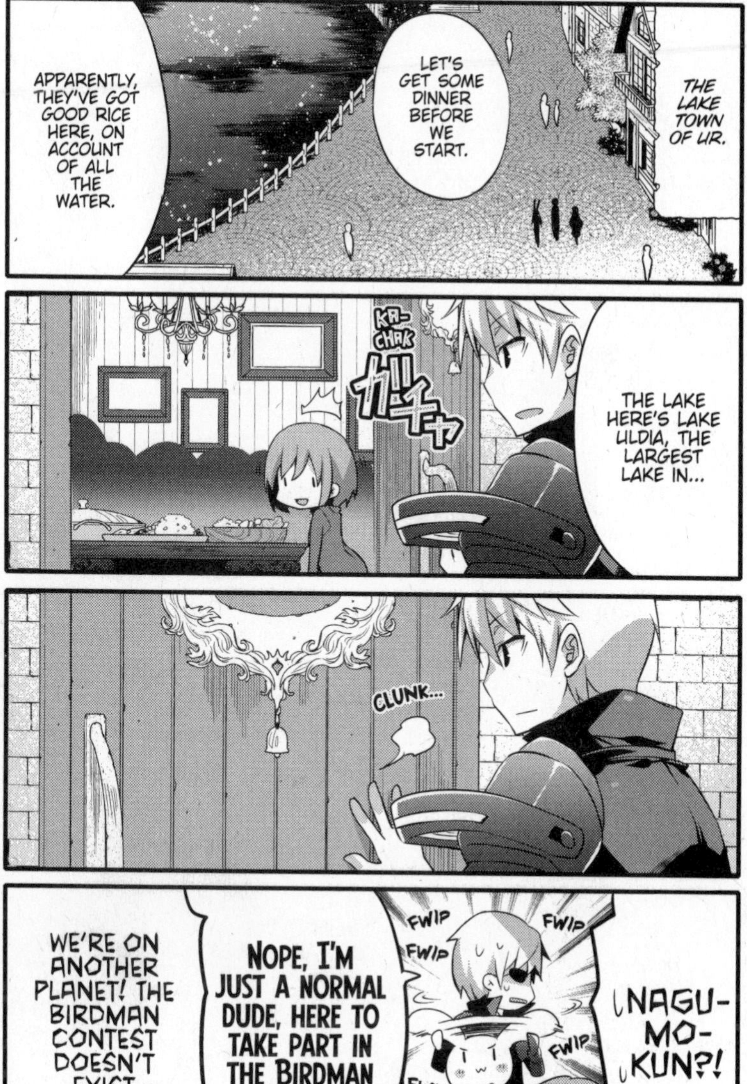
THE LAKE TOWN OF UR.
LET'S GET SOME DINNER BEFORE WE START.
APPARENTLY, THEY'VE GOT GOOD RICE HERE, ON ACCOUNT OF ALL THE WATER.
THE LAKE HERE'S LAKE ULDIA, THE LARGEST LAKE IN...
KA-CHAK
CLUNK...
NAGUMO-KUN?!
FWIP
FWIP
FWIP
FWIP
FWIP
NOPE, I'M JUST A NORMAL DUDE, HERE TO TAKE PART IN THE BIRDMAN CONTEST.
WE'RE ON ANOTHER PLANET! THE BIRDMAN CONTEST DOESN'T EXIST HERE!!

ED

BET HE'D BE COMPETING FOR DISTANCE.

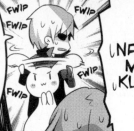

FROM COMMONPLACE SOAP OPERA TO WORLD'S STRONGEST

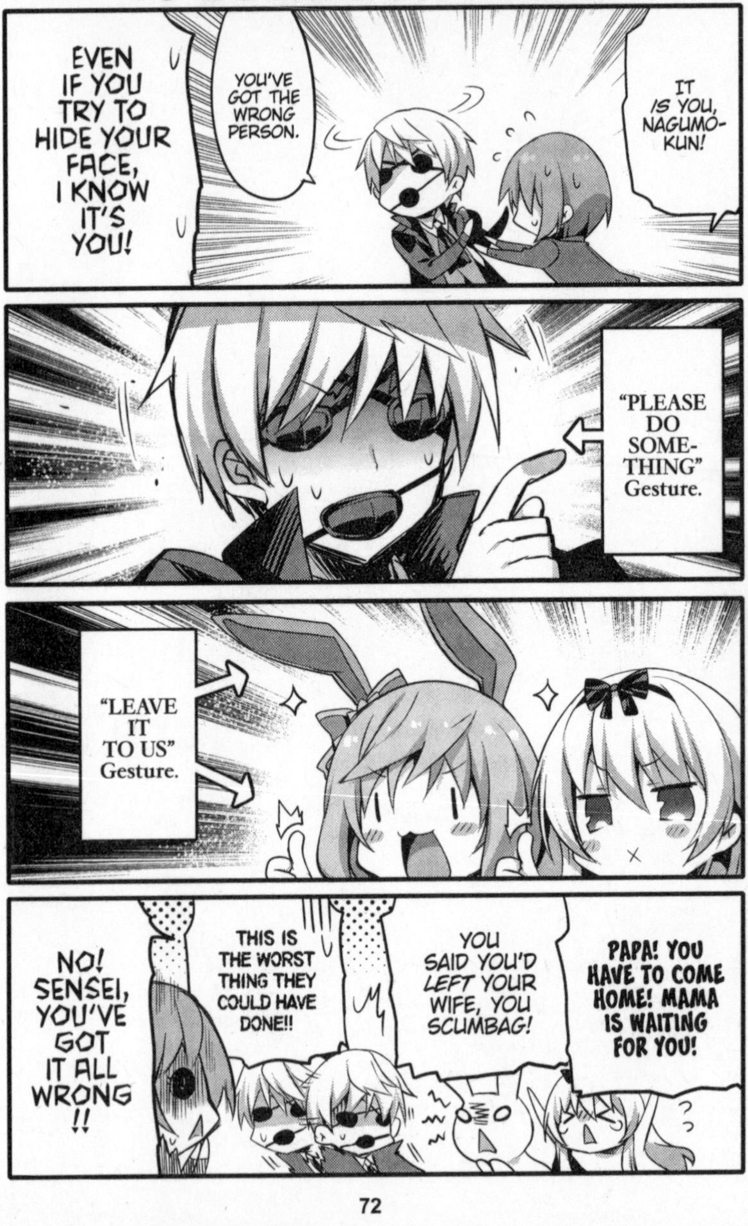
IT IS YOU, NAGUMO-KUN!
YOU'VE GOT THE WRONG PERSON.
EVEN IF YOU TRY TO HIDE YOUR FACE, I KNOW IT'S YOU!
"PLEASE DO SOME-THING" Gesture.
"LEAVE IT TO US" Gesture.
PAPA! YOU HAVE TO COME HOME! MAMA IS WAITING FOR YOU!
YOU SAID YOU'D *LEFT* YOUR WIFE, YOU SCUMBAG!
THIS IS THE WORST THING THEY COULD HAVE DONE!!
NO! SENSEI, YOU'VE GOT IT ALL WRONG!!

THIS WAS THE ONE THING I WAS AFRAID OF...

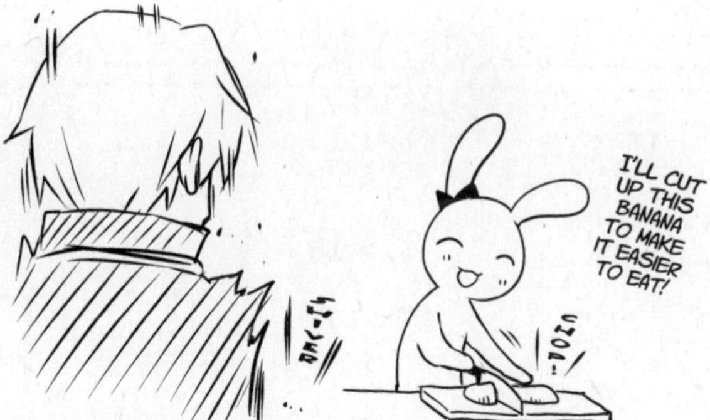
I'LL CUT UP THIS BANANA TO MAKE IT EASIER TO EAT!

ARIFURETA:

ARIFURETA SHOKUGYOU DE SEKAISAIKYOU

*. I ❤ Isekai *

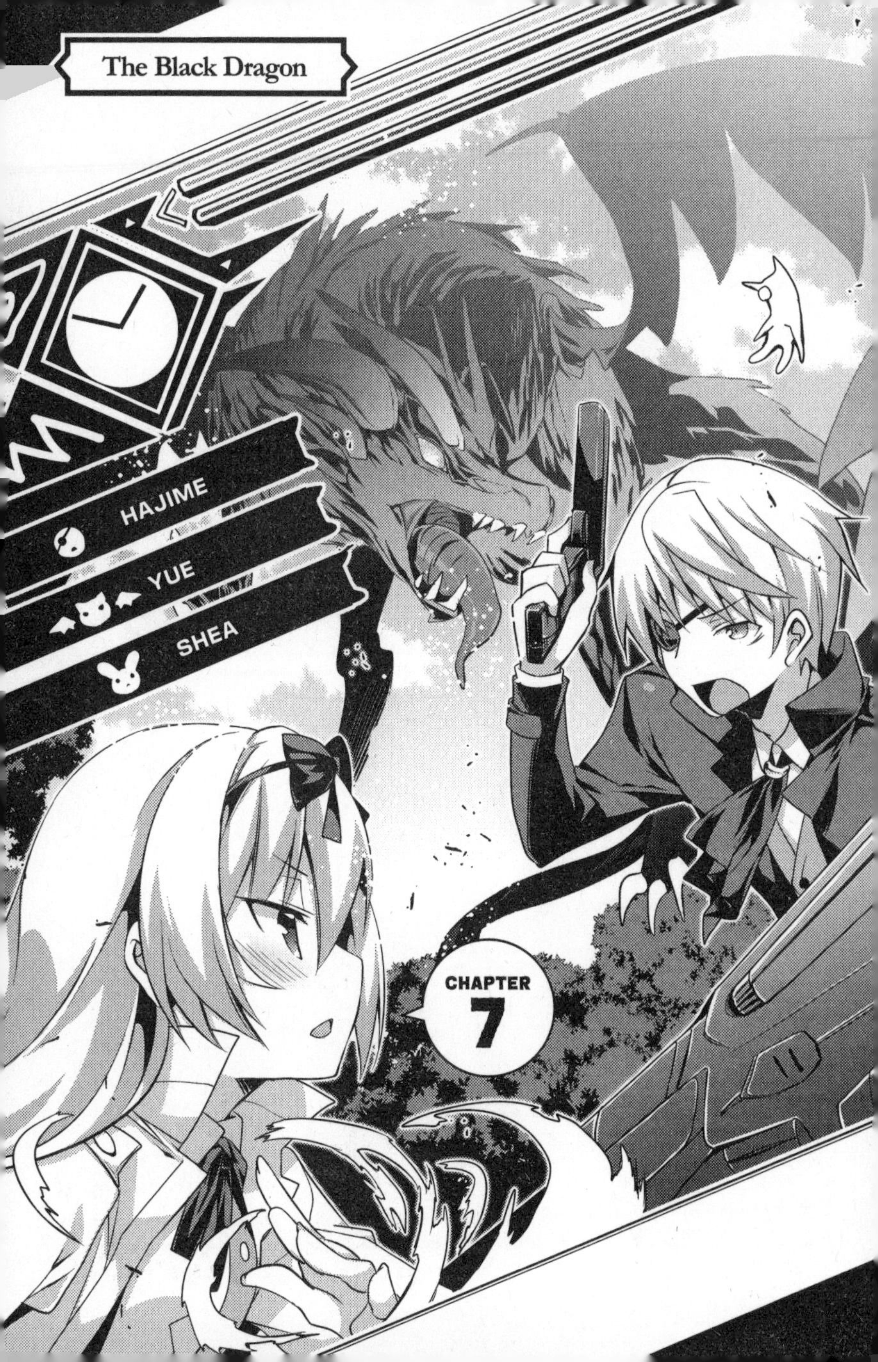
The Black Dragon
HAJIME
YUE
SHEA
CHAPTER
7

HE'S OBSESSED WITH IT

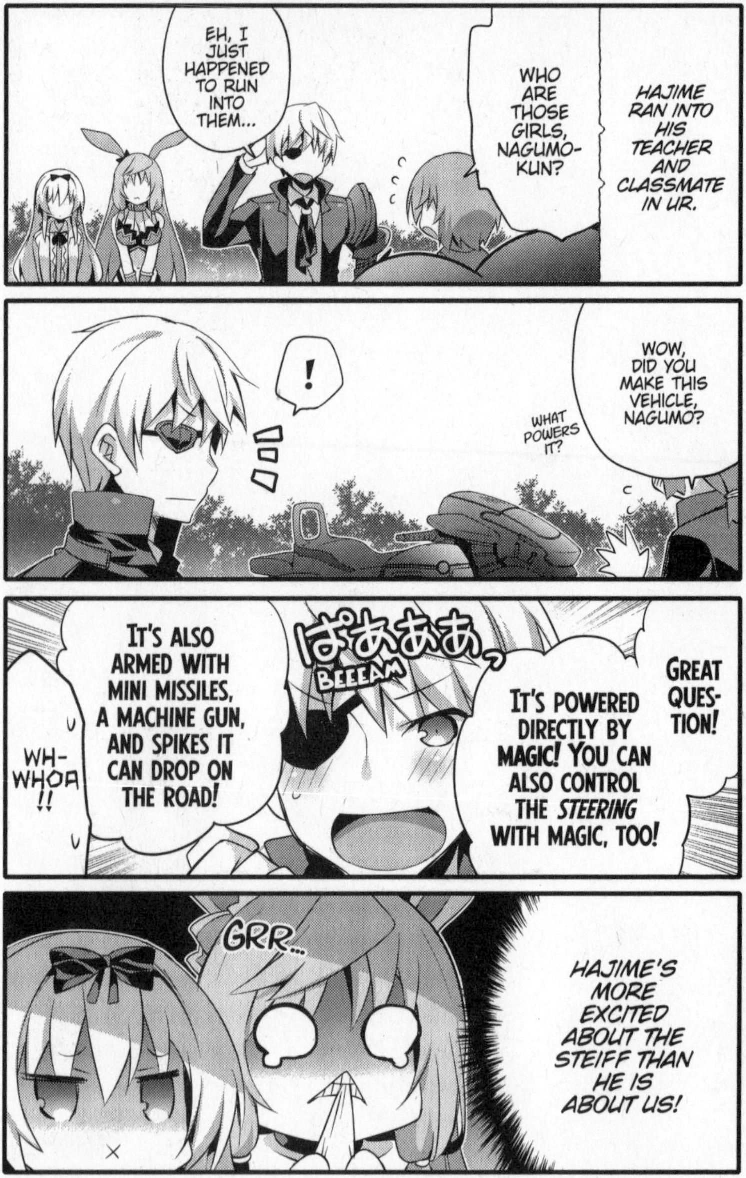

HAJIME RAN INTO HIS TEACHER AND CLASSMATE IN UR.
WHO ARE THOSE GIRLS, NAGUMO-KUN?
EH, I JUST HAPPENED TO RUN INTO THEM...
WOW, DID YOU MAKE THIS VEHICLE, NAGUMO?
WHAT POWERS IT?
!
GREAT QUES-TION!
IT'S POWERED DIRECTLY BY MAGIC! YOU CAN ALSO CONTROL THE *STEERING* WITH MAGIC, TOO!
ぱあああっ
BEEEAM
IT'S ALSO ARMED WITH MINI MISSILES, A MACHINE GUN, AND SPIKES IT CAN DROP ON THE ROAD!
WH-WHOA!!
HAJIME'S MORE EXCITED ABOUT THE STEIFF THAN HE IS ABOUT US!
GRR...

ED IT SURE IS FUN TALKING ABOUT YOUR PASSIONS!

A LETTER FROM NAGUMO HAJIME

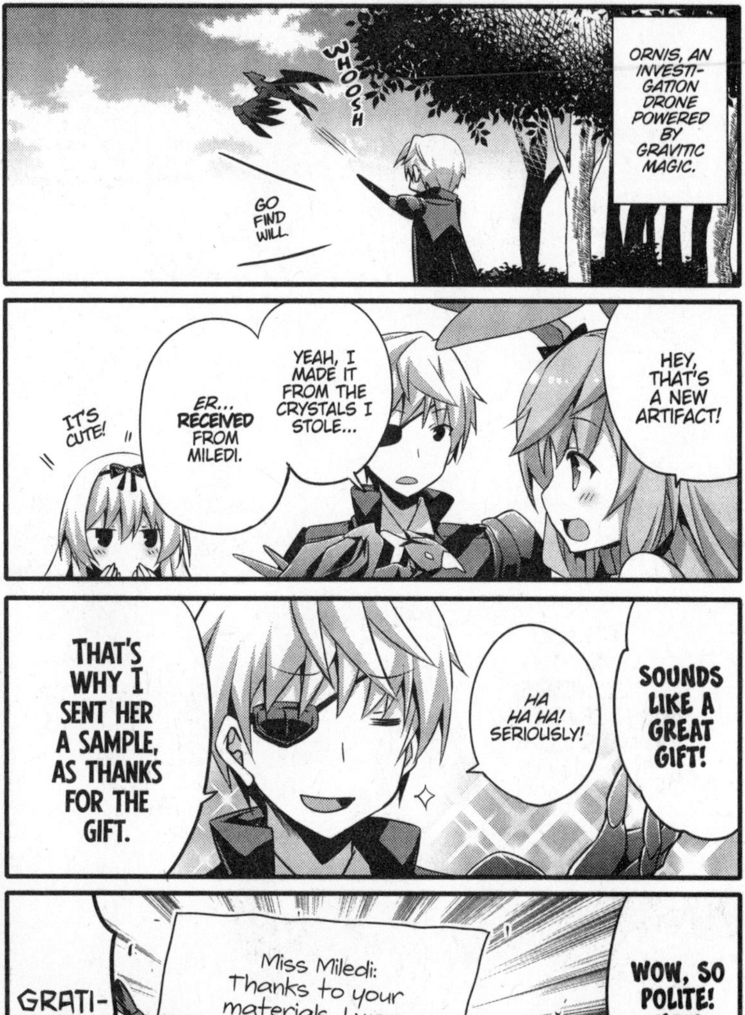
ORNIS, AN INVESTI-GATION DRONE POWERED BY GRAVITIC MAGIC.
WHOOOSH
GO FIND WILL.
HEY, THAT'S A NEW ARTIFACT!
YEAH, I MADE IT FROM THE CRYSTALS I STOLE...
ER... RECEIVED FROM MILEDI.
IT'S CUTE!
SOUNDS LIKE A GREAT GIFT!
HA HA HA! SERIOUSLY!
THAT'S WHY I SENT HER A SAMPLE, AS THANKS FOR THE GIFT.
WOW, SO POLITE! HOW MATURE!
Miss Miledi: Thanks to your materials, I was able to make a wondrous artifact. I've sent a sample to express my gratitude.
GRATI-TUDE, MY BUTT!!

ED HE SURE DOES WHAT HE WANTS...

HE'S NOT VERY ACCOMMODATING

ED

GUESS THERE ARE MOMMA'S BOYS IN PARALLEL WORLDS, TOO!

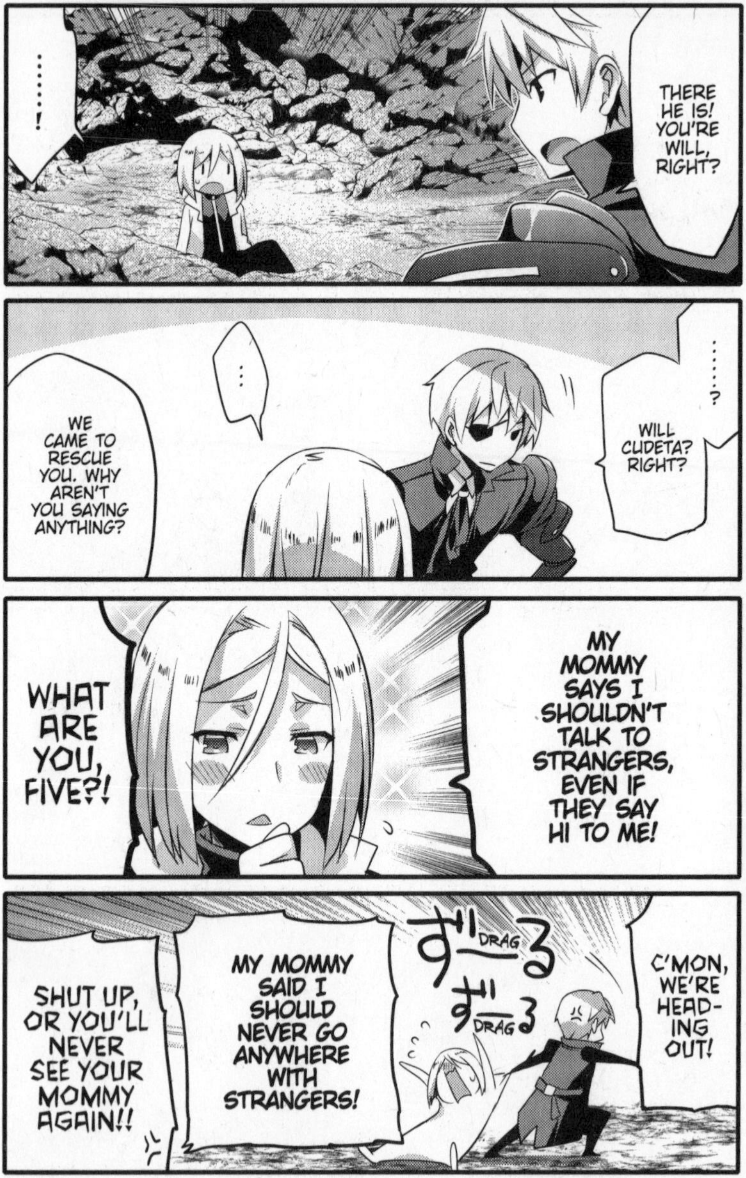

THERE HE IS! YOU'RE WILL, RIGHT?
……!
……?
WILL CUDETA? RIGHT?
…
WE CAME TO RESCUE YOU. WHY AREN'T YOU SAYING ANYTHING?
MY MOMMY SAYS I SHOULDN'T TALK TO STRANGERS, EVEN IF THEY SAY HI TO ME!
WHAT ARE YOU, FIVE?!
C'MON, WE'RE HEAD-ING OUT!
ずーる DRAG
ずーる DRAG
MY MOMMY SAID I SHOULD NEVER GO ANYWHERE WITH STRANGERS!
SHUT UP, OR YOU'LL NEVER SEE YOUR MOMMY AGAIN!!

MOMMY YUE

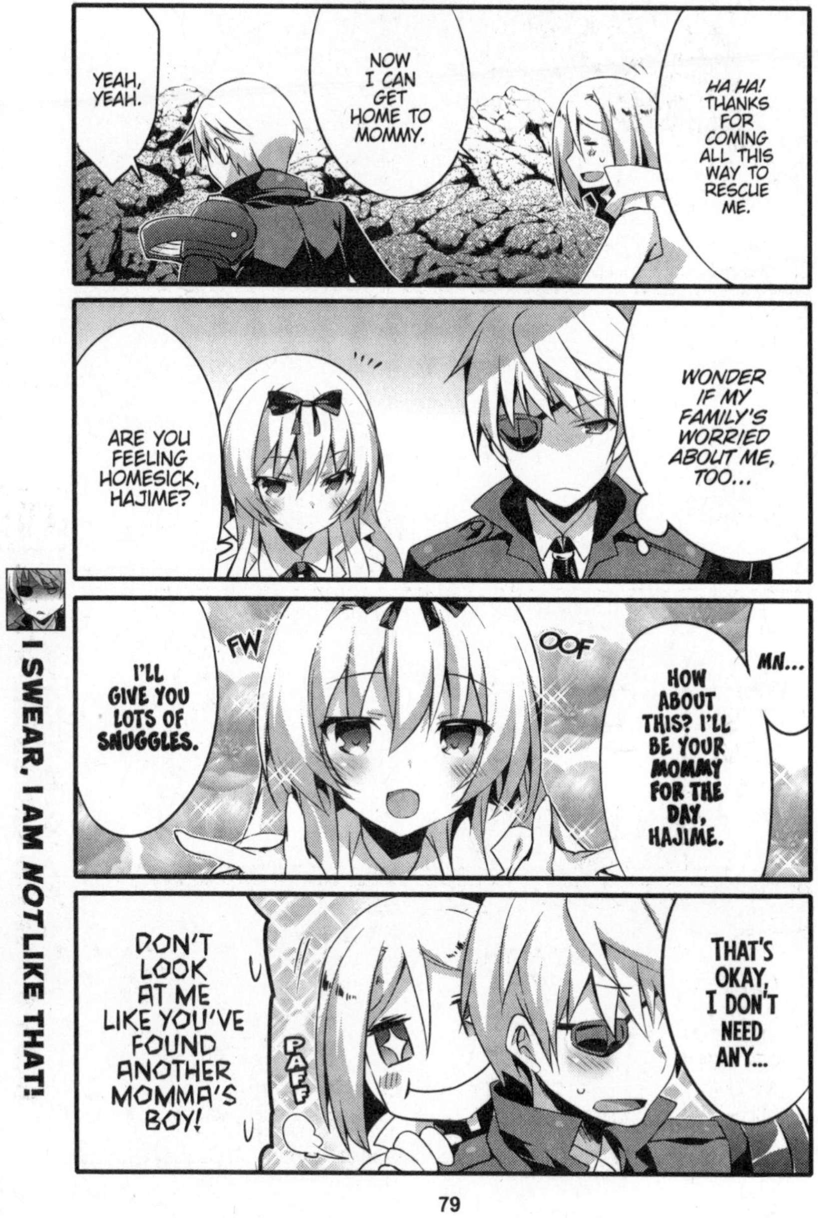
HA HA! THANKS FOR COMING ALL THIS WAY TO RESCUE ME.
NOW I CAN GET HOME TO MOMMY.
YEAH, YEAH.
WONDER IF MY FAMILY'S WORRIED ABOUT ME, TOO...
ARE YOU FEELING HOMESICK, HAJIME?
MN...
HOW ABOUT THIS? I'LL BE YOUR MOMMY FOR THE DAY, HAJIME.
FW OOF
I'LL GIVE YOU LOTS OF SNUGGLES.
THAT'S OKAY, I DON'T NEED ANY...
PAFF
DON'T LOOK AT ME LIKE YOU'VE FOUND ANOTHER MOMMA'S BOY!
I SWEAR, I AM NOT LIKE THAT!

MOMMY SHEA

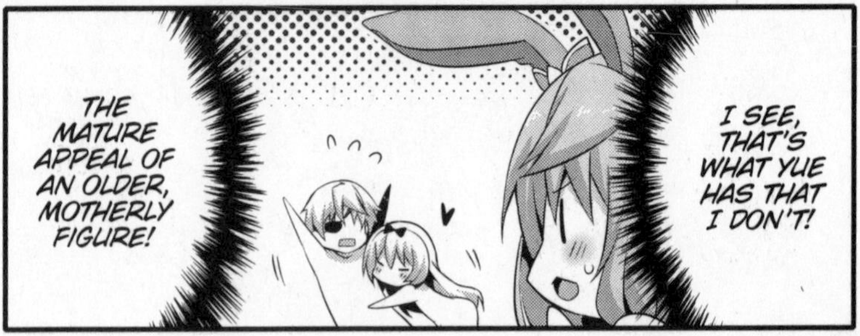
I SEE, THAT'S WHAT YUE HAS THAT I DON'T!
THE MATURE APPEAL OF AN OLDER, MOTHERLY FIGURE!

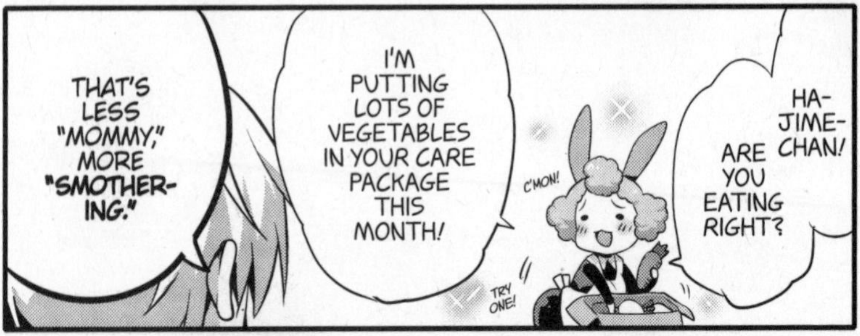
HA-JIME-CHAN!
ARE YOU EATING RIGHT?
C'MON!
TRY ONE!
I'M PUTTING LOTS OF VEGETABLES IN YOUR CARE PACKAGE THIS MONTH!
THAT'S LESS "MOMMY," MORE "SMOTHERING."

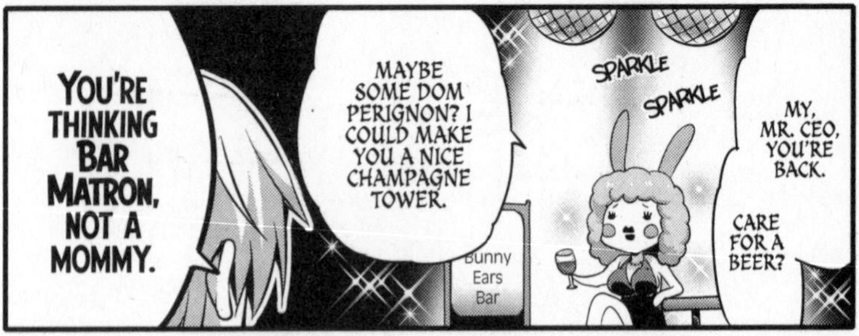
MY, MR. CEO, YOU'RE BACK.
CARE FOR A BEER?
SPARKLE
SPARKLE
Bunny Ears Bar
MAYBE SOME DOM PERIGNON? I COULD MAKE YOU A NICE CHAMPAGNE TOWER.
YOU'RE THINKING BAR MATRON, NOT A MOMMY.

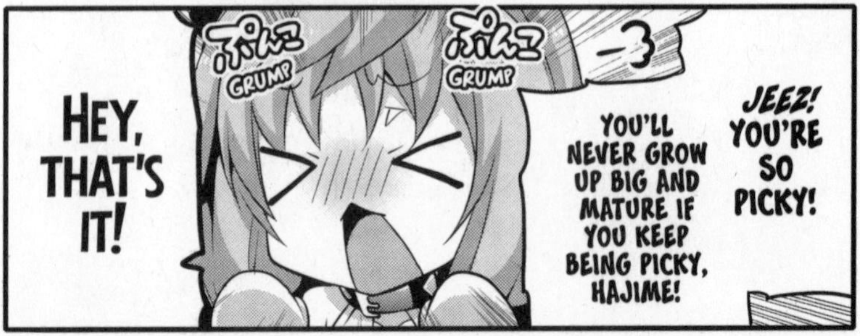
JEEZ! YOU'RE SO PICKY!
YOU'LL NEVER GROW UP BIG AND MATURE IF YOU KEEP BEING PICKY, HAJIME!
GRUMP
GRUMP
HEY, THAT'S IT!

MOMMY HAJIME

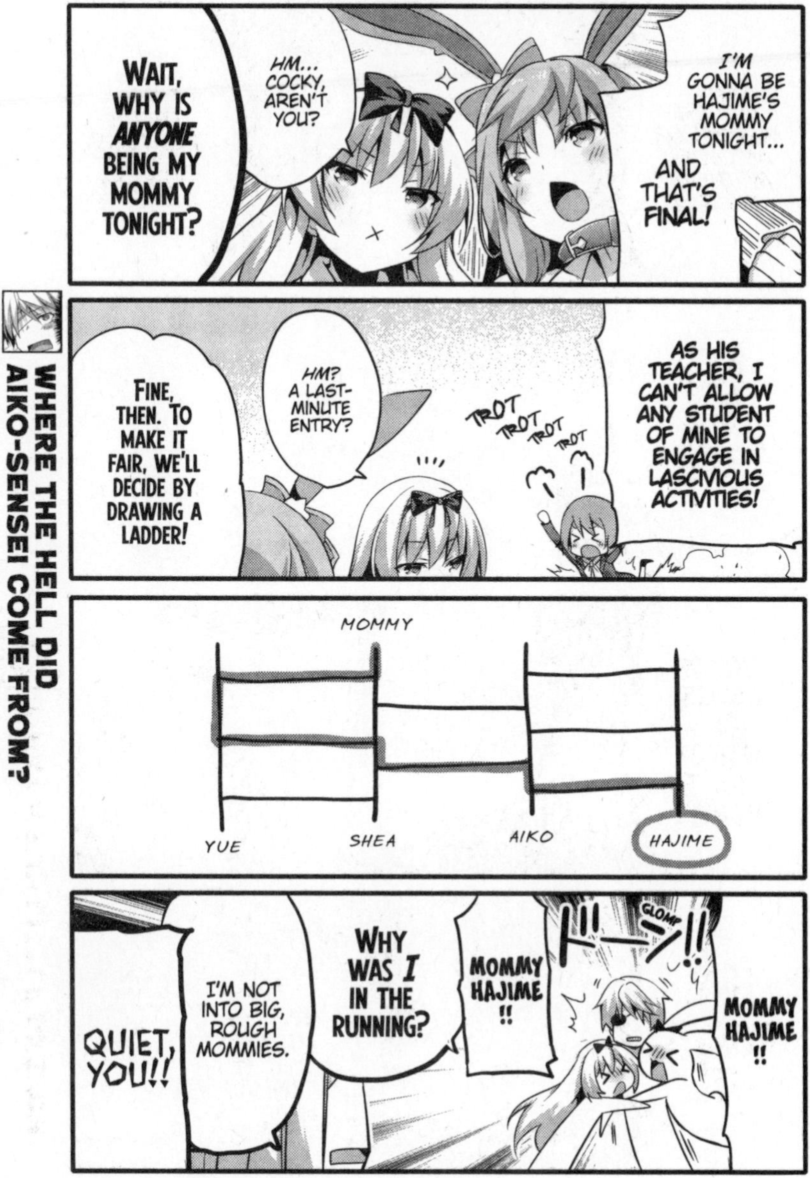
I'M GONNA BE HAJIME'S MOMMY TONIGHT...
AND THAT'S FINAL!
HM... COCKY, AREN'T YOU?
WAIT, WHY IS *ANYONE* BEING MY MOMMY TONIGHT?
AS HIS TEACHER, I CAN'T ALLOW ANY STUDENT OF MINE TO ENGAGE IN LASCIVIOUS ACTIVITIES!
TROT TROT TROT TROT
HM? A LAST-MINUTE ENTRY?
FINE, THEN. TO MAKE IT FAIR, WE'LL DECIDE BY DRAWING A LADDER!
MOMMY
YUE
SHEA
AIKO
HAJIME
MOMMY HAJIME!!
GLOMP
MOMMY HAJIME!!
WHY WAS *I* IN THE RUNNING?
I'M NOT INTO BIG, ROUGH MOMMIES.
QUIET, YOU!!
WHERE THE HELL DID AIKO-SENSEI COME FROM?

THE DRAGON AWAKENS

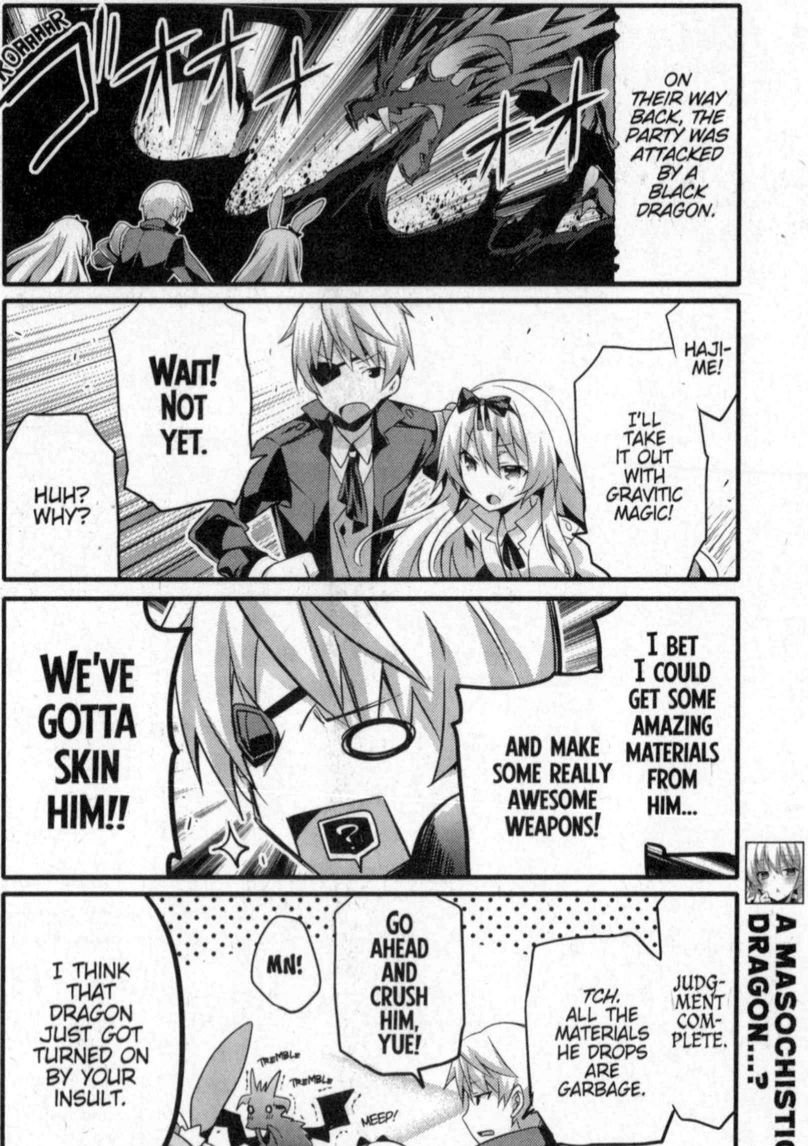
ON THEIR WAY BACK, THE PARTY WAS ATTACKED BY A BLACK DRAGON.
FROAAAAR
HAJI-ME!
I'LL TAKE IT OUT WITH GRAVITIC MAGIC!
WAIT! NOT YET.
HUH? WHY?
I BET I COULD GET SOME AMAZING MATERIALS FROM HIM...
AND MAKE SOME REALLY AWESOME WEAPONS!
WE'VE GOTTA SKIN HIM!!
JUDG-MENT COM-PLETE.
TCH. ALL THE MATERIALS HE DROPS ARE GARBAGE.
GO AHEAD AND CRUSH HIM, YUE!
MN!
MEEP!
TREMBLE
TREMBLE
I THINK THAT DRAGON JUST GOT TURNED ON BY YOUR INSULT.
A MASOCHISTIC DRAGON...?

THE INTERVIEW

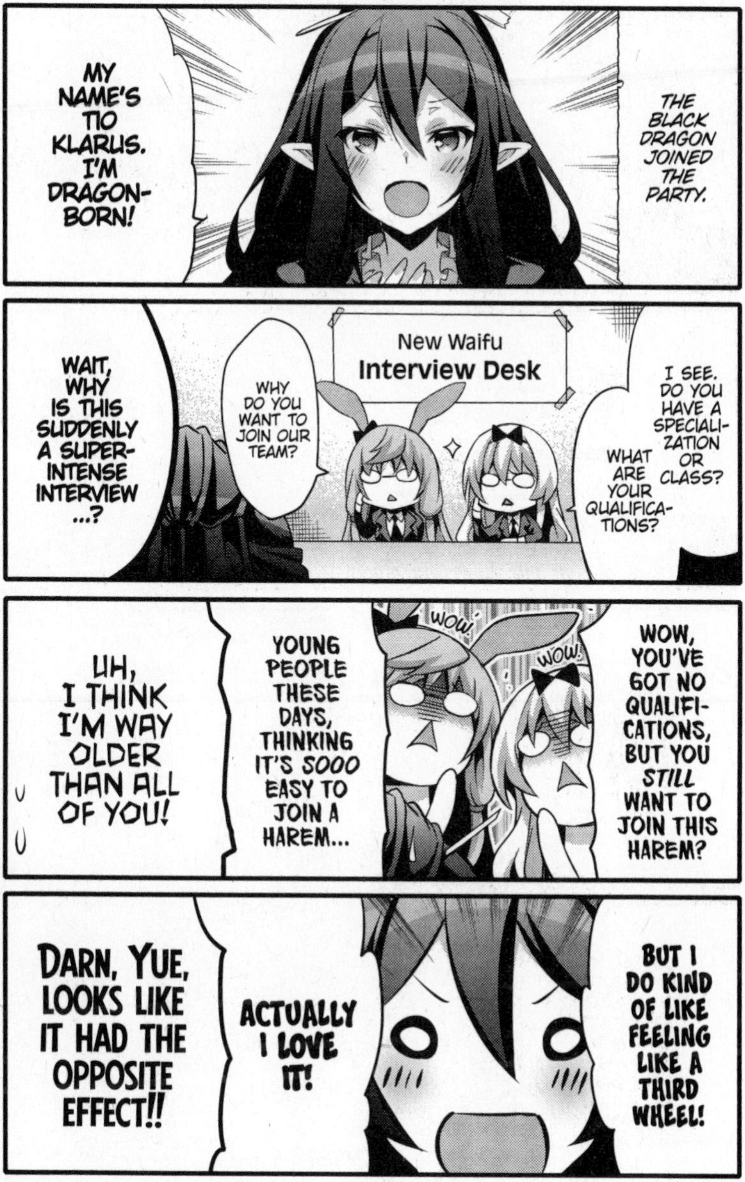

THE BLACK DRAGON JOINED THE PARTY.
MY NAME'S TIO KLARUS. I'M DRAGONBORN!
I SEE. DO YOU HAVE A SPECIALIZATION OR CLASS?
WHAT ARE YOUR QUALIFICATIONS?
New Waifu Interview Desk
WHY DO YOU WANT TO JOIN OUR TEAM?
WAIT, WHY IS THIS SUDDENLY A SUPER-INTENSE INTERVIEW ...?
WOW, YOU'VE GOT NO QUALIFICATIONS, BUT YOU STILL WANT TO JOIN THIS HAREM?
WOW!
WOW!
YOUNG PEOPLE THESE DAYS, THINKING IT'S SOOO EASY TO JOIN A HAREM...
UH, I THINK I'M WAY OLDER THAN ALL OF YOU!
BUT I DO KIND OF LIKE FEELING LIKE A THIRD WHEEL!
ACTUALLY I LOVE IT!
DARN, YUE, LOOKS LIKE IT HAD THE OPPOSITE EFFECT!!

ED SHE'S NOT THE TYPE TO BE DISCOURAGED.

HE'S MAKING GREAT PROGRESS

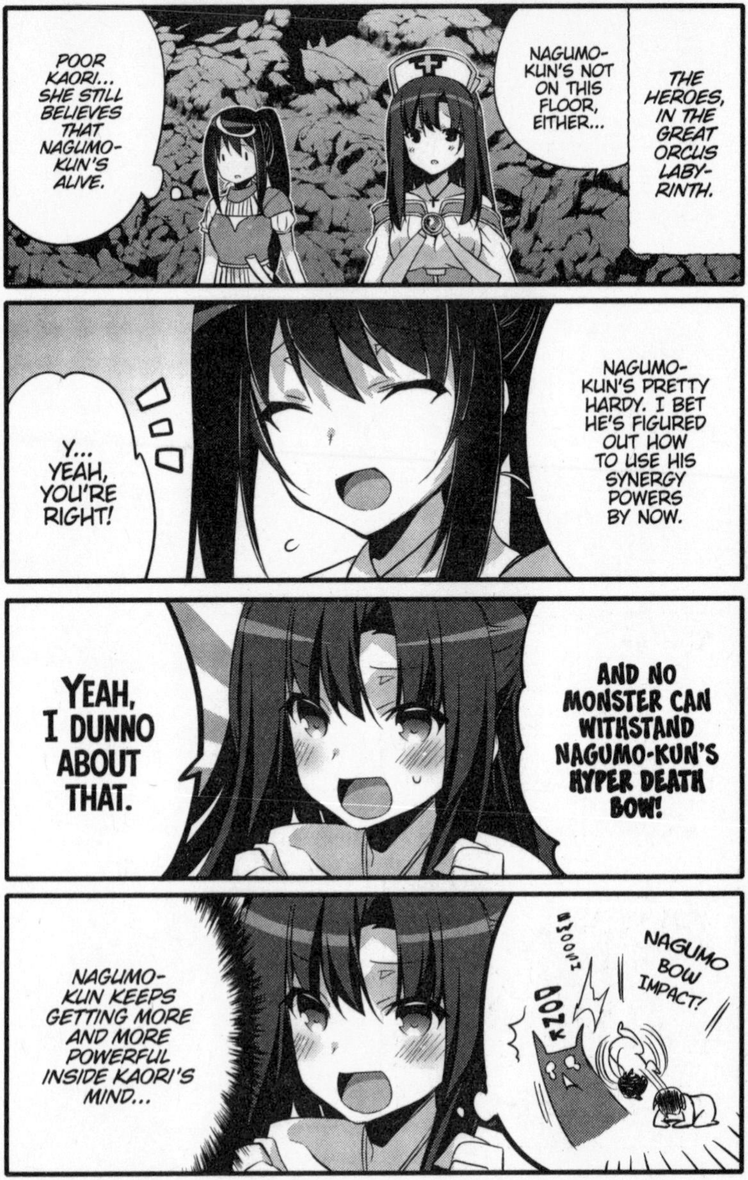
THE HEROES, IN THE GREAT ORCUS LABYRINTH.
NAGUMO-KUN'S NOT ON THIS FLOOR, EITHER...
POOR KAORI... SHE STILL BELIEVES THAT NAGUMO-KUN'S ALIVE.
NAGUMO-KUN'S PRETTY HARDY. I BET HE'S FIGURED OUT HOW TO USE HIS SYNERGY POWERS BY NOW.
Y... YEAH, YOU'RE RIGHT!
AND NO MONSTER CAN WITHSTAND NAGUMO-KUN'S HYPER DEATH BOW!
YEAH, I DUNNO ABOUT THAT.
NAGUMO BOW IMPACT!
NAGUMO-KUN KEEPS GETTING MORE AND MORE POWERFUL INSIDE KAORI'S MIND...

ED THE LONGER SHE'S WITHOUT HIM, THE GRANDER HER FANTASIES GROW...

Resume

Applying for: Hajime's Wife

Tio Klarus

Education and Work Experience

Dragonborn Princess
↓
Master's Sex Slave

Reason for Application

I want to

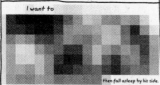

then fall asleep by his side.

Hobbies and Skills

ARIFURETA:

ARIFURETA SHOKUGYOU DE SEKAISAIKYOU

I ♥ Isekai

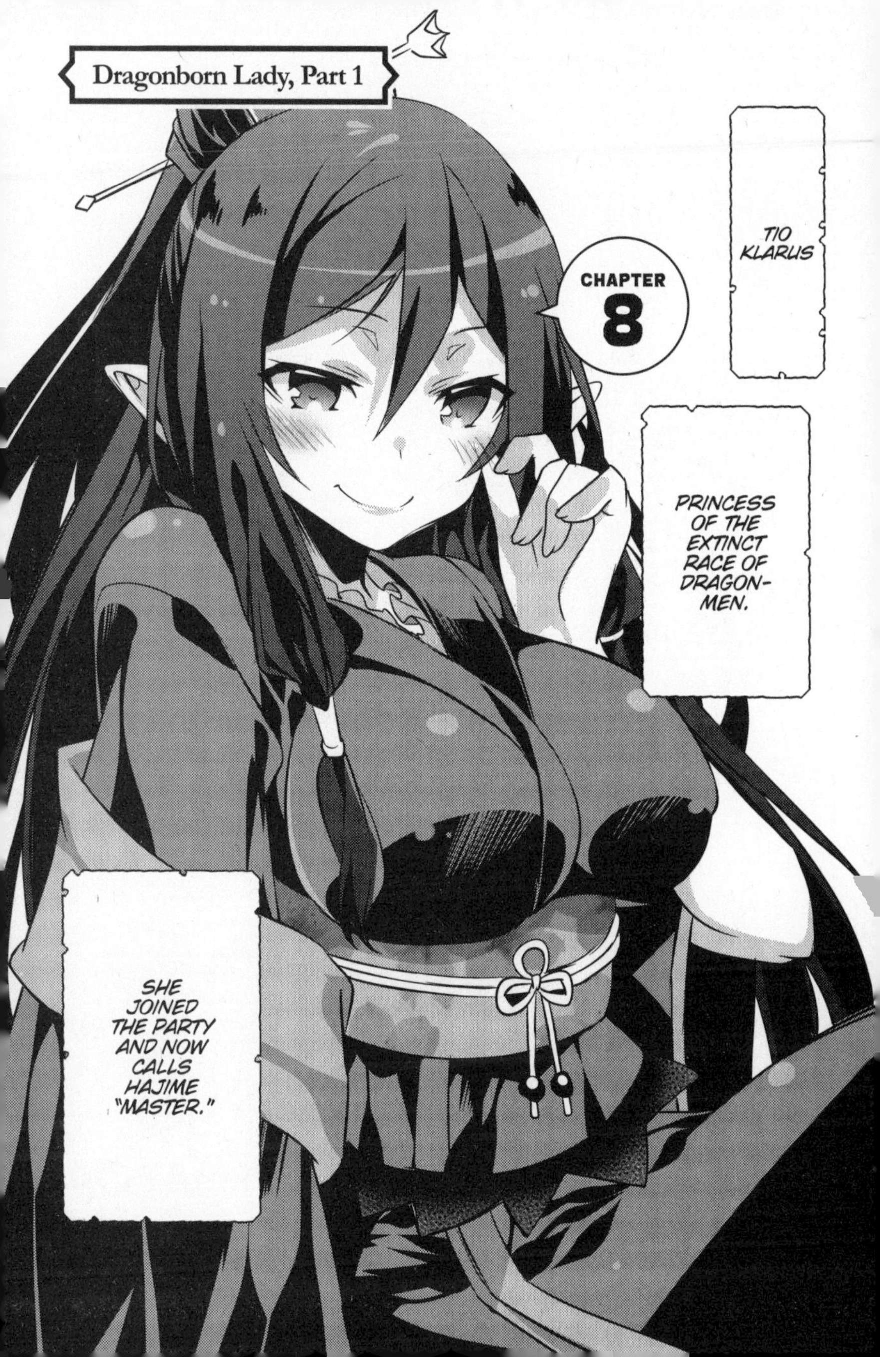
Dragonborn Lady, Part 1
CHAPTER 8
TIO KLARUS
PRINCESS OF THE EXTINCT RACE OF DRAGON-MEN.
SHE JOINED THE PARTY AND NOW CALLS HAJIME "MASTER."

MORE RIVALS, YAY!

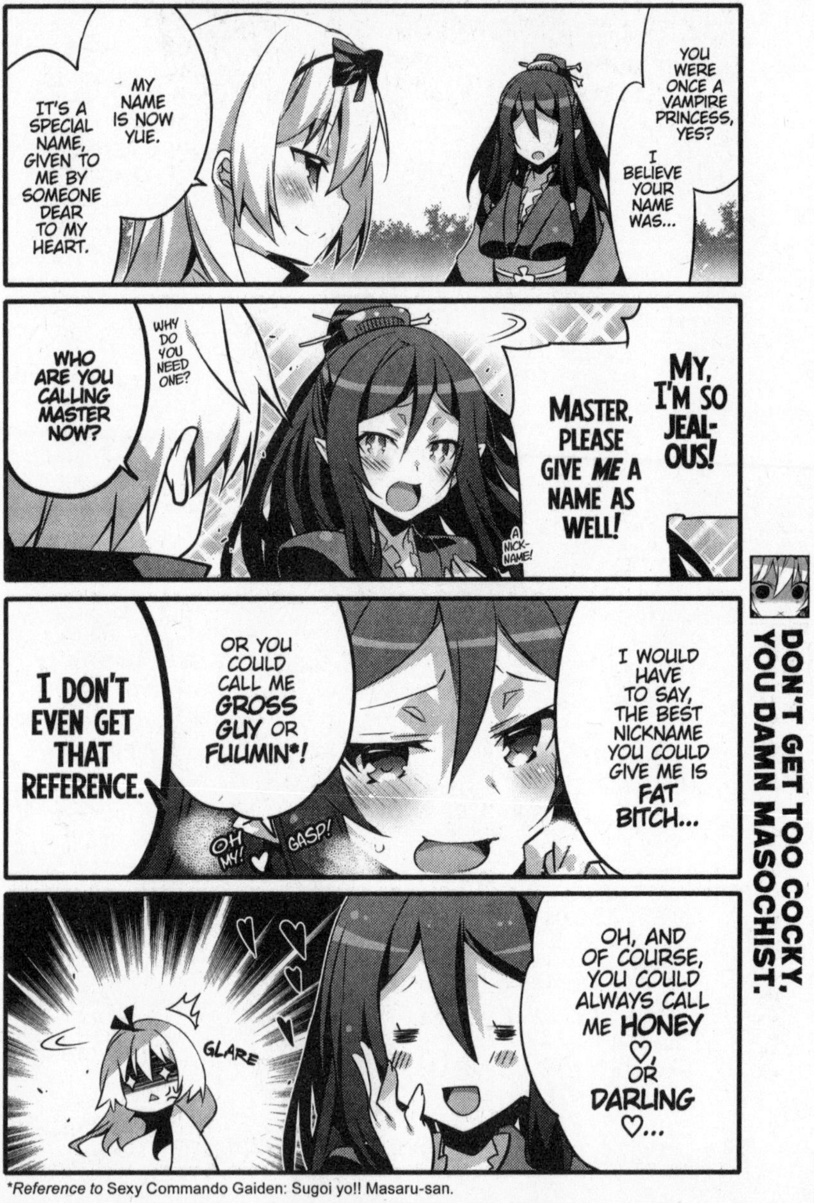
YOU WERE ONCE A VAMPIRE PRINCESS, YES?
I BELIEVE YOUR NAME WAS...
MY NAME IS NOW YUE.
IT'S A SPECIAL NAME, GIVEN TO ME BY SOMEONE DEAR TO MY HEART.
MY, I'M SO JEALOUS!
MASTER, PLEASE GIVE ME A NAME AS WELL!
A NICKNAME!
WHY DO YOU NEED ONE?
WHO ARE YOU CALLING MASTER NOW?
I WOULD HAVE TO SAY, THE BEST NICKNAME YOU COULD GIVE ME IS FAT BITCH...
GASP!
OH MY! ♡
OR YOU COULD CALL ME GROSS GUY OR FUUMIN*!
I DON'T EVEN GET THAT REFERENCE.
OH, AND OF COURSE, YOU COULD ALWAYS CALL ME HONEY ♡, OR DARLING ♡...
GLARE

DON'T GET TOO COCKY, YOU DAMN MASOCHIST.

*Reference to Sexy Commando Gaiden: Sugoi yo!! Masaru-san.

THE POWERFUL RACE OF DRAGONMEN

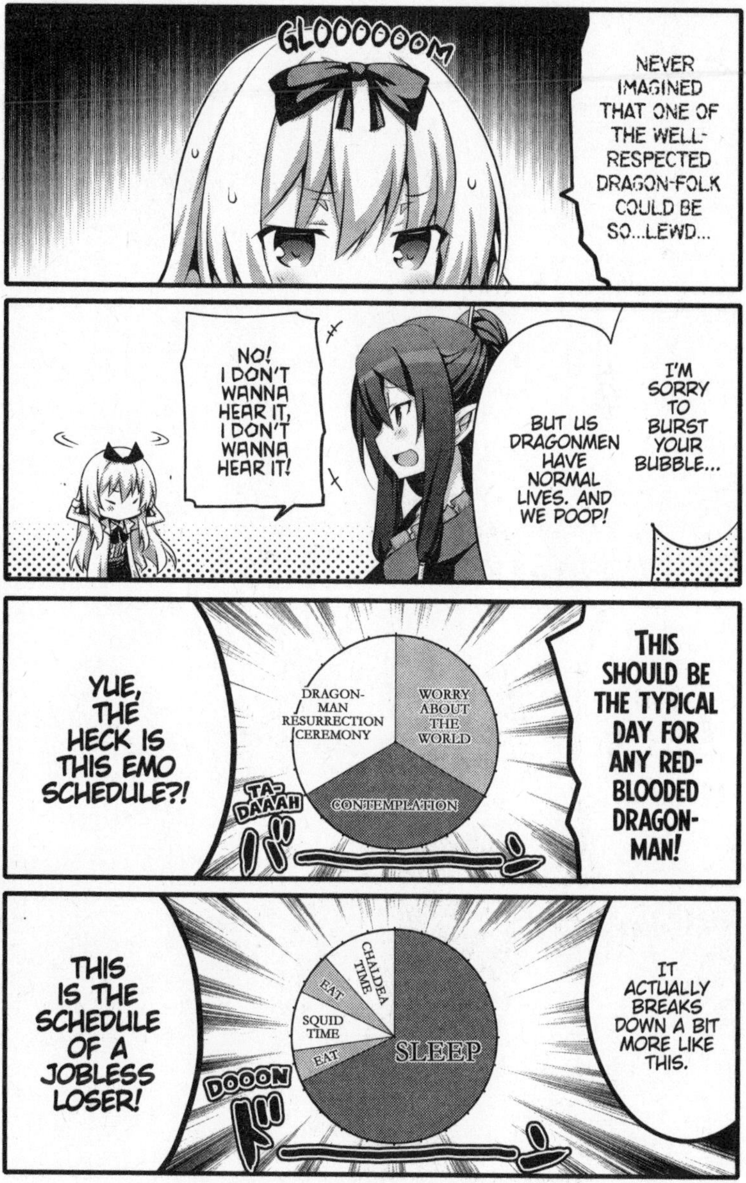
GLOOOOOOM
NEVER IMAGINED THAT ONE OF THE WELL-RESPECTED DRAGON-FOLK COULD BE SO...LEWD...
I'M SORRY TO BURST YOUR BUBBLE...
BUT US DRAGONMEN HAVE NORMAL LIVES. AND WE POOP!
NO! I DON'T WANNA HEAR IT, I DON'T WANNA HEAR IT!
THIS SHOULD BE THE TYPICAL DAY FOR ANY RED-BLOODED DRAGON-MAN!
WORRY ABOUT THE WORLD
DRAGON-MAN RESURRECTION CEREMONY
CONTEMPLATION
TA-DAAAH
YUE, THE HECK IS THIS EMO SCHEDULE?!
IT ACTUALLY BREAKS DOWN A BIT MORE LIKE THIS.
SLEEP
CHALDEA TIME
EAT
SQUID TIME
EAT
DOOON
THIS IS THE SCHEDULE OF A JOBLESS LOSER!

ED I WISH I COULD LIVE LIKE THAT!

NICE GROWTH

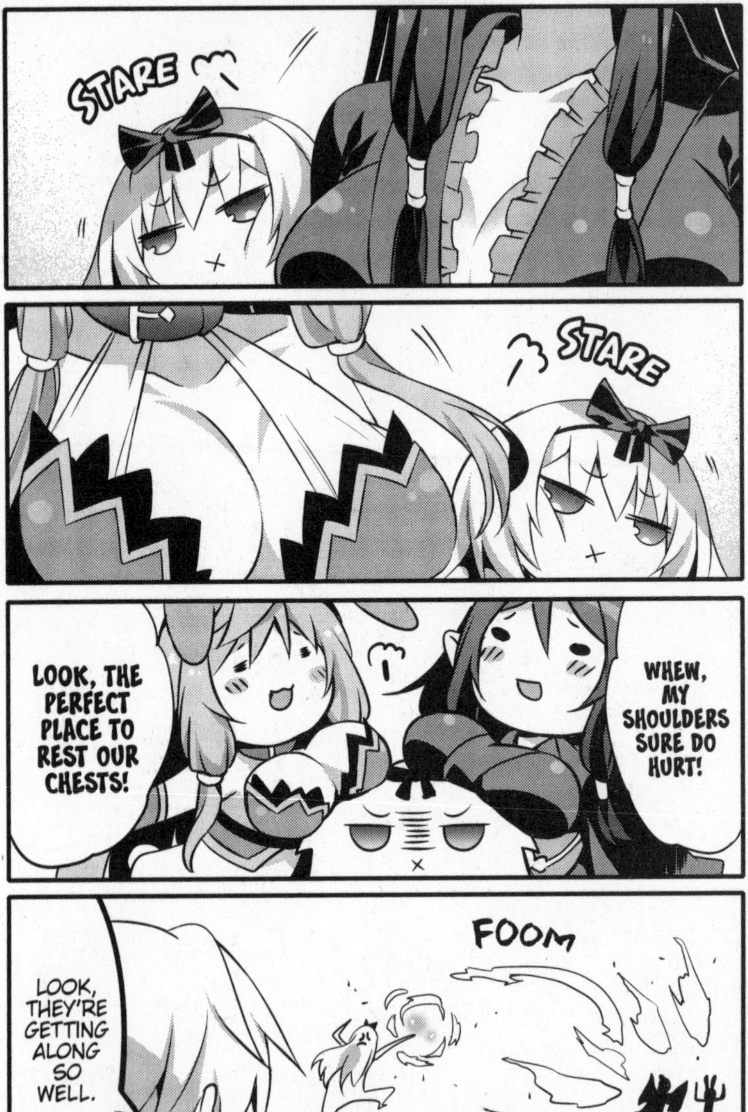
STARE
STARE
WHEW, MY SHOULDERS SURE DO HURT!
LOOK, THE PERFECT PLACE TO REST OUR CHESTS!
FOOM
LOOK, THEY'RE GETTING ALONG SO WELL.

ED I'VE GOT TWO HANDS YOU CAN USE AS A BOOB REST.

TELL THEM WHILE IT'S STILL FRESH

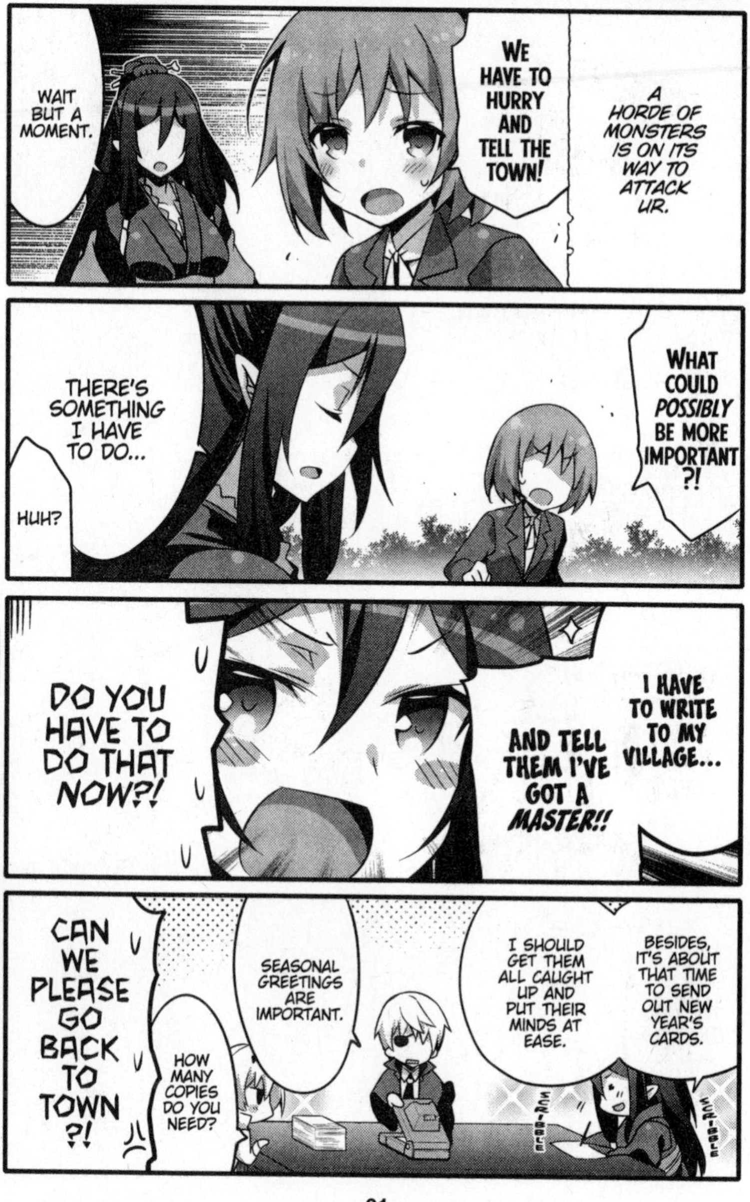

A HORDE OF MONSTERS IS ON ITS WAY TO ATTACK UR.
WE HAVE TO HURRY AND TELL THE TOWN!
WAIT BUT A MOMENT.
WHAT COULD *POSSIBLY* BE MORE IMPORTANT?!
THERE'S SOMETHING I HAVE TO DO...
HUH?
I HAVE TO WRITE TO MY VILLAGE...
AND TELL THEM I'VE GOT A *MASTER*!!
DO YOU HAVE TO DO THAT *NOW*?!
BESIDES, IT'S ABOUT THAT TIME TO SEND OUT NEW YEAR'S CARDS.
SCRIBBLE
I SHOULD GET THEM ALL CAUGHT UP AND PUT THEIR MINDS AT EASE.
SCRIBBLE
SEASONAL GREETINGS ARE IMPORTANT.
HOW MANY COPIES DO YOU NEED?
CAN WE PLEASE GO BACK TO TOWN?!

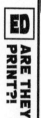

ED ARE THEY PRETENDING TO PRINT?!

THE LIMITS OF HIS HUMANITY

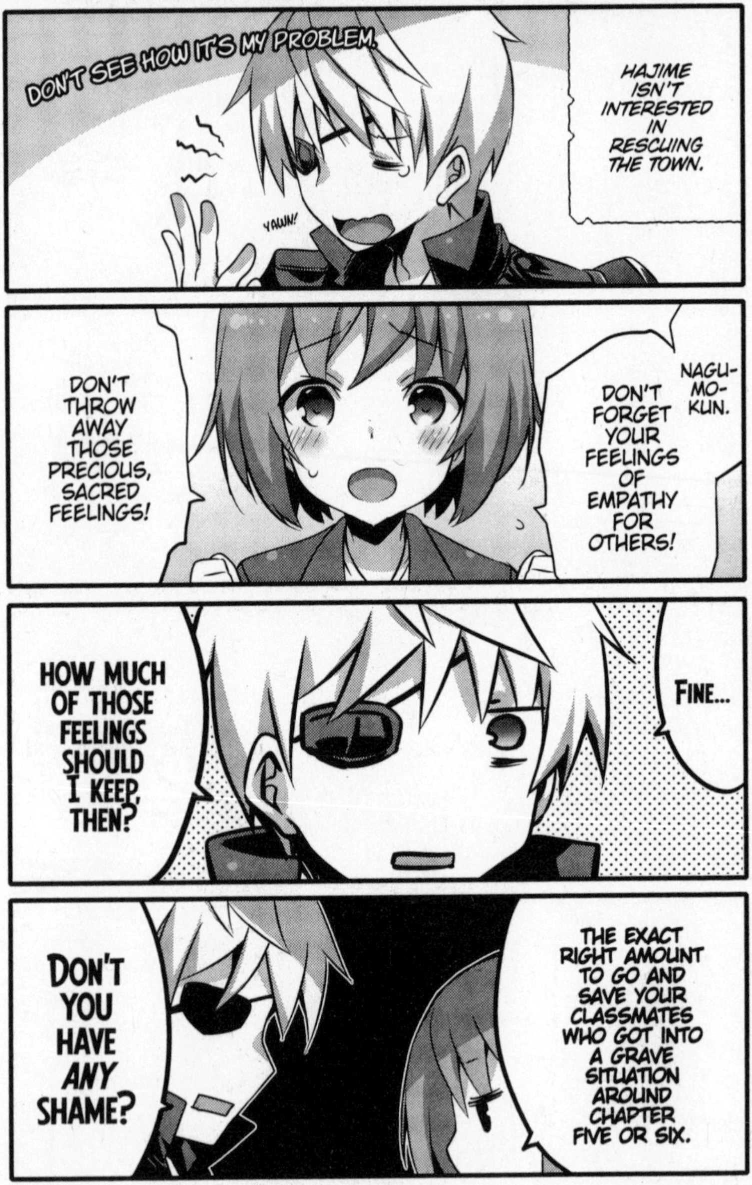
HAJIME ISN'T INTERESTED IN RESCUING THE TOWN.
DON'T SEE HOW IT'S MY PROBLEM.
YAWN!
NAGUMO-KUN.
DON'T FORGET YOUR FEELINGS OF EMPATHY FOR OTHERS!
DON'T THROW AWAY THOSE PRECIOUS, SACRED FEELINGS!
FINE...
HOW MUCH OF THOSE FEELINGS SHOULD I KEEP, THEN?
THE EXACT RIGHT AMOUNT TO GO AND SAVE YOUR CLASSMATES WHO GOT INTO A GRAVE SITUATION AROUND CHAPTER FIVE OR SIX.
DON'T YOU HAVE *ANY* SHAME?

ED SENSEI IS A PERSON, TOO!

LET'S PRESERVE THIS DRAWING

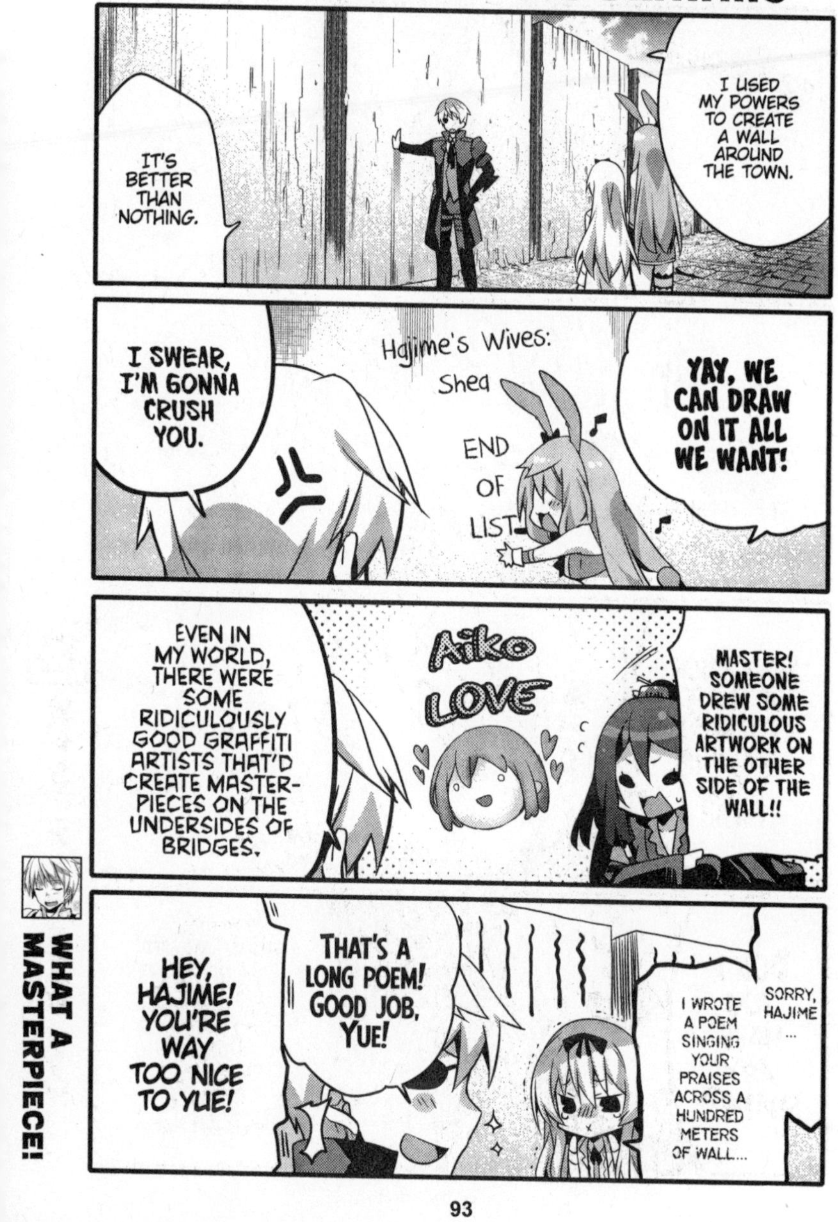
I USED MY POWERS TO CREATE A WALL AROUND THE TOWN.
IT'S BETTER THAN NOTHING.
YAY, WE CAN DRAW ON IT ALL WE WANT!
Hajime's Wives: Shea
END OF LIST
I SWEAR, I'M GONNA CRUSH YOU.
MASTER! SOMEONE DREW SOME RIDICULOUS ARTWORK ON THE OTHER SIDE OF THE WALL!!
Aiko
LOVE
EVEN IN MY WORLD, THERE WERE SOME RIDICULOUSLY GOOD GRAFFITI ARTISTS THAT'D CREATE MASTER-PIECES ON THE UNDERSIDES OF BRIDGES.
SORRY, HAJIME...
I WROTE A POEM SINGING YOUR PRAISES ACROSS A HUNDRED METERS OF WALL...
THAT'S A LONG POEM! GOOD JOB, YUE!
HEY, HAJIME! YOU'RE WAY TOO NICE TO YUE!

WHAT A MASTERPIECE!

SERVED WITH AFTERNOON FRAGRANCE AND HERBAL TEA

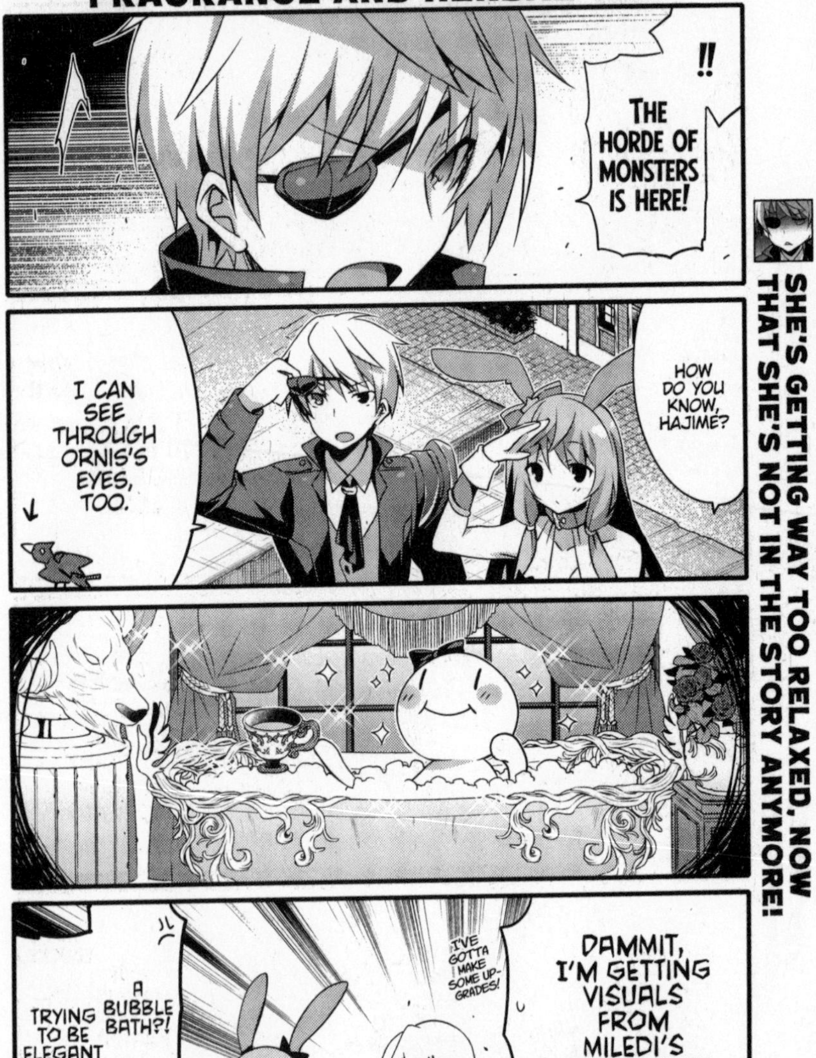
!!
THE HORDE OF MONSTERS IS HERE!
HOW DO YOU KNOW, HAJIME?
I CAN SEE THROUGH ORNIS'S EYES, TOO.
DAMMIT, I'M GETTING VISUALS FROM MILEDI'S ORNIS MIXED IN WITH EVERYTHING!
I'VE GOTTA MAKE SOME UP-GRADES!
A BUBBLE BATH?!
TRYING TO BE ELEGANT OR SOME-THING?!
SHE'S GETTING WAY TOO RELAXED, NOW THAT SHE'S NOT IN THE STORY ANYMORE!

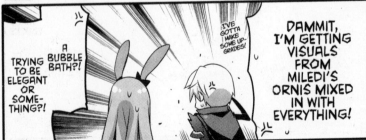

THE GRASS IS ALWAYS GREENER

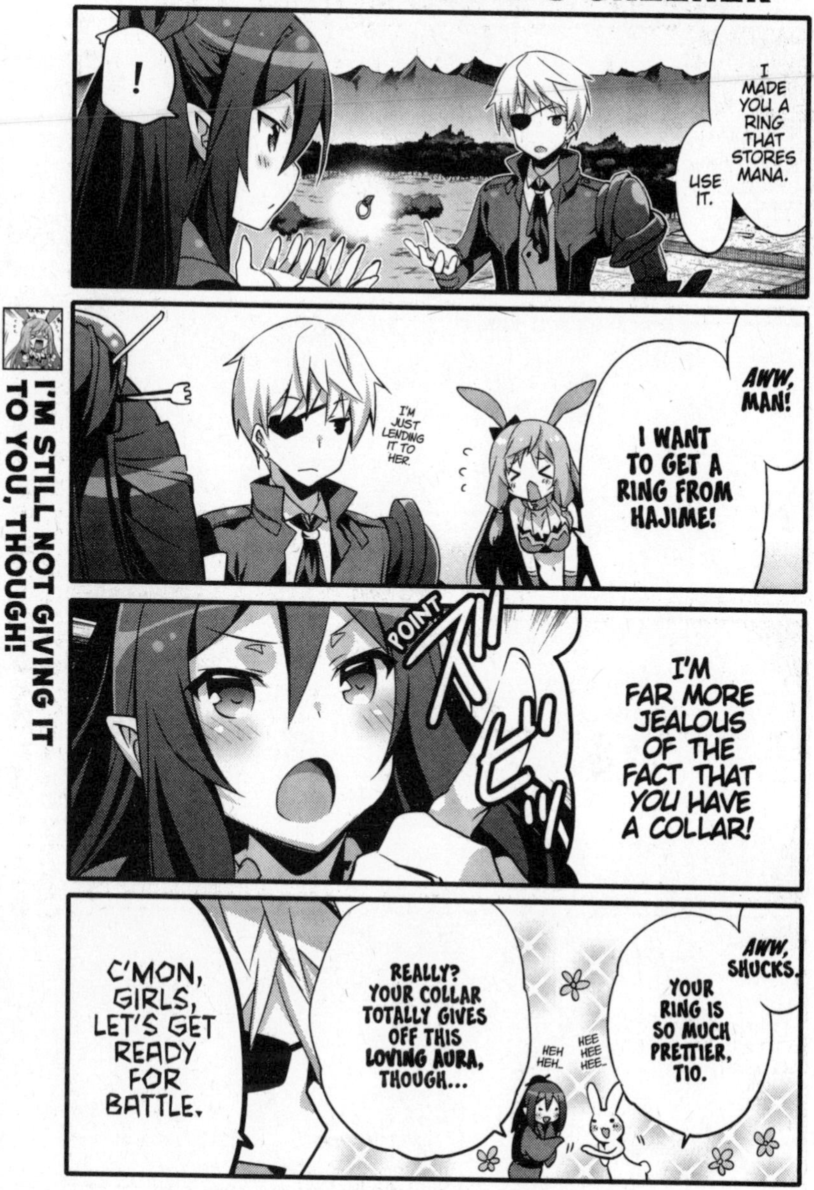
I MADE YOU A RING THAT STORES MANA.
USE IT.
!
AWW, MAN!
I WANT TO GET A RING FROM HAJIME!
I'M JUST LENDING IT TO HER.
POINT
I'M FAR MORE JEALOUS OF THE FACT THAT YOU HAVE A COLLAR!
AWW, SHUCKS.
YOUR RING IS SO MUCH PRETTIER, TIO.
HEE HEE HEE...
HEH HEH...
REALLY? YOUR COLLAR TOTALLY GIVES OFF THIS LOVING AURA, THOUGH...
C'MON, GIRLS, LET'S GET READY FOR BATTLE.
I'M STILL NOT GIVING IT TO YOU, THOUGH!

THEY AUCTIONED IT FOR THIRTY MILLION

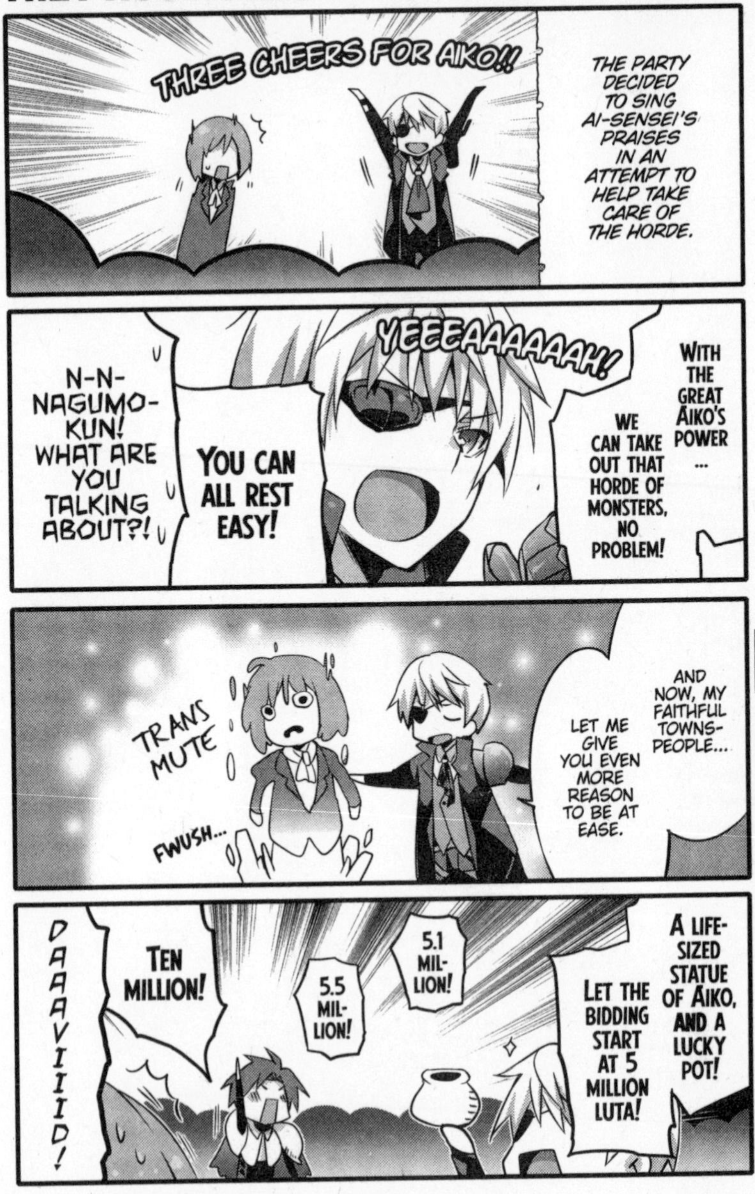
THE PARTY DECIDED TO SING AI-SENSEI'S PRAISES IN AN ATTEMPT TO HELP TAKE CARE OF THE HORDE.
THREE CHEERS FOR AIKO!!
WITH THE GREAT AIKO'S POWER ...
WE CAN TAKE OUT THAT HORDE OF MONSTERS, NO PROBLEM!
YEEEAAAAAAH!
YOU CAN ALL REST EASY!
N-N-NAGUMO-KUN! WHAT ARE YOU TALKING ABOUT?!
AND NOW, MY FAITHFUL TOWNSPEOPLE...
LET ME GIVE YOU EVEN MORE REASON TO BE AT EASE.
TRANS MUTE
FWUSH...
A LIFE-SIZED STATUE OF AIKO, AND A LUCKY POT!
LET THE BIDDING START AT 5 MILLION LUTA!
5.1 MILLION!
5.5 MILLION!
TEN MILLION!
DAAAAVIIIID!

ED IT'S LIKE AN AUCTION AT MAXXX*AXXBI.

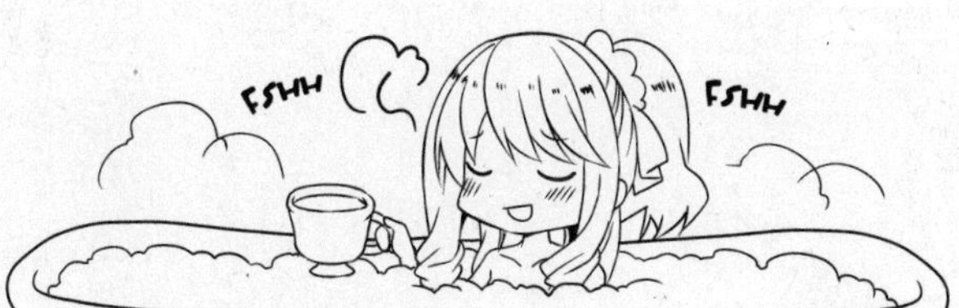
FSHH
FSHH

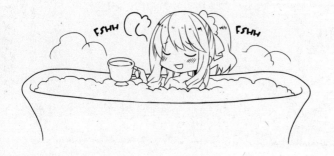

ARIFURETA:
ARIFURETA SHOKUGYOU DE SEKAISAIKYOU

. I ♥ Isekai *.*

CHAPTER 9

Dragonborn Lady, Part 2

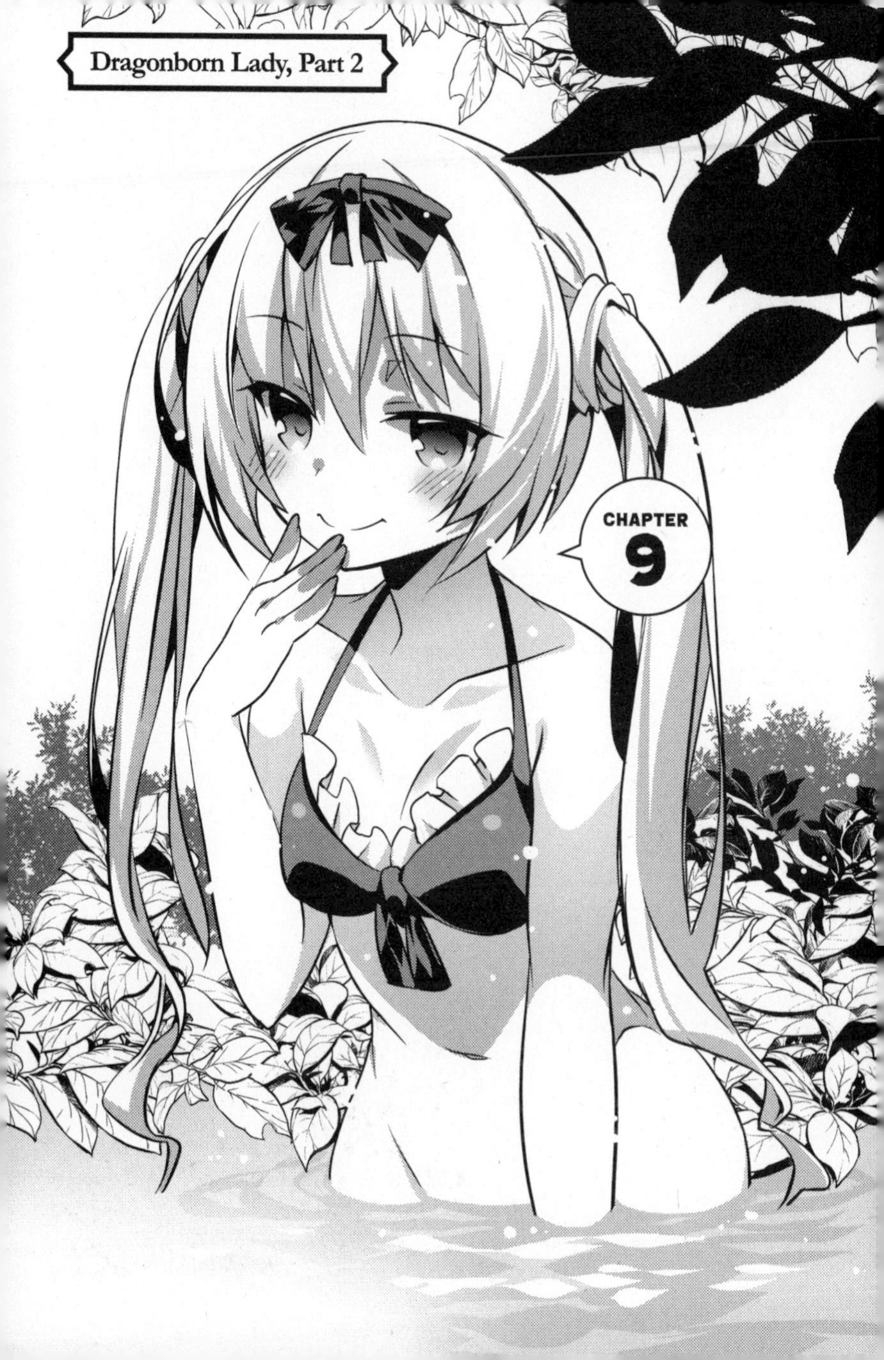

ARTIFACTS CAN DO EVERYTHING

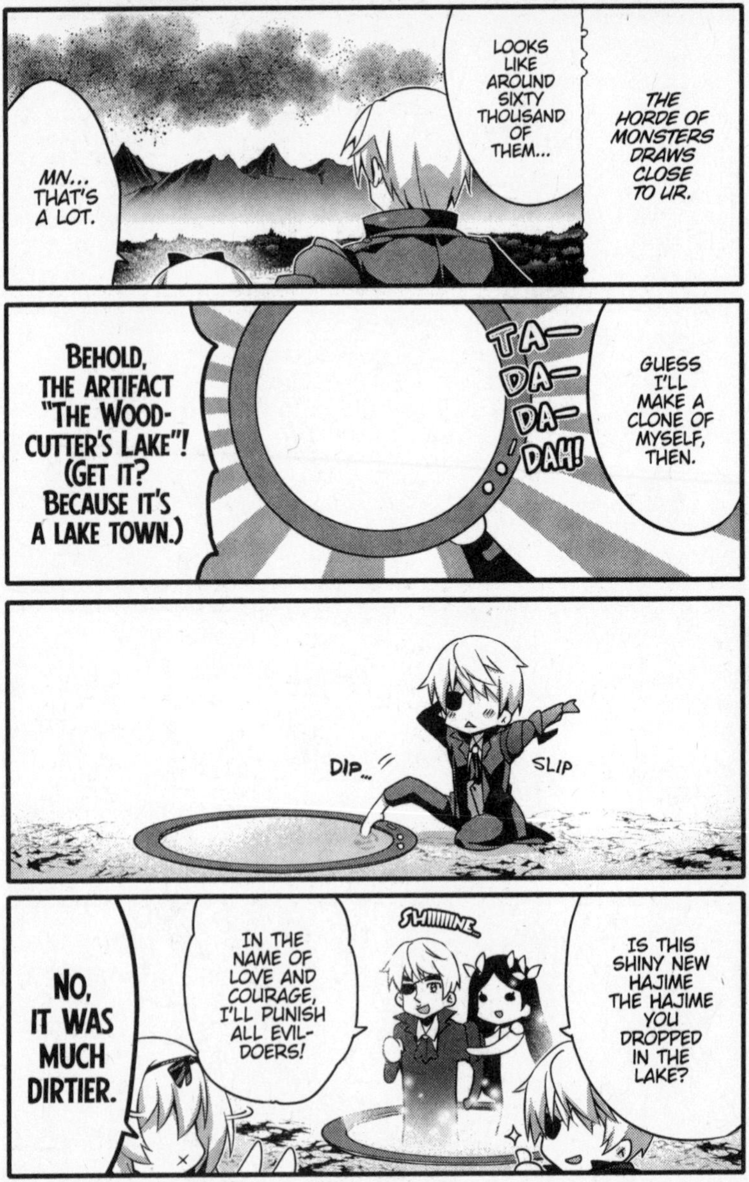
THE HORDE OF MONSTERS DRAWS CLOSE TO UR.
LOOKS LIKE AROUND SIXTY THOUSAND OF THEM...
MN... THAT'S A LOT.
GUESS I'LL MAKE A CLONE OF MYSELF, THEN.
TA-DA-DA-DAH!
BEHOLD, THE ARTIFACT "THE WOOD-CUTTER'S LAKE"! (GET IT? BECAUSE IT'S A LAKE TOWN.)
SLIP
DIP...
IS THIS SHINY NEW HAJIME THE HAJIME YOU DROPPED IN THE LAKE?
SHIIIIIINE
IN THE NAME OF LOVE AND COURAGE, I'LL PUNISH ALL EVIL-DOERS!
NO, IT WAS MUCH DIRTIER.

ED THAT'S A SEXY POSE THERE IN PANEL 3.

A MORE HEROIC HAJIME

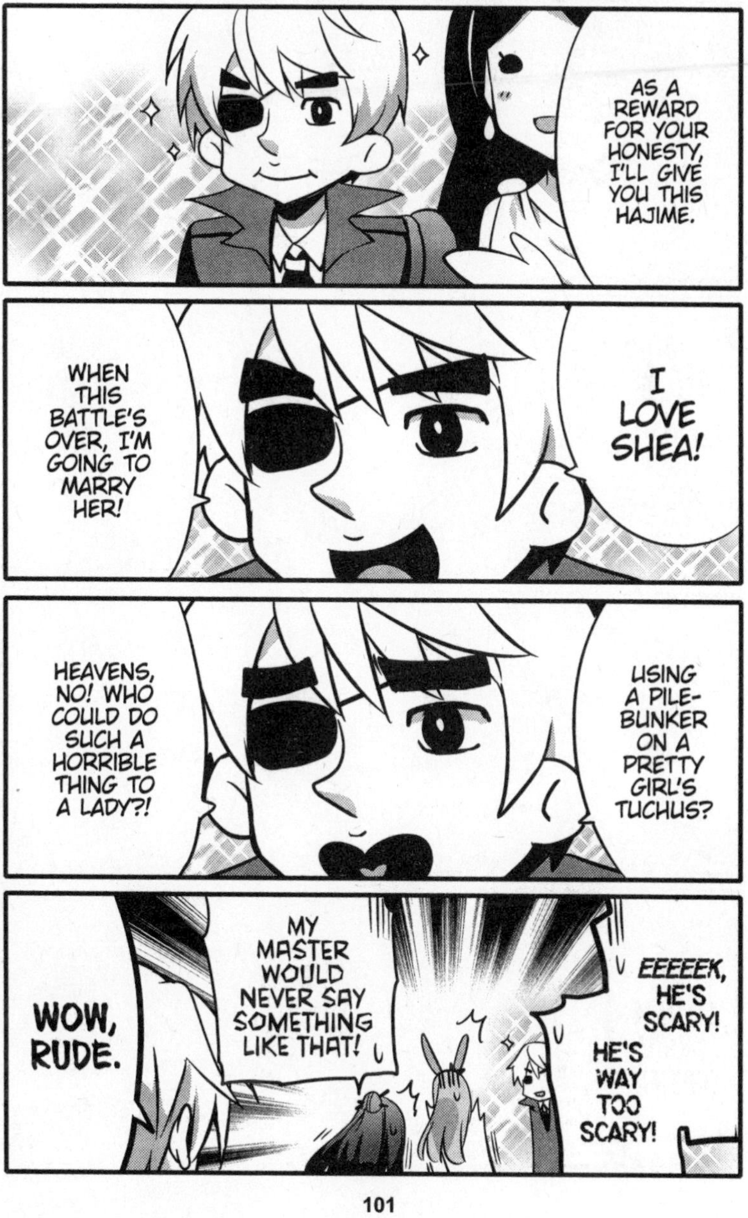
AS A REWARD FOR YOUR HONESTY, I'LL GIVE YOU THIS HAJIME.
I LOVE SHEA!
WHEN THIS BATTLE'S OVER, I'M GOING TO MARRY HER!
USING A PILE-BUNKER ON A PRETTY GIRL'S TUCHUS?
HEAVENS, NO! WHO COULD DO SUCH A HORRIBLE THING TO A LADY?!
EEEEEK, HE'S SCARY!
HE'S WAY TOO SCARY!
MY MASTER WOULD NEVER SAY SOMETHING LIKE THAT!
WOW, RUDE.

ED HIS EYES ARE INTENSE!

TRAUMATIZED DRAGON

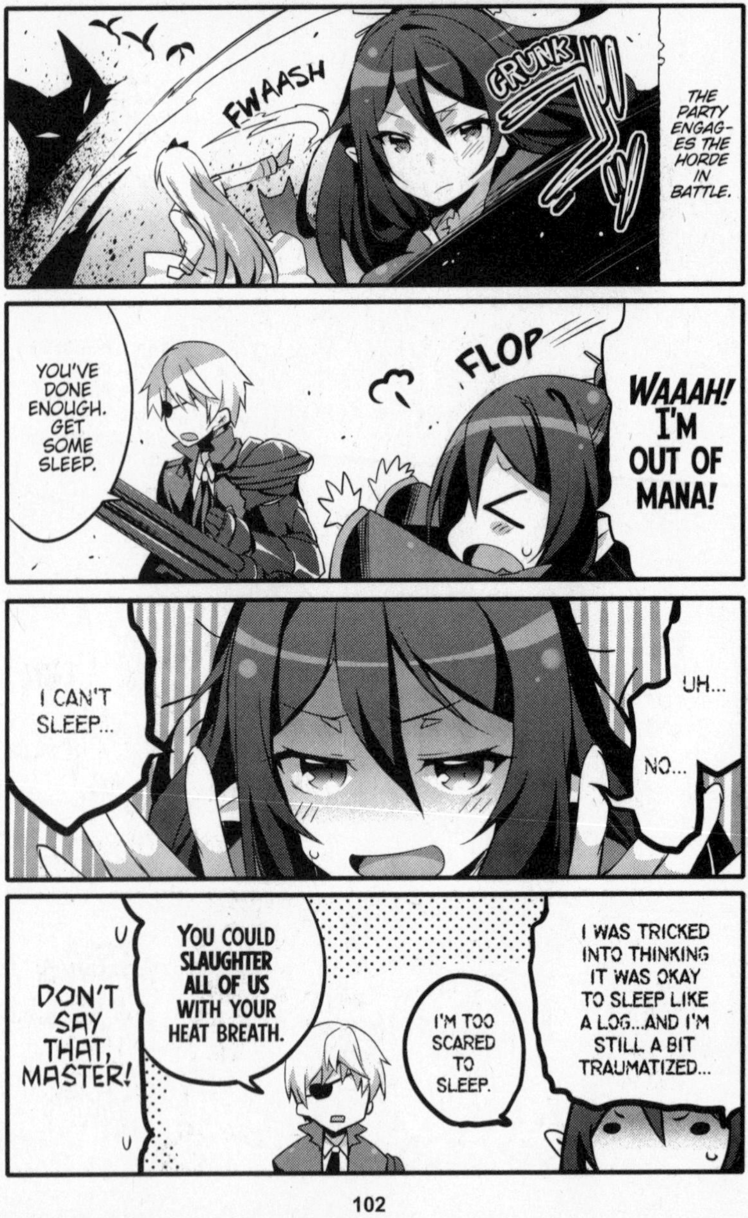
THE PARTY ENGAGES THE HORDE IN BATTLE.
GRUNK
FWAASH
WAAAH! I'M OUT OF MANA!
FLOP
YOU'VE DONE ENOUGH. GET SOME SLEEP.
UH...
NO...
I CAN'T SLEEP...
I WAS TRICKED INTO THINKING IT WAS OKAY TO SLEEP LIKE A LOG...AND I'M STILL A BIT TRAUMATIZED...
I'M TOO SCARED TO SLEEP.
YOU COULD SLAUGHTER ALL OF US WITH YOUR HEAT BREATH.
DON'T SAY THAT, MASTER!

ED

EVEN A CRAZY PERVERT HAS MOMENTS OF CLARITY.

CAPTURED

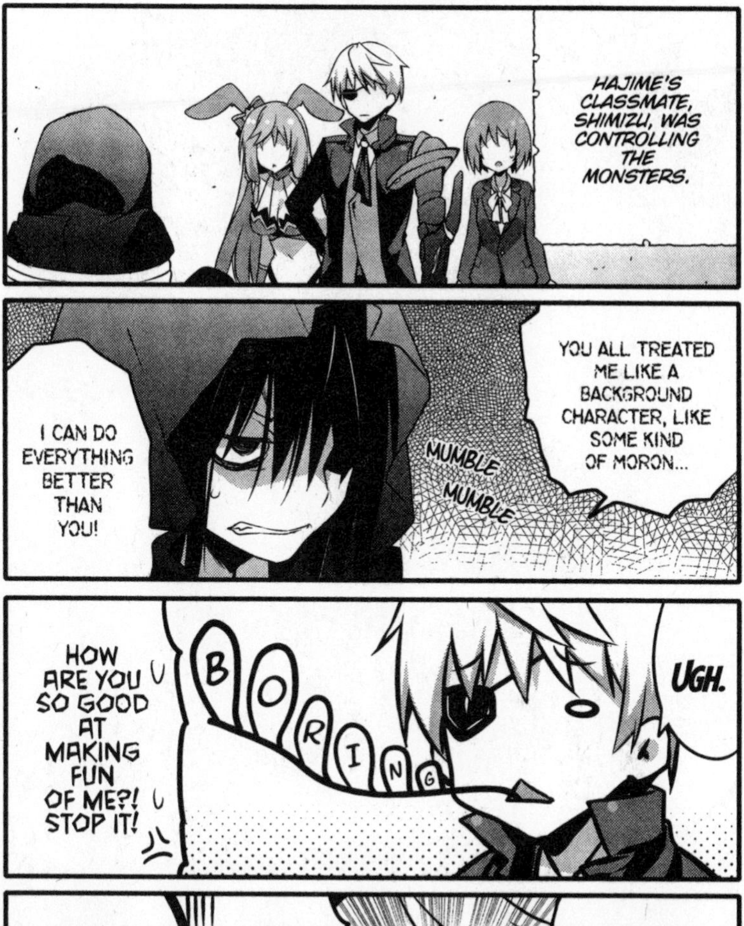
HAJIME'S CLASSMATE, SHIMIZU, WAS CONTROLLING THE MONSTERS.
YOU ALL TREATED ME LIKE A BACKGROUND CHARACTER, LIKE SOME KIND OF MORON...
MUMBLE
MUMBLE
I CAN DO EVERYTHING BETTER THAN YOU!
UGH.
BORING
HOW ARE YOU SO GOOD AT MAKING FUN OF ME?! STOP IT!
DON'T WORRY! IF WE HELP HIM GROW A HEART, WE CAN REFORM HIM!!
EEP! THERE ARE TWO OF HIM?!
HAJIME, WHY HAVEN'T YOU GOTTEN RID OF HIM YET?

GO AHEAD, MAKE FUN OF THEM

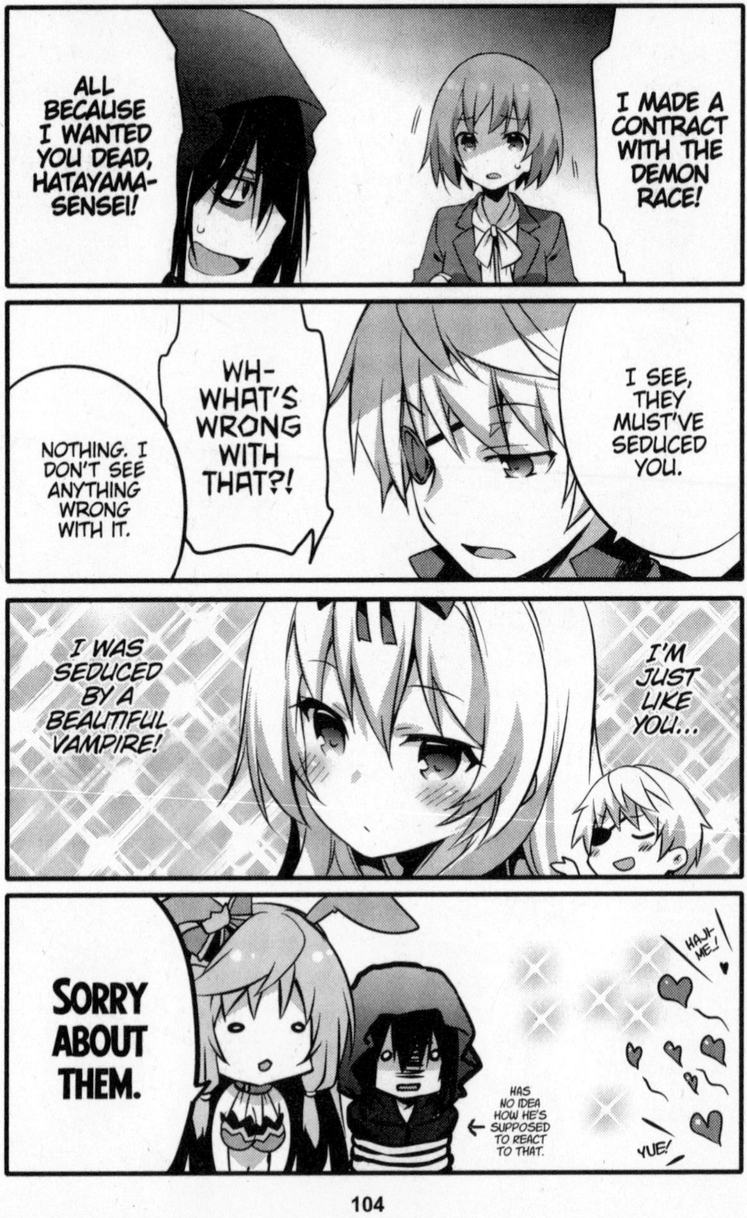
I MADE A CONTRACT WITH THE DEMON RACE!
ALL BECAUSE I WANTED YOU DEAD, HATAYAMA-SENSEI!
I SEE, THEY MUST'VE SEDUCED YOU.
WH-WHAT'S WRONG WITH THAT?!
NOTHING. I DON'T SEE ANYTHING WRONG WITH IT.
I'M JUST LIKE YOU...
I WAS SEDUCED BY A BEAUTIFUL VAMPIRE!
HAJIME!
YUE!
HAS NO IDEA HOW HE'S SUPPOSED TO REACT TO THAT.
SORRY ABOUT THEM.

ED BEEN A WHILE SINCE WE SAW THAT JOKE!

ENGLISH AND GERMAN

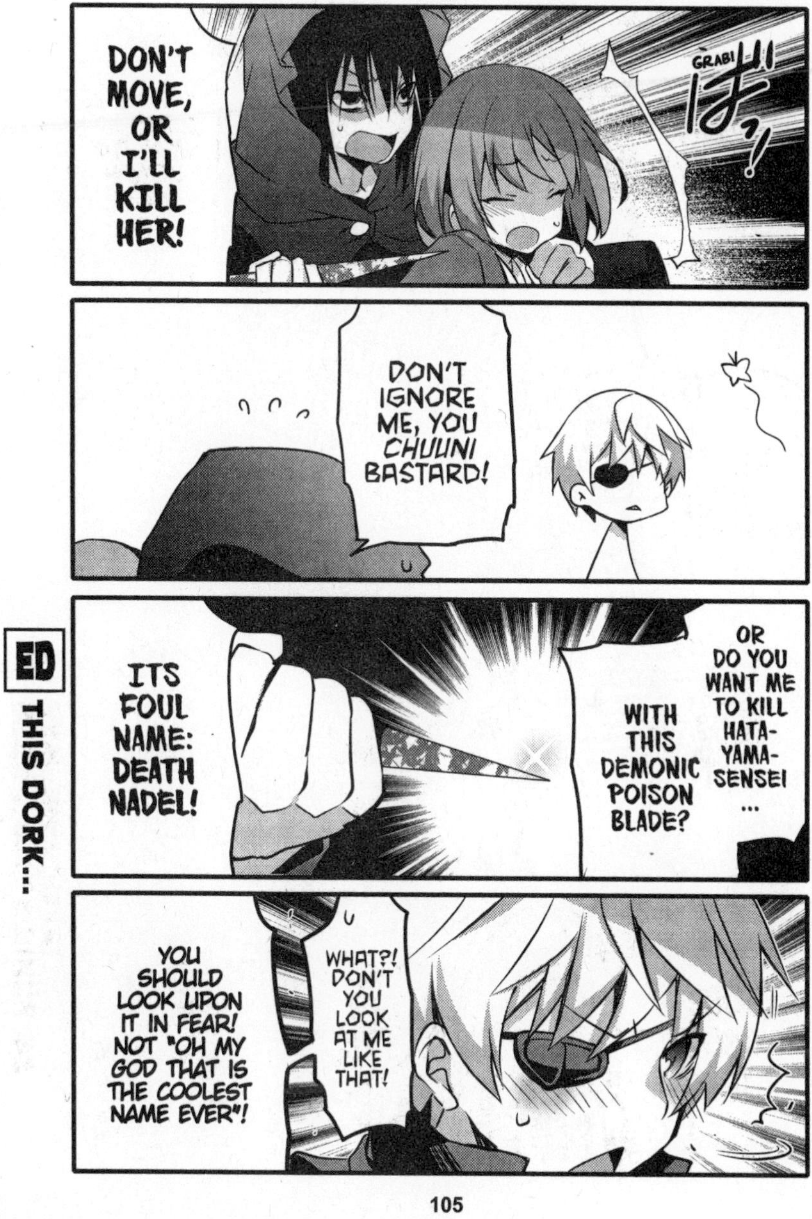

GRAB!
DON'T MOVE, OR I'LL KILL HER!
DON'T IGNORE ME, YOU CHUUNI BASTARD!
OR DO YOU WANT ME TO KILL HATA-YAMA-SENSEI...
WITH THIS DEMONIC POISON BLADE?
ITS FOUL NAME: DEATH NADEL!
WHAT?! DON'T YOU LOOK AT ME LIKE THAT!
YOU SHOULD LOOK UPON IT IN FEAR! NOT "OH MY GOD THAT IS THE COOLEST NAME EVER"!

ED THIS DORK...

JUST LIKE ME!

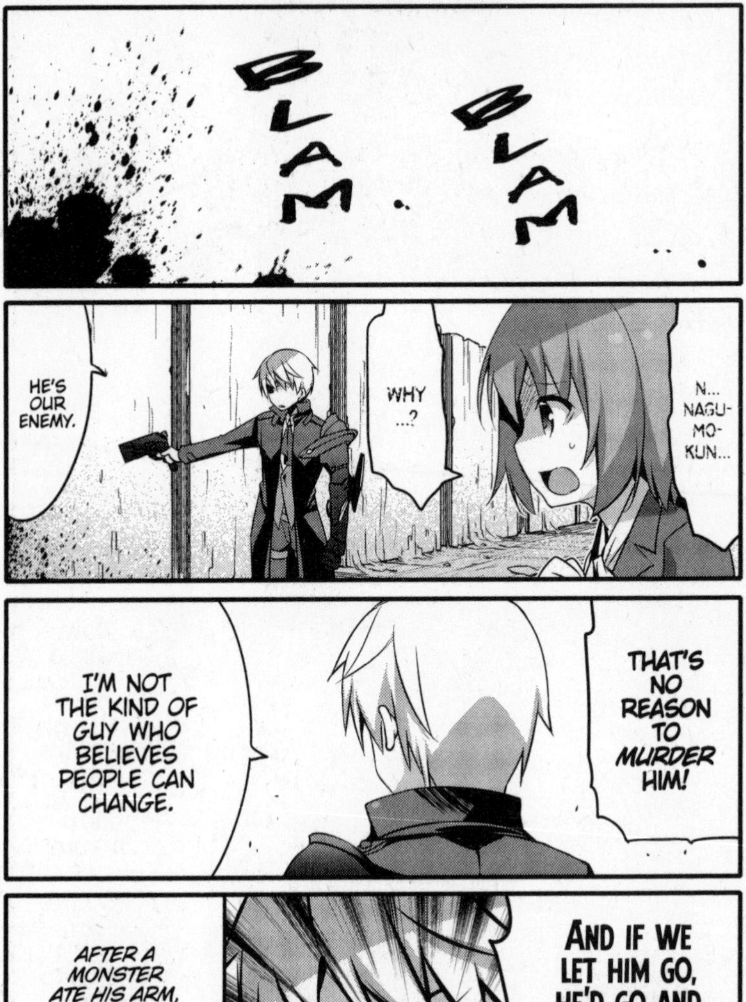
BLAM BLAM...
N... NAGU-MO-KUN...
WHY ...?
HE'S OUR ENEMY.
THAT'S NO REASON TO *MURDER* HIM!
I'M NOT THE KIND OF GUY WHO BELIEVES PEOPLE CAN CHANGE.
AND IF WE LET HIM GO, HE'D GO AND GET STRONGER, THEN COME BACK FOR REVENGE!!
AFTER A MONSTER ATE HIS ARM, HE WENT AND GOT STRONGER, THEN CAME BACK FOR REVENGE.

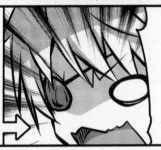

BUNNY DUMPLING

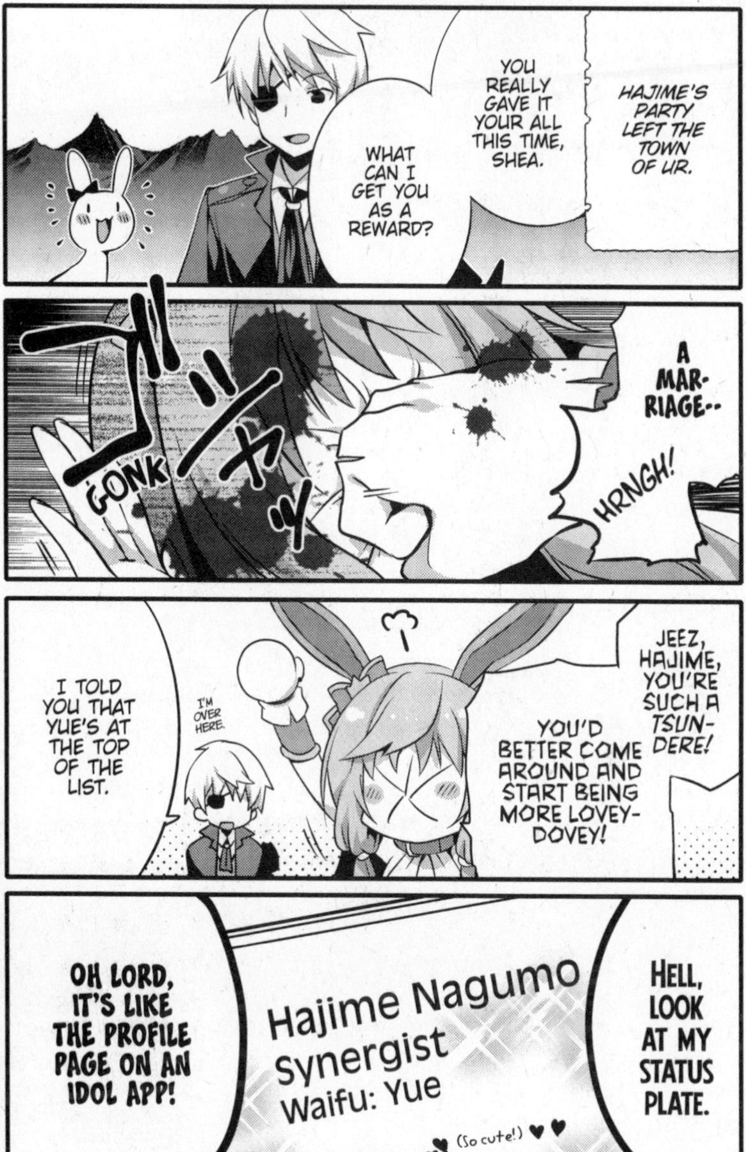
HAJIME'S PARTY LEFT THE TOWN OF UR.
YOU REALLY GAVE IT YOUR ALL THIS TIME, SHEA.
WHAT CAN I GET YOU AS A REWARD?
A MARRIAGE--
HRNGH!
GONK
JEEZ, HAJIME, YOU'RE SUCH A TSUNDERE!
YOU'D BETTER COME AROUND AND START BEING MORE LOVEY-DOVEY!
I'M OVER HERE.
I TOLD YOU THAT YUE'S AT THE TOP OF THE LIST.
HELL, LOOK AT MY STATUS PLATE.
Hajime Nagumo
Synergist
Waifu: Yue
(So cute!)
OH LORD, IT'S LIKE THE PROFILE PAGE ON AN IDOL APP!

ED WHO KNEW STATUS PLATES HAD A BOX FOR YOUR WAIFU?

BLABBERMOUTH BUNNY

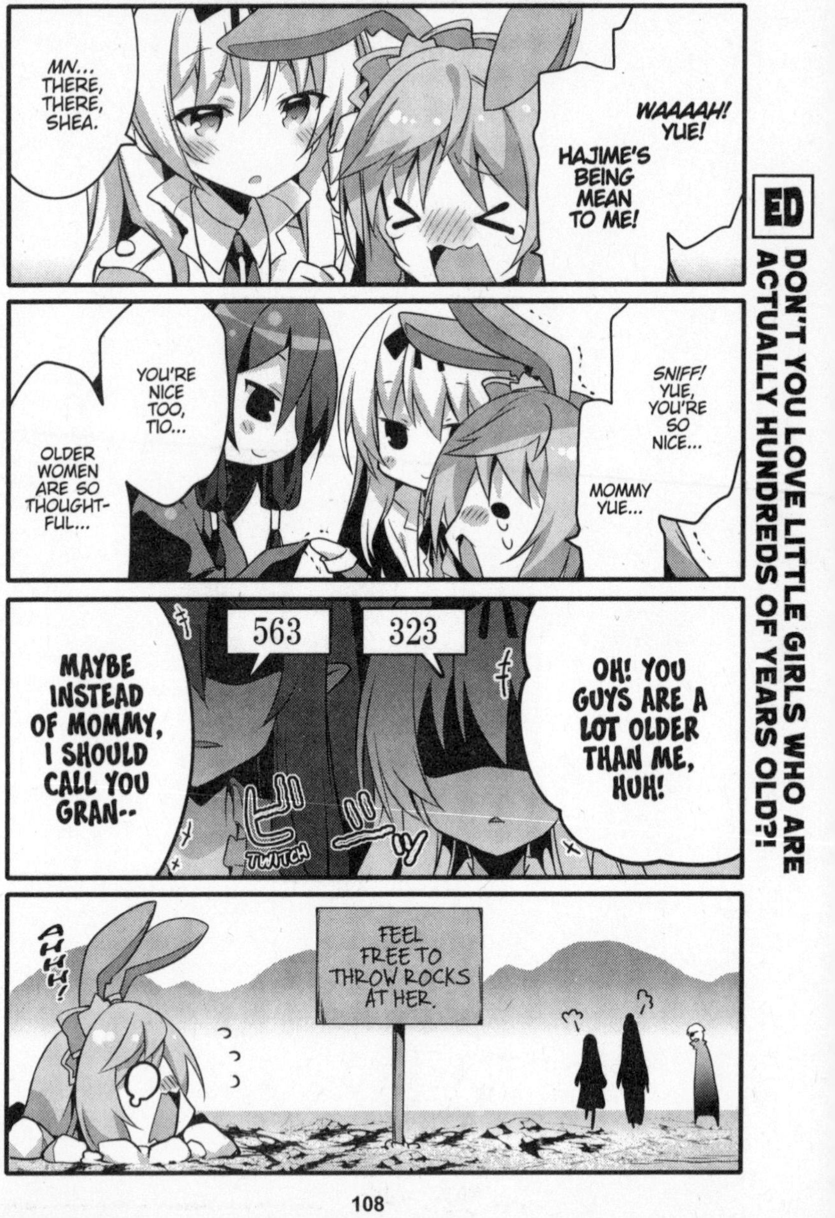
WAAAAH! YUE!
HAJIME'S BEING MEAN TO ME!
MN... THERE, THERE, SHEA.
SNIFF! YUE, YOU'RE SO NICE...
MOMMY YUE...
YOU'RE NICE TOO, TIO...
OLDER WOMEN ARE SO THOUGHTFUL...
OH! YOU GUYS ARE A LOT OLDER THAN ME, HUH!
323
563
MAYBE INSTEAD OF MOMMY, I SHOULD CALL YOU GRAN--
TWITCH
AHHH!
FEEL FREE TO THROW ROCKS AT HER.

Ants.

ARIFURETA:
ARIFURETA SHOKUGYOU DE SEKAISAIKYOU

I ♥ Isekai

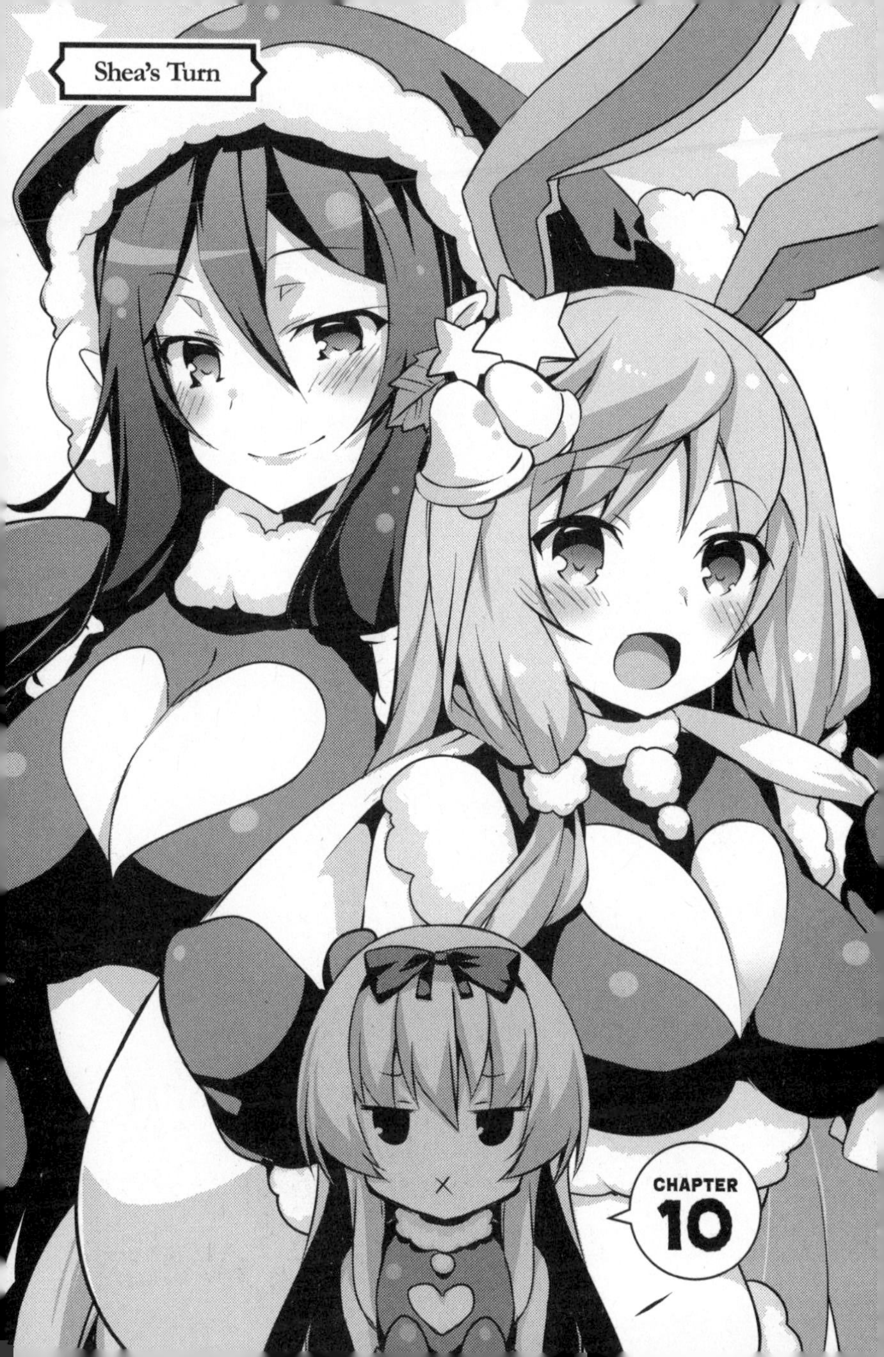
Shea's Turn
CHAPTER
10

COMES WITH HEATER AND FRIDGE

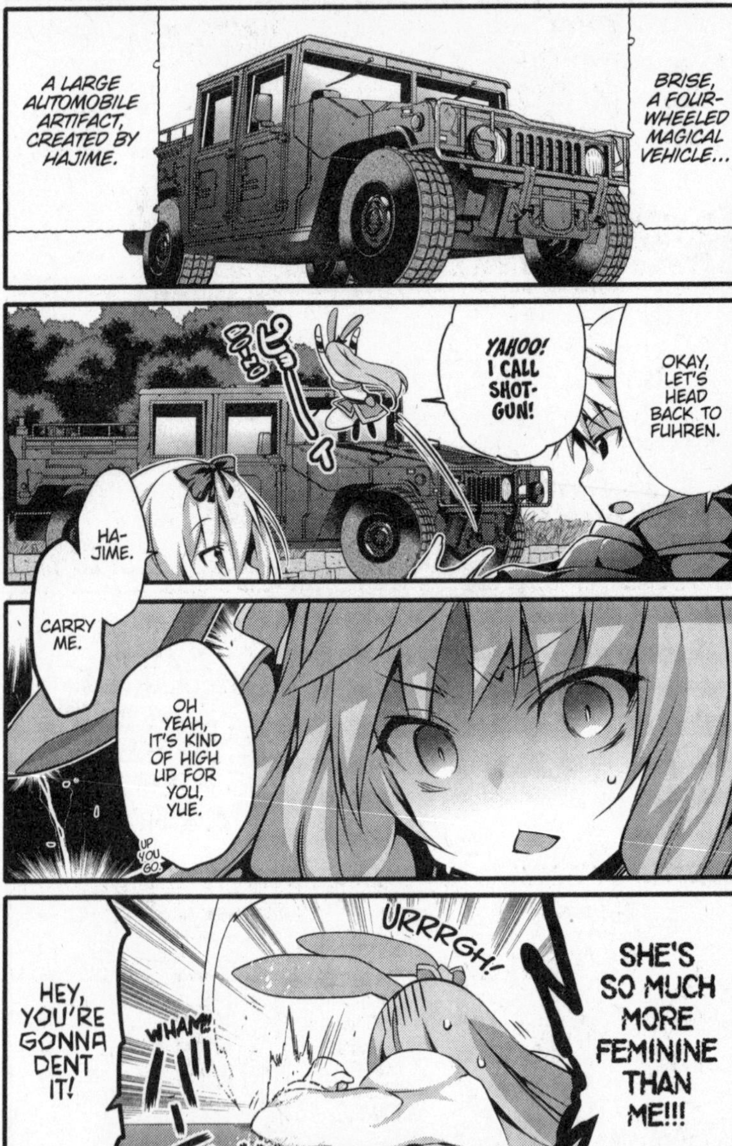
BRISE, A FOUR-WHEELED MAGICAL VEHICLE...
A LARGE AUTOMOBILE ARTIFACT, CREATED BY HAJIME.
OKAY, LET'S HEAD BACK TO FUHREN.
YAHOO! I CALL SHOT-GUN!
HA-JIME.
CARRY ME.
OH YEAH, IT'S KIND OF HIGH UP FOR YOU, YUE.
UP YOU GO.
SHE'S SO MUCH MORE FEMININE THAN ME!!!
URRRGH!
WHAM!!
HEY, YOU'RE GONNA DENT IT!

ED PUT YOUR MUSCLY BODY AWAY FIRST!

BUNNY FANGIRL

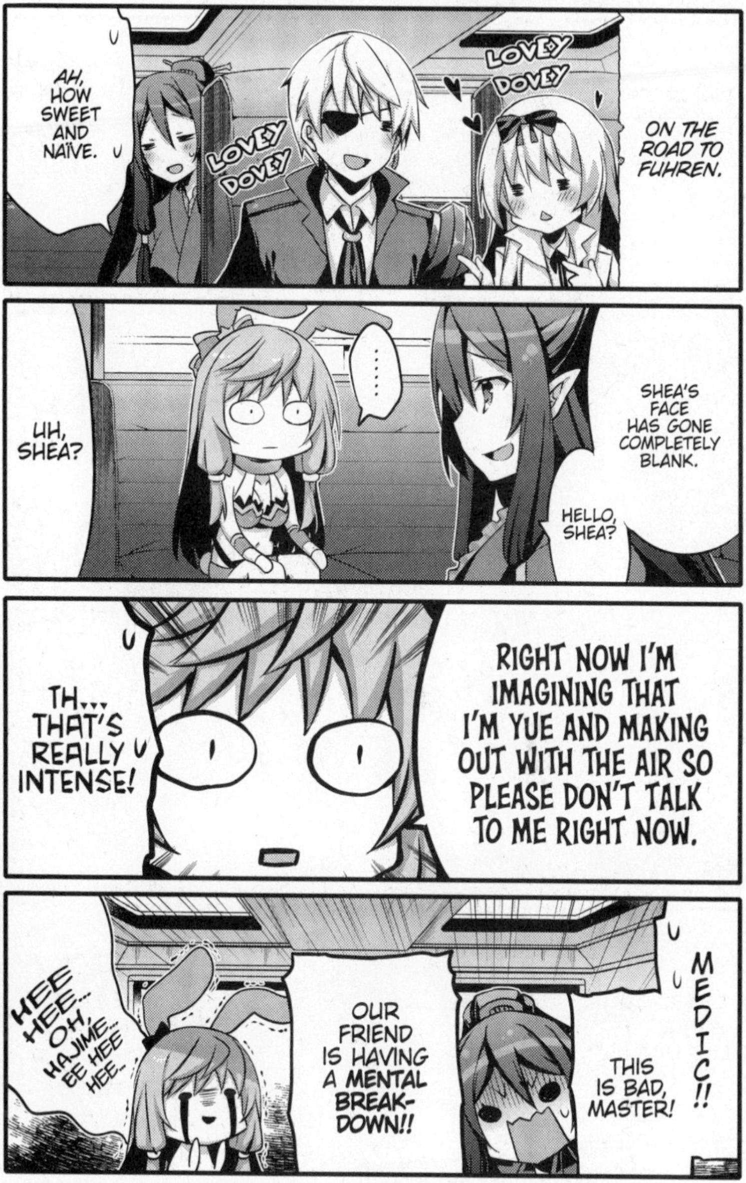
ON THE ROAD TO FUHREN.
LOVEY DOVEY
LOVEY DOVEY
AH, HOW SWEET AND NAÏVE.
SHEA'S FACE HAS GONE COMPLETELY BLANK.
HELLO, SHEA?
......
UH, SHEA?
RIGHT NOW I'M IMAGINING THAT I'M YUE AND MAKING OUT WITH THE AIR SO PLEASE DON'T TALK TO ME RIGHT NOW.
TH... THAT'S REALLY INTENSE!
MEDIC!!
THIS IS BAD, MASTER!
OUR FRIEND IS HAVING A MENTAL BREAK-DOWN!!
HEE HEE... OH, HAJIME... EE HEE HEE...

ED A NEW DOOR HAS BEEN OPENED!

DON'T FORGET ME

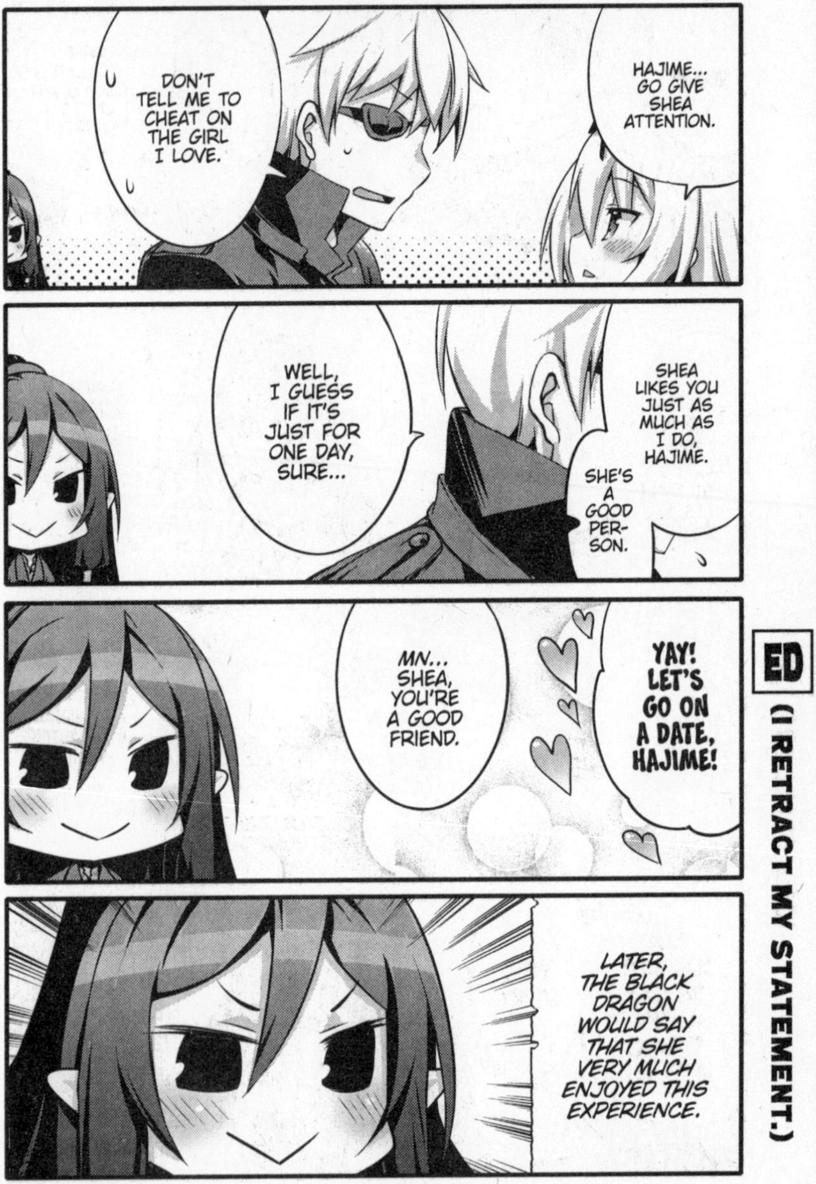
HAJIME... GO GIVE SHEA ATTENTION.
DON'T TELL ME TO CHEAT ON THE GIRL I LOVE.
SHEA LIKES YOU JUST AS MUCH AS I DO, HAJIME.
SHE'S A GOOD PER-SON.
WELL, I GUESS IF IT'S JUST FOR ONE DAY, SURE...
YAY! LET'S GO ON A DATE, HAJIME!
MN... SHEA, YOU'RE A GOOD FRIEND.
LATER, THE BLACK DRAGON WOULD SAY THAT SHE VERY MUCH ENJOYED THIS EXPERIENCE.
ED
(I RETRACT MY STATEMENT.)

WHAT DID THEY MEAN?

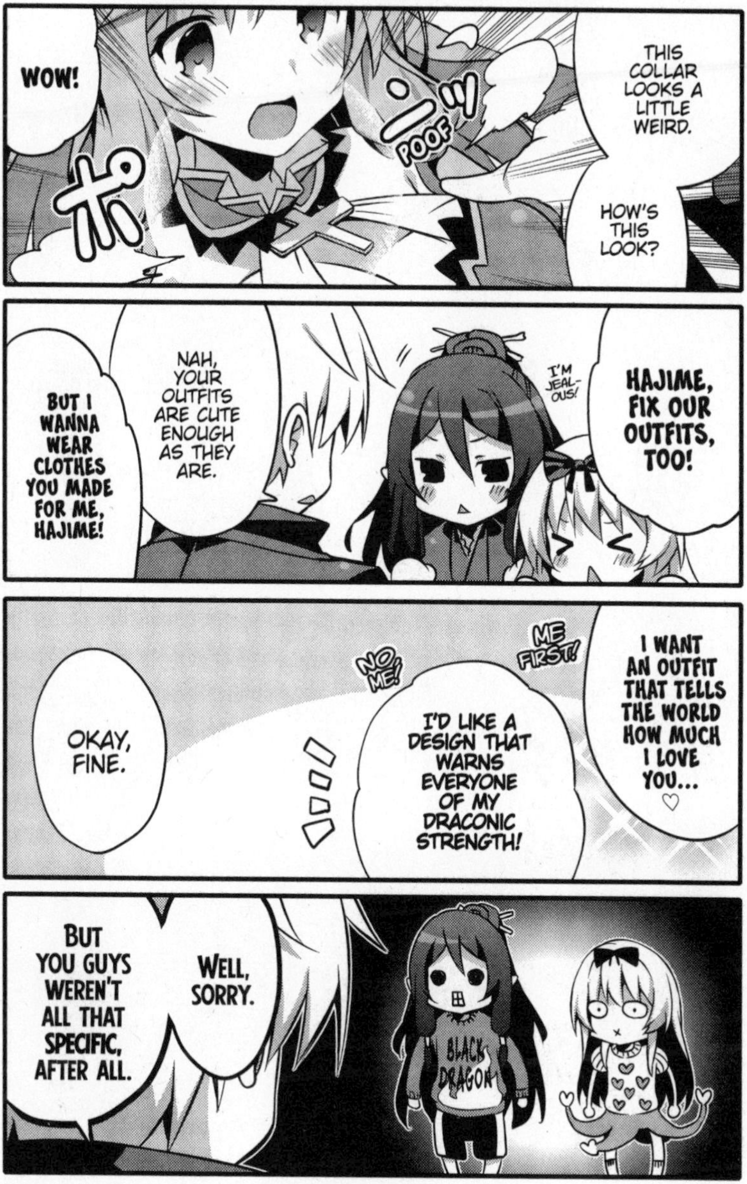

THIS COLLAR LOOKS A LITTLE WEIRD.
HOW'S THIS LOOK?
POOF
WOW!
HAJIME, FIX OUR OUTFITS, TOO!
I'M JEALOUS!
NAH, YOUR OUTFITS ARE CUTE ENOUGH AS THEY ARE.
BUT I WANNA WEAR CLOTHES YOU MADE FOR ME, HAJIME!
I WANT AN OUTFIT THAT TELLS THE WORLD HOW MUCH I LOVE YOU...♡
ME FIRST!
NO, ME!
I'D LIKE A DESIGN THAT WARNS EVERYONE OF MY DRACONIC STRENGTH!
OKAY, FINE.
WELL, SORRY.
BUT YOU GUYS WEREN'T ALL THAT SPECIFIC, AFTER ALL.
BLACK DRAGON

I CAN'T EXPLAIN IT

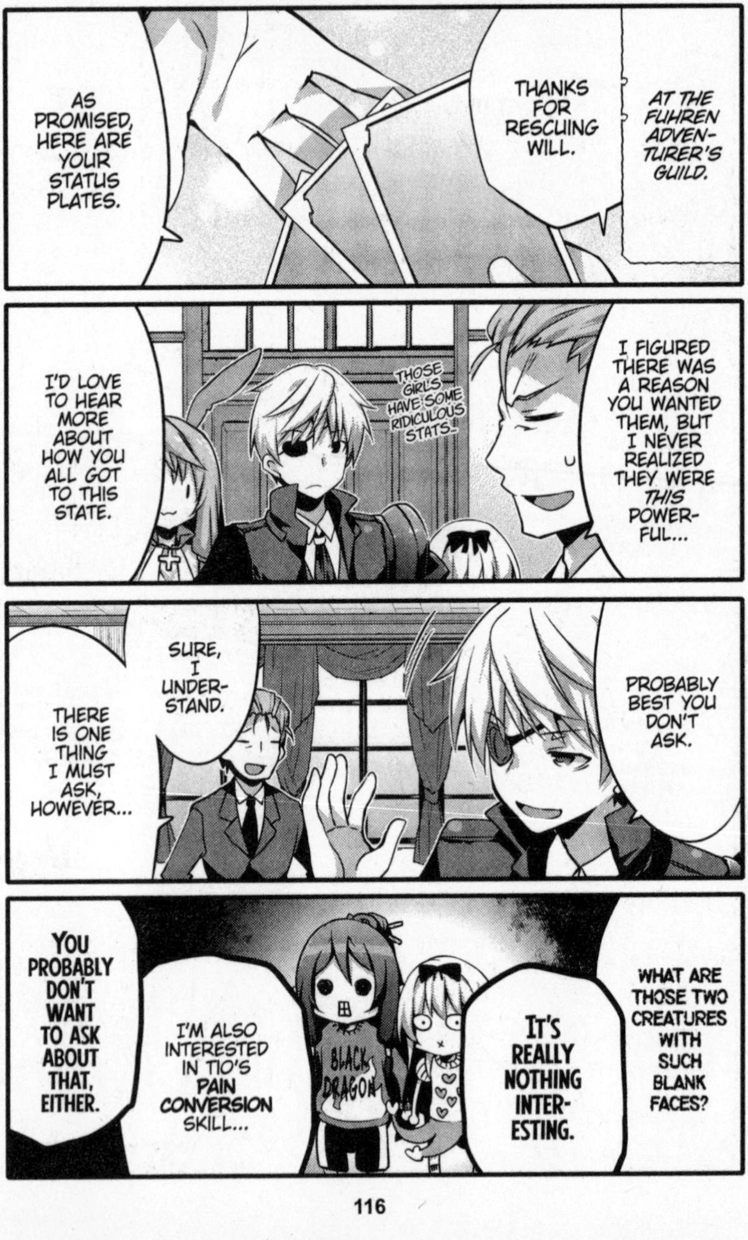
AT THE FUHREN ADVENTURER'S GUILD.
THANKS FOR RESCUING WILL.
AS PROMISED, HERE ARE YOUR STATUS PLATES.
I FIGURED THERE WAS A REASON YOU WANTED THEM, BUT I NEVER REALIZED THEY WERE *THIS* POWERFUL...
THOSE GIRLS HAVE SOME RIDICULOUS STATS!
I'D LOVE TO HEAR MORE ABOUT HOW YOU ALL GOT TO THIS STATE.
PROBABLY BEST YOU DON'T ASK.
SURE, I UNDERSTAND.
THERE IS ONE THING I MUST ASK, HOWEVER...
WHAT ARE THOSE TWO CREATURES WITH SUCH BLANK FACES?
IT'S REALLY NOTHING INTERESTING.
BLACK DRAGON
I'M ALSO INTERESTED IN TIO'S **PAIN CONVERSION** SKILL...
YOU PROBABLY DON'T WANT TO ASK ABOUT THAT, EITHER.

ED THEY'RE STILL EXPERIENCING THAT DEBUFF...

GAMER LOGIC

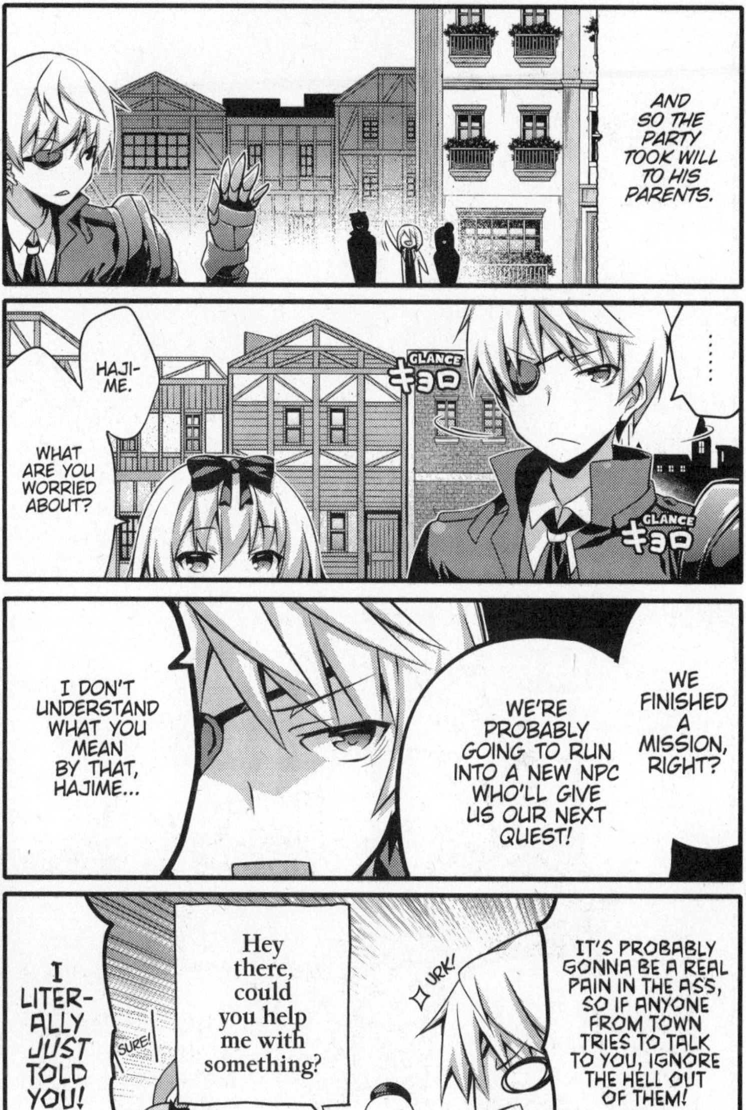
AND SO THE PARTY TOOK WILL TO HIS PARENTS.
......
GLANCE キョロ
GLANCE キョロ
HAJI-ME.
WHAT ARE YOU WORRIED ABOUT?
WE FINISHED A MISSION, RIGHT?
WE'RE PROBABLY GOING TO RUN INTO A NEW NPC WHO'LL GIVE US OUR NEXT QUEST!
I DON'T UNDERSTAND WHAT YOU MEAN BY THAT, HAJIME...
IT'S PROBABLY GONNA BE A REAL PAIN IN THE ASS, SO IF ANYONE FROM TOWN TRIES TO TALK TO YOU, IGNORE THE HELL OUT OF THEM!
URK!
Hey there, could you help me with something?
SURE!
I LITERALLY JUST TOLD YOU!

ED

HE'S NOT WRONG, YOU KNOW!

THIS COULD BE OUR NEW HOME

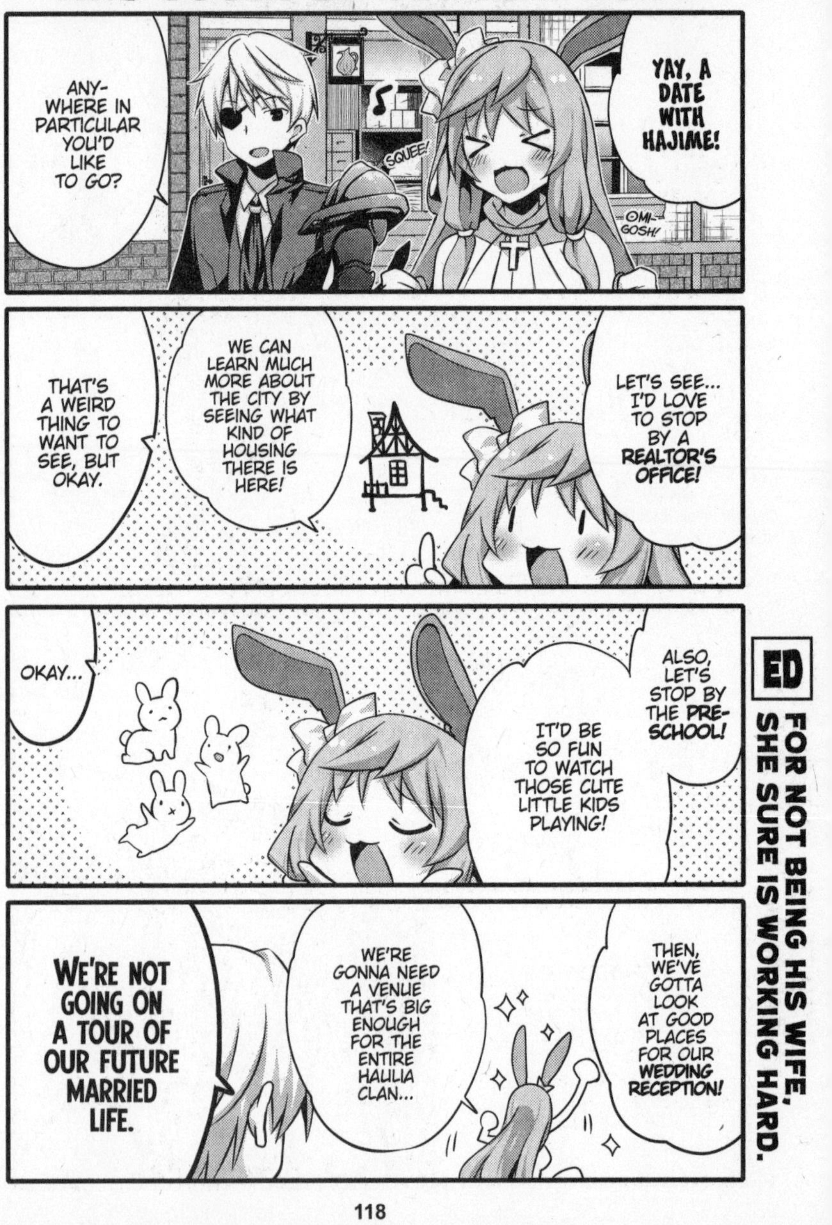
YAY, A DATE WITH HAJIME!
SQUEE!
OMI-GOSH!
ANY-WHERE IN PARTICULAR YOU'D LIKE TO GO?
LET'S SEE... I'D LOVE TO STOP BY A REALTOR'S OFFICE!
WE CAN LEARN MUCH MORE ABOUT THE CITY BY SEEING WHAT KIND OF HOUSING THERE IS HERE!
THAT'S A WEIRD THING TO WANT TO SEE, BUT OKAY.
ALSO, LET'S STOP BY THE PRE-SCHOOL!
IT'D BE SO FUN TO WATCH THOSE CUTE LITTLE KIDS PLAYING!
OKAY...
THEN, WE'VE GOTTA LOOK AT GOOD PLACES FOR OUR WEDDING RECEPTION!
WE'RE GONNA NEED A VENUE THAT'S BIG ENOUGH FOR THE ENTIRE HAULIA CLAN...
WE'RE NOT GOING ON A TOUR OF OUR FUTURE MARRIED LIFE.

ED FOR NOT BEING HIS WIFE, SHE SURE IS WORKING HARD.

SHEA'S BEING ATTACKED FOR NO REASON!

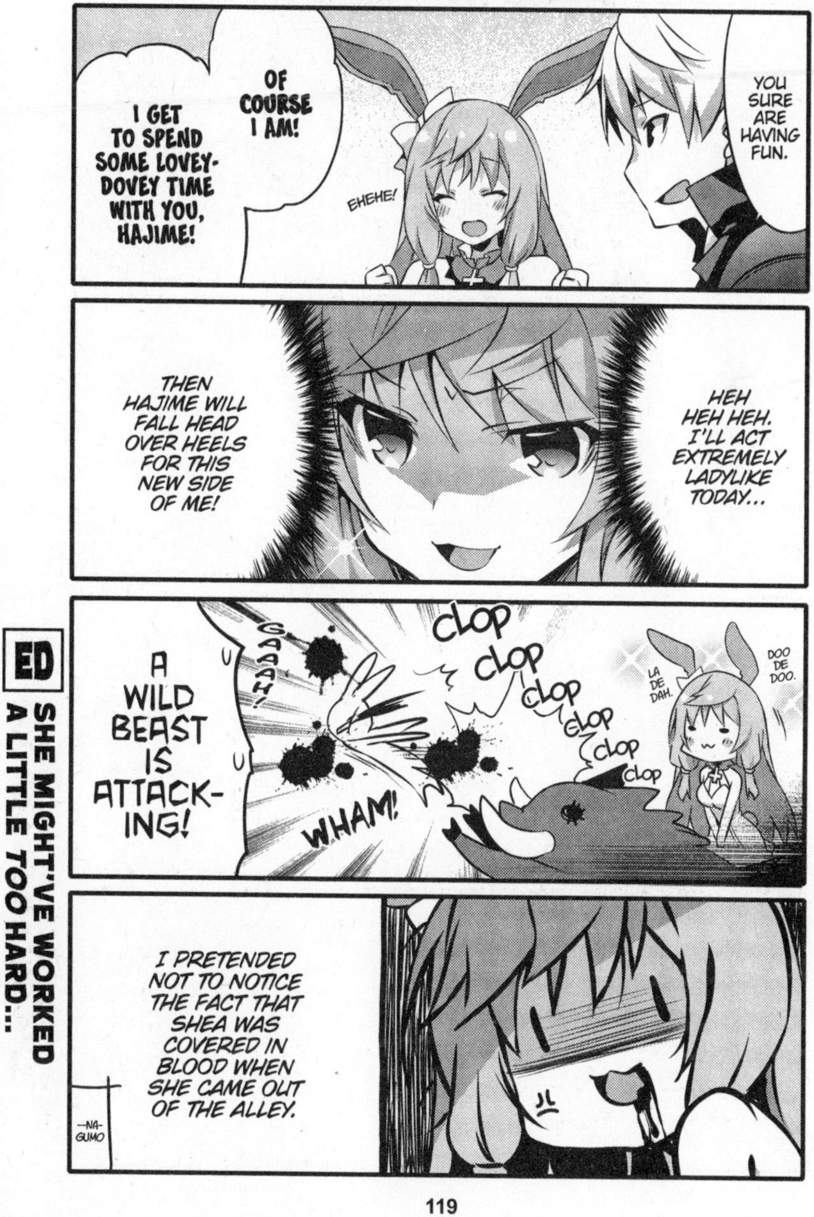

YOU SURE ARE HAVING FUN.
OF COURSE I AM!
EHEHE!
I GET TO SPEND SOME LOVEY-DOVEY TIME WITH YOU, HAJIME!
HEH HEH HEH. I'LL ACT EXTREMELY LADYLIKE TODAY...
THEN HAJIME WILL FALL HEAD OVER HEELS FOR THIS NEW SIDE OF ME!
DOO DE DOO.
LA DE DAH.
CLOP CLOP CLOP CLOP CLOP CLOP
GAAAH!
A WILD BEAST IS ATTACKING!
WHAM!
I PRETENDED NOT TO NOTICE THE FACT THAT SHEA WAS COVERED IN BLOOD WHEN SHE CAME OUT OF THE ALLEY.
—NAGUMO
ED
SHE MIGHT'VE WORKED A LITTLE TOO HARD...

HIS REAL WIFE DOESN'T WORRY

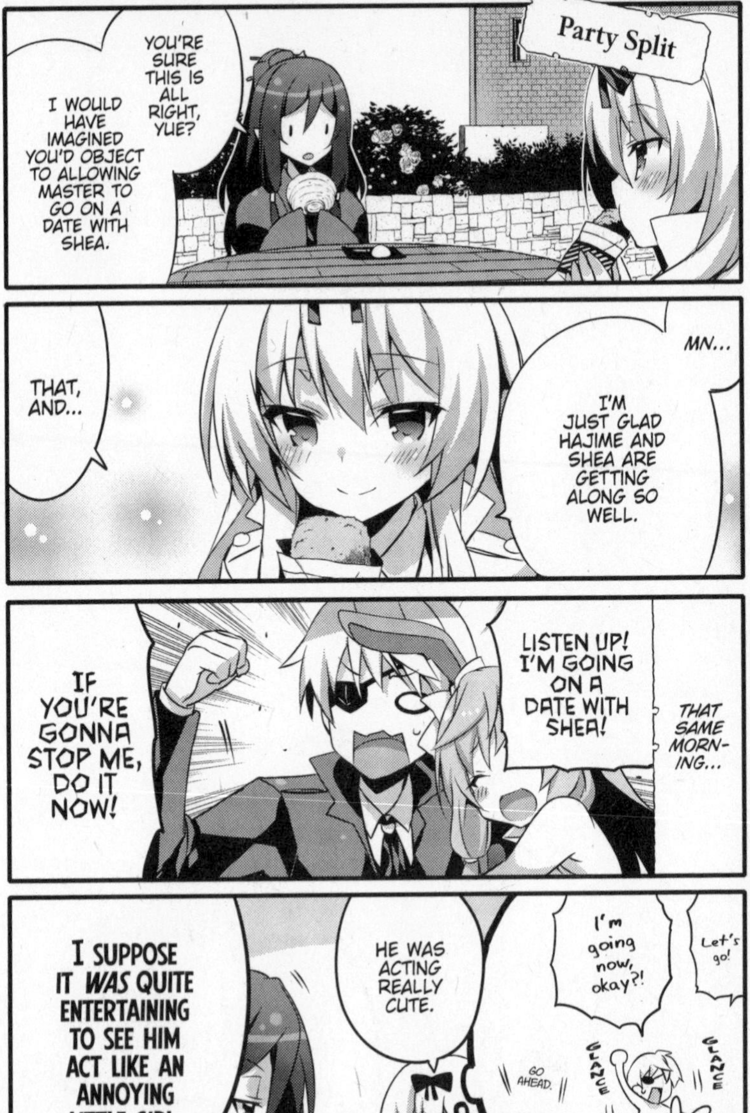
Party Split
YOU'RE SURE THIS IS ALL RIGHT, YUE?
I WOULD HAVE IMAGINED YOU'D OBJECT TO ALLOWING MASTER TO GO ON A DATE WITH SHEA.
MN...
I'M JUST GLAD HAJIME AND SHEA ARE GETTING ALONG SO WELL.
THAT, AND...
THAT SAME MORNING...
LISTEN UP! I'M GOING ON A DATE WITH SHEA!
IF YOU'RE GONNA STOP ME, DO IT NOW!
Let's go!
I'm going now, okay?!
GLANCE
GLANCE
GO AHEAD.
HE WAS ACTING REALLY CUTE.
AHHH...
I SUPPOSE IT *WAS* QUITE ENTERTAINING TO SEE HIM ACT LIKE AN ANNOYING LITTLE GIRL.

ED MAYBE SHE'S A BIT TOO CALM ABOUT IT...

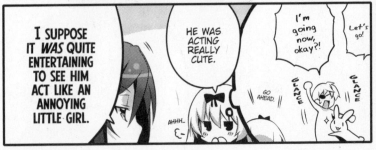

ARIFURETA:

ARIFURETA SHOKUGYOU DE SEKAISAIKYOU

I ♥ Isekai

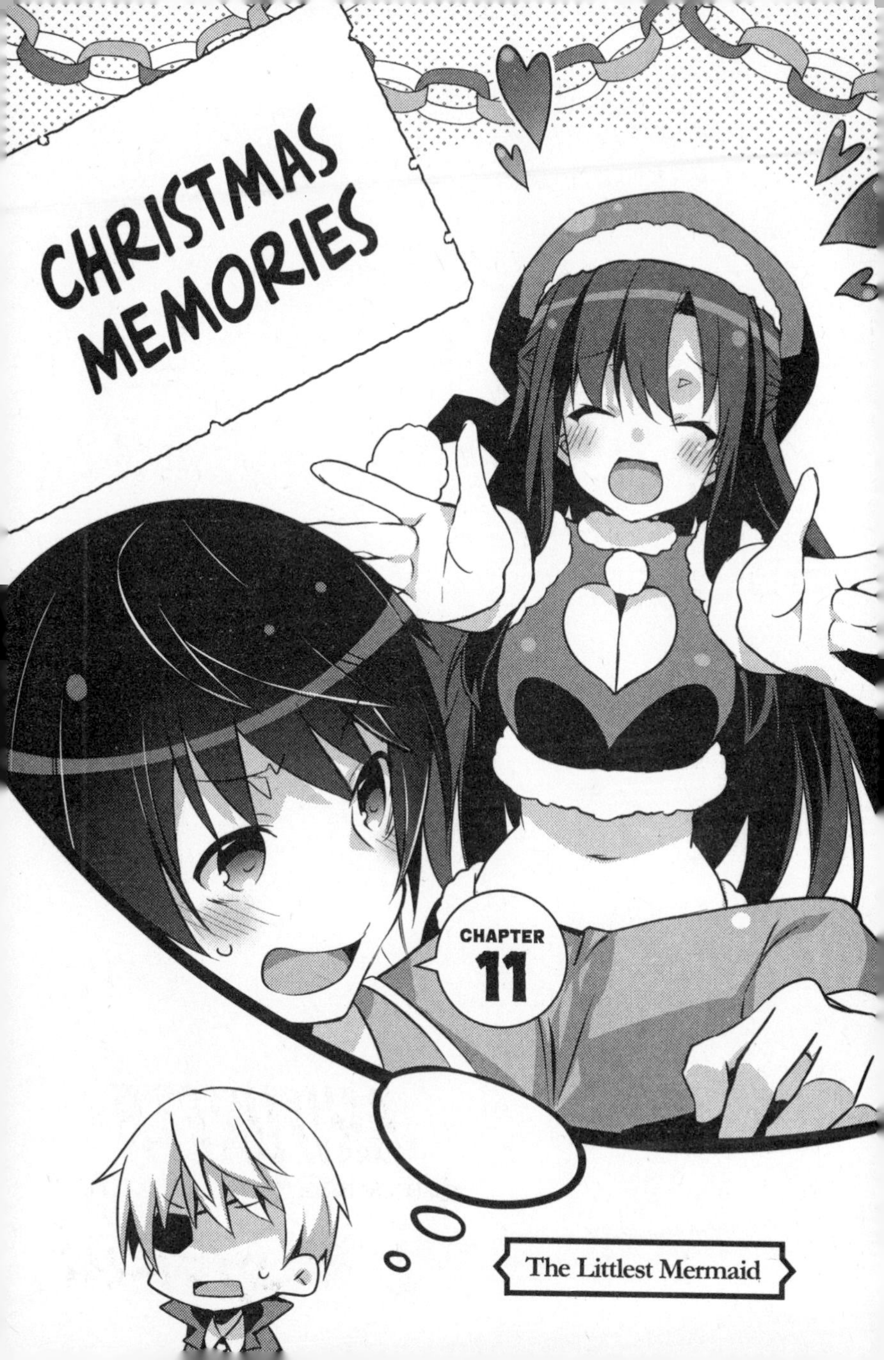

CHRISTMAS MEMORIES
CHAPTER 11
The Littlest Mermaid

FOLLOWING YUE'S EXAMPLE

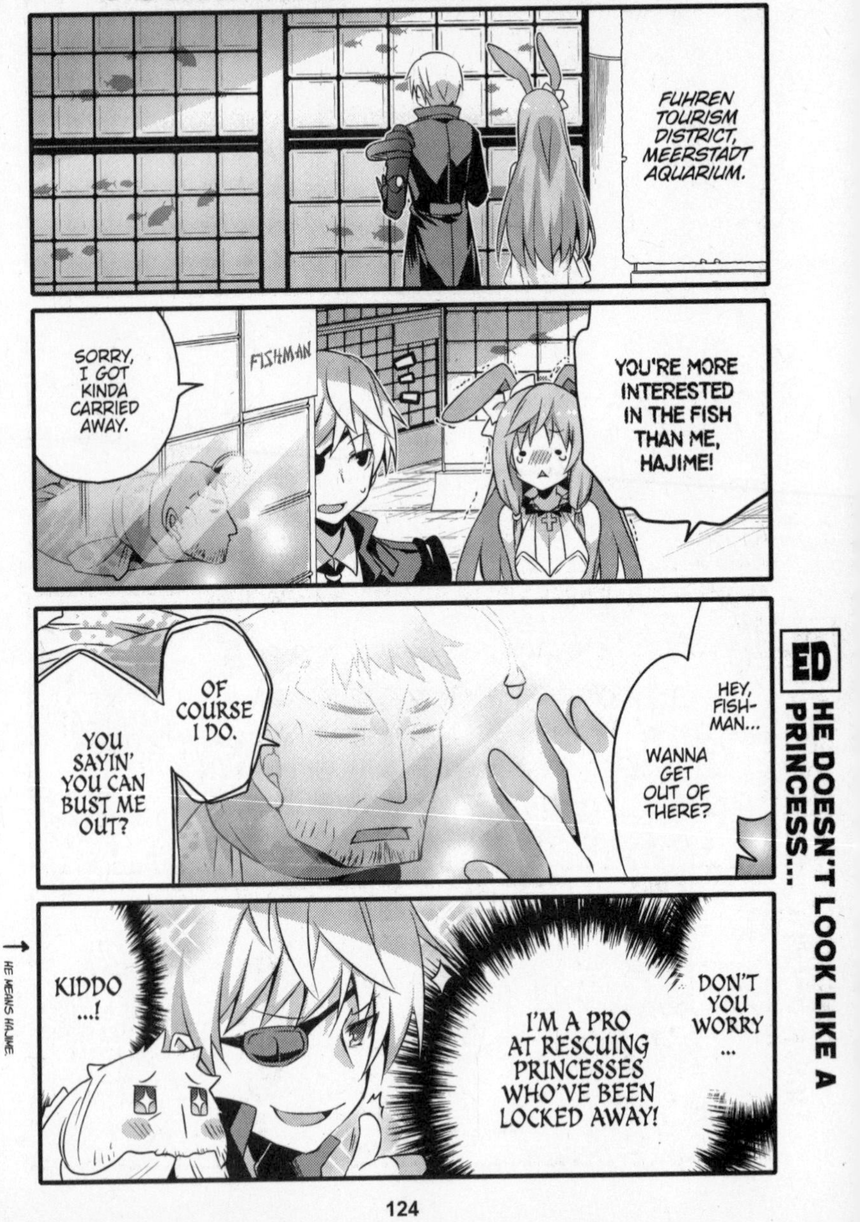
FUHREN TOURISM DISTRICT, MEERSTADT AQUARIUM.
YOU'RE MORE INTERESTED IN THE FISH THAN ME, HAJIME!
FISHMAN
SORRY, I GOT KINDA CARRIED AWAY.
HEY, FISH-MAN...
WANNA GET OUT OF THERE?
YOU SAYIN' YOU CAN BUST ME OUT?
OF COURSE I DO.
DON'T YOU WORRY...
I'M A PRO AT RESCUING PRINCESSES WHO'VE BEEN LOCKED AWAY!
KIDDO...!

ED HE DOESN'T LOOK LIKE A PRINCESS...

← HE MEANS HAJIME.

SHEA'S APOLOGY MEAL

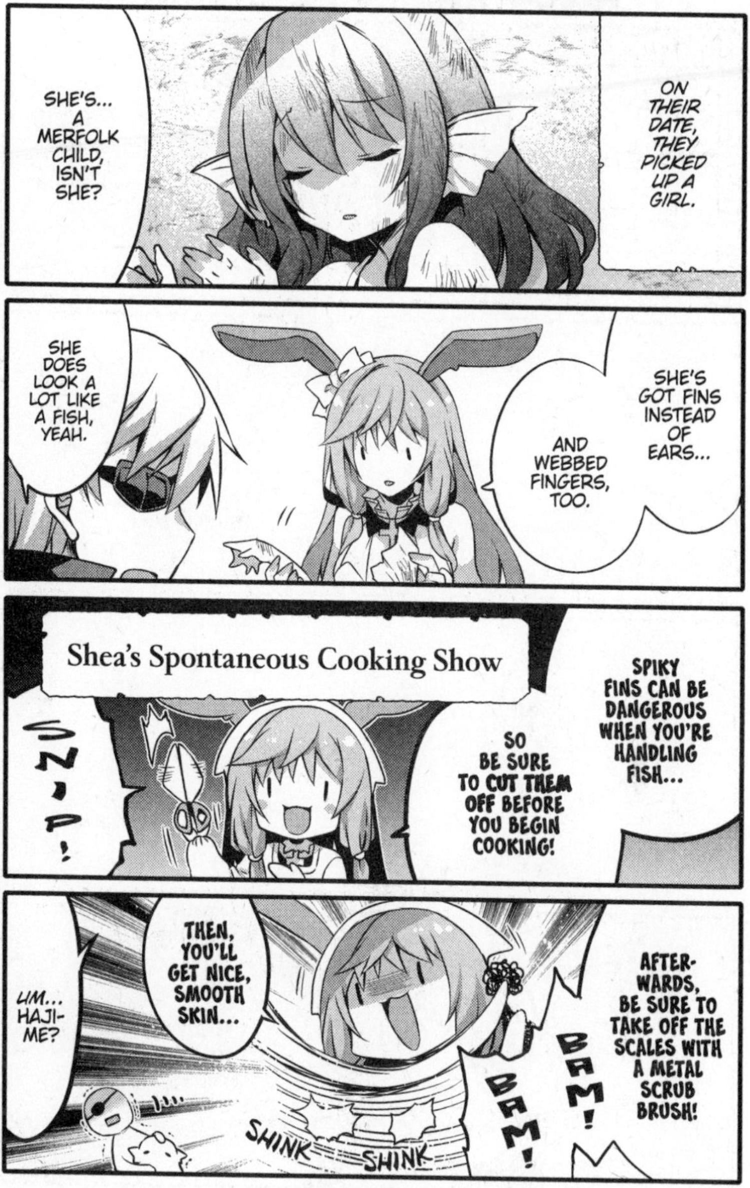
ON THEIR DATE, THEY PICKED UP A GIRL.
SHE'S... A MERFOLK CHILD, ISN'T SHE?
SHE'S GOT FINS INSTEAD OF EARS...
AND WEBBED FINGERS, TOO.
SHE DOES LOOK A LOT LIKE A FISH, YEAH.
Shea's Spontaneous Cooking Show
SPIKY FINS CAN BE DANGEROUS WHEN YOU'RE HANDLING FISH...
SO BE SURE TO CUT THEM OFF BEFORE YOU BEGIN COOKING!
SNIP!
AFTER-WARDS, BE SURE TO TAKE OFF THE SCALES WITH A METAL SCRUB BRUSH!
BAM!
BAM!
THEN, YOU'LL GET NICE, SMOOTH SKIN...
UM... HAJI-ME?
SHINK SHINK

ED

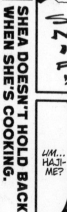

SHEA DOESN'T HOLD BACK WHEN SHE'S COOKING.

CONCERN

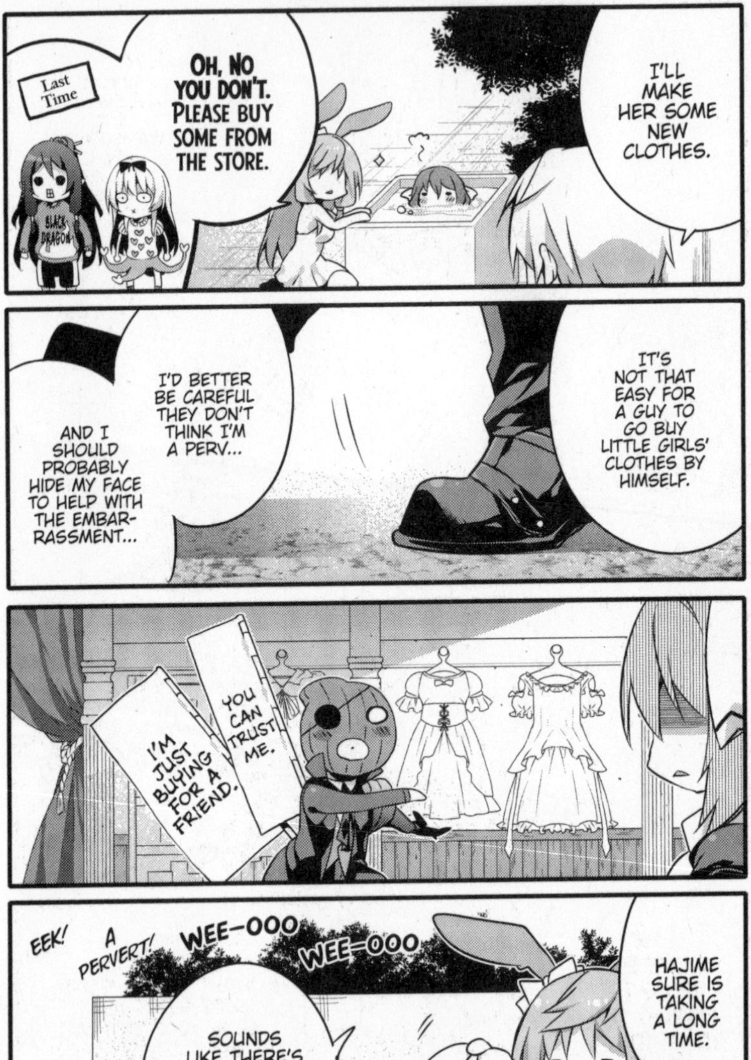
Last Time
I'LL MAKE HER SOME NEW CLOTHES.
OH, NO YOU DON'T. PLEASE BUY SOME FROM THE STORE.
IT'S NOT THAT EASY FOR A GUY TO GO BUY LITTLE GIRLS' CLOTHES BY HIMSELF.
I'D BETTER BE CAREFUL THEY DON'T THINK I'M A PERV...
AND I SHOULD PROBABLY HIDE MY FACE TO HELP WITH THE EMBARRASSMENT...
YOU CAN TRUST ME.
I'M JUST BUYING FOR A FRIEND.
HAJIME SURE IS TAKING A LONG TIME.
WEE-OOO
WEE-OOO
A PERVERT!
EEK!
SOUNDS LIKE THERE'S A REAL RUCKUS GOING ON, TOO.
MYUU...

ED GOOD WORK, HAJIME. TOTALLY HIT THE MARK.

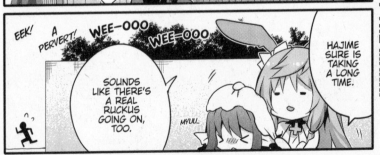

THE FIRST STEP TO GIFTED EDUCATION

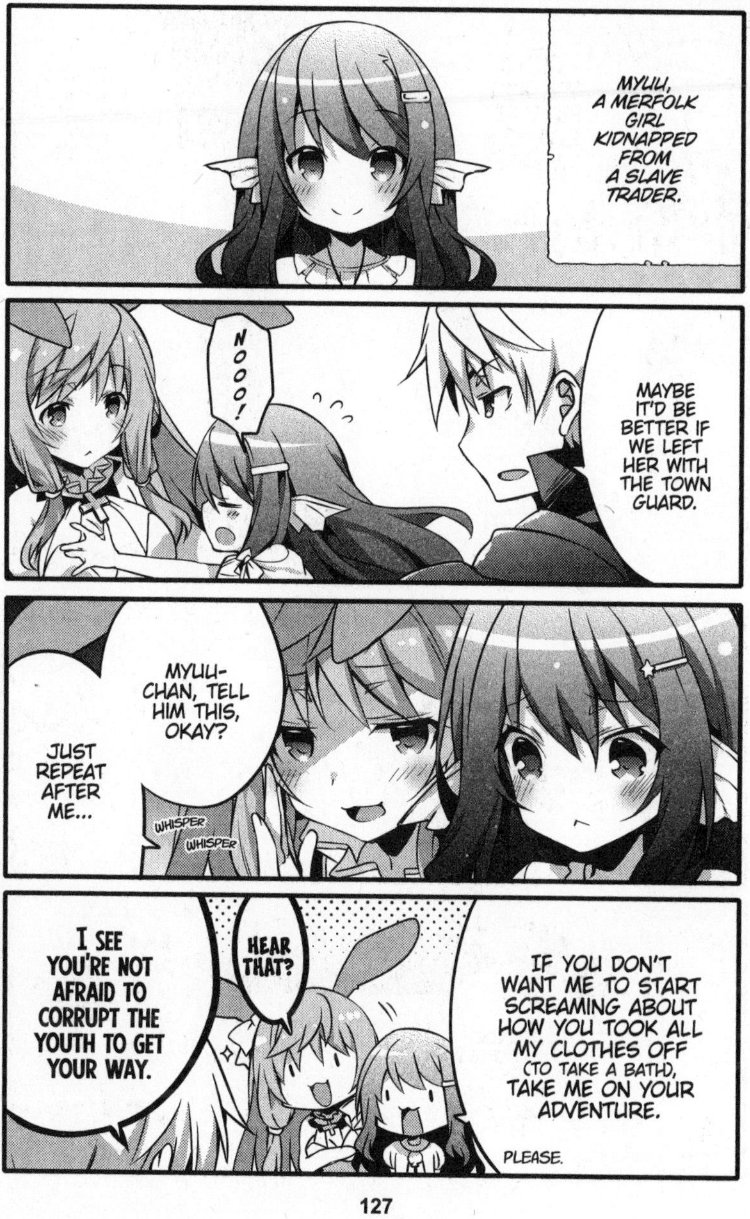
MYUU, A MERFOLK GIRL KIDNAPPED FROM A SLAVE TRADER.
MAYBE IT'D BE BETTER IF WE LEFT HER WITH THE TOWN GUARD.
NOOOO!
MYUU-CHAN, TELL HIM THIS, OKAY?
JUST REPEAT AFTER ME...
WHISPER
WHISPER
IF YOU DON'T WANT ME TO START SCREAMING ABOUT HOW YOU TOOK ALL MY CLOTHES OFF (TO TAKE A BATH), TAKE ME ON YOUR ADVENTURE.
PLEASE.
HEAR THAT?
I SEE YOU'RE NOT AFRAID TO CORRUPT THE YOUTH TO GET YOUR WAY.

← POLICE.

ED I BELIEVE THAT'S CALLED BLACKMAIL.

AAAAND INTERRUPTED

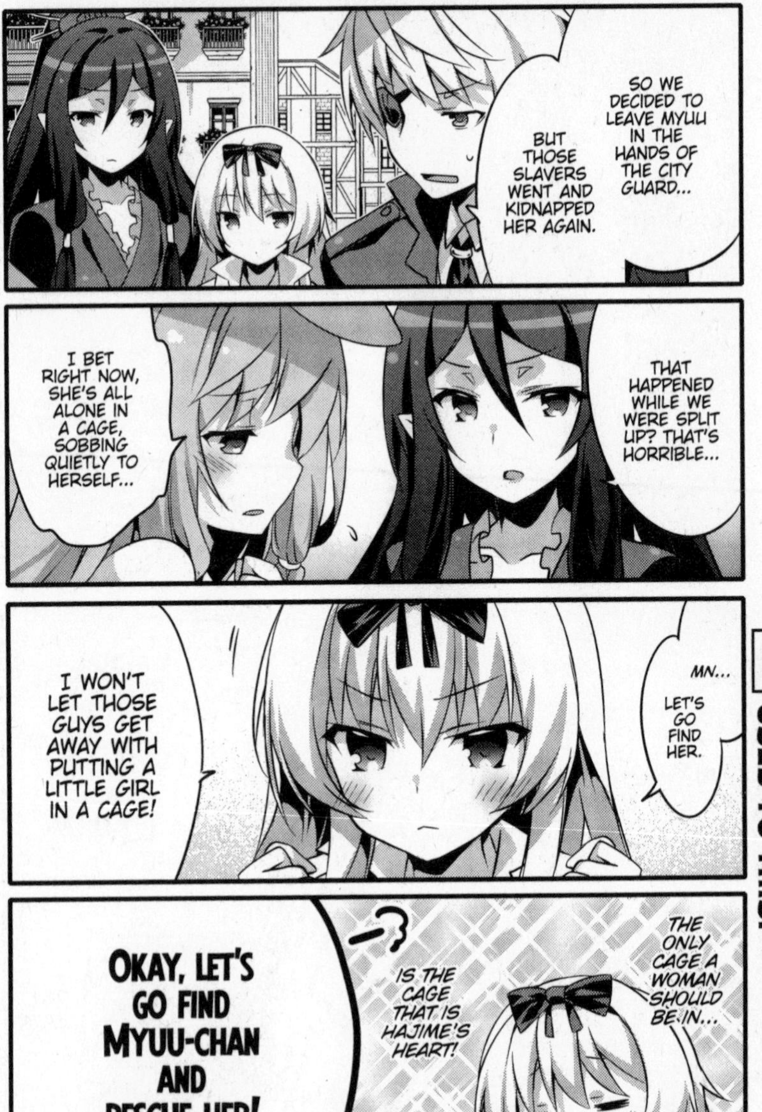
SO WE DECIDED TO LEAVE MYUU IN THE HANDS OF THE CITY GUARD...
BUT THOSE SLAVERS WENT AND KIDNAPPED HER AGAIN.
THAT HAPPENED WHILE WE WERE SPLIT UP? THAT'S HORRIBLE...
I BET RIGHT NOW, SHE'S ALL ALONE IN A CAGE, SOBBING QUIETLY TO HERSELF...
MN...
LET'S GO FIND HER.
I WON'T LET THOSE GUYS GET AWAY WITH PUTTING A LITTLE GIRL IN A CAGE!
THE ONLY CAGE A WOMAN SHOULD BE IN...
IS THE CAGE THAT IS HAJIME'S HEART!
OKAY, LET'S GO FIND MYUU-CHAN AND RESCUE HER!

ED EVERYONE ELSE HAS GOTTEN USED TO THIS.

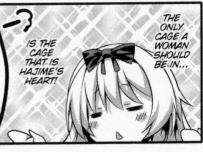

(°Д°#)

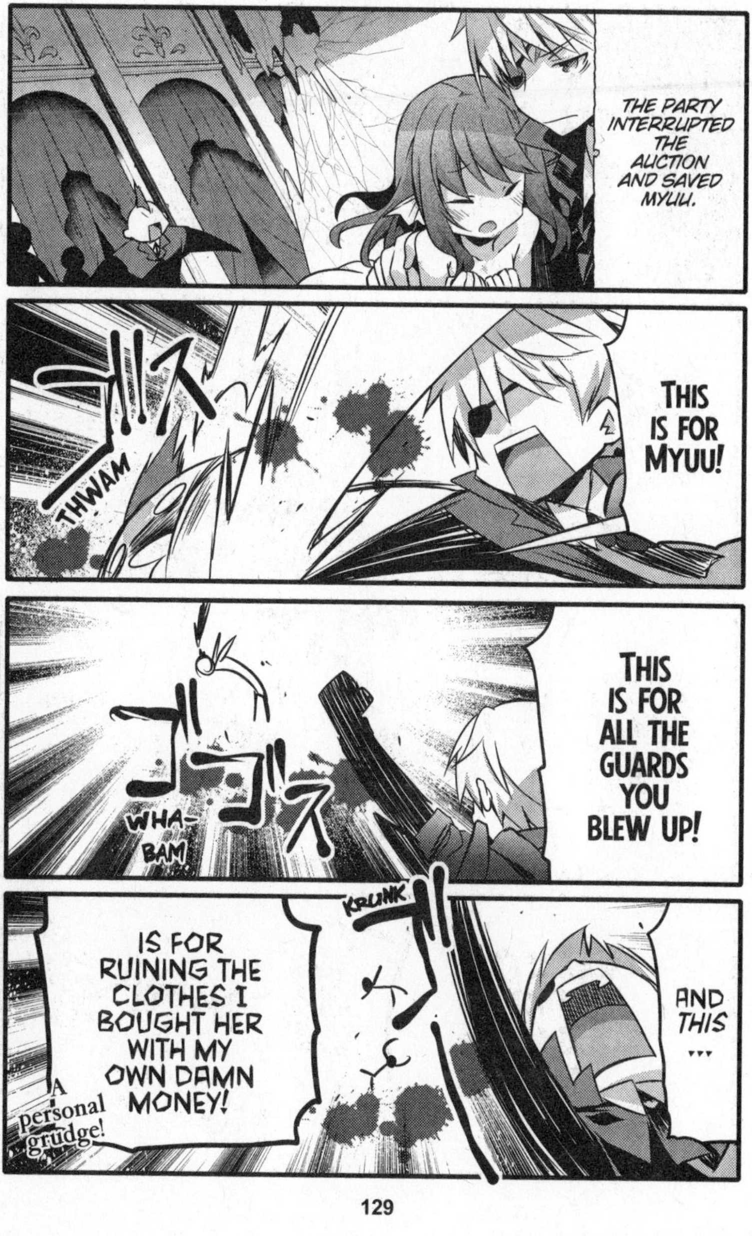
THE PARTY INTERRUPTED THE AUCTION AND SAVED MYUU.
THIS IS FOR MYUU!
THWAM
THIS IS FOR ALL THE GUARDS YOU BLEW UP!
WHA-BAM
AND THIS...
KRUNK
IS FOR RUINING THE CLOTHES I BOUGHT HER WITH MY OWN DAMN MONEY!
A personal grudge!

ED HIS FEELINGS ARE MORE IMPORTANT THAN ALL THAT!

WHO'S RESPONSIBLE?

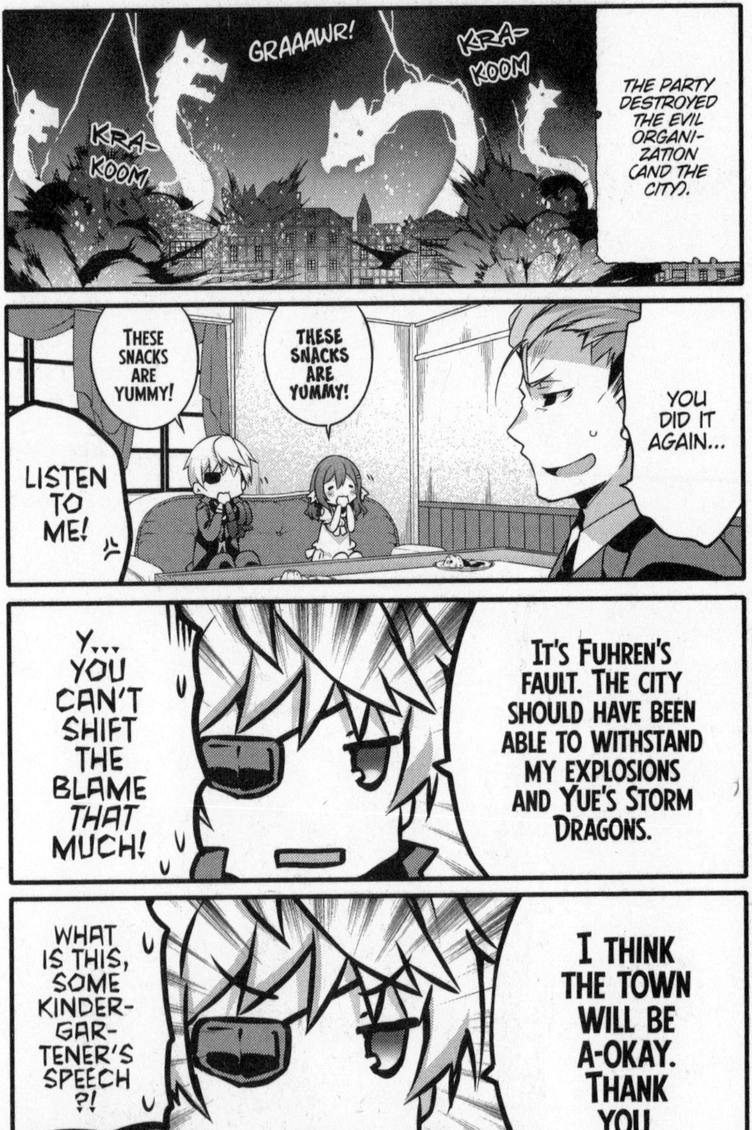

THE PARTY DESTROYED THE EVIL ORGANIZATION (AND THE CITY).
KRA-KOOM
GRAAAWR!
KRA-KOOM
YOU DID IT AGAIN...
THESE SNACKS ARE YUMMY!
THESE SNACKS ARE YUMMY!
LISTEN TO ME!
IT'S FUHREN'S FAULT. THE CITY SHOULD HAVE BEEN ABLE TO WITHSTAND MY EXPLOSIONS AND YUE'S STORM DRAGONS.
Y... YOU CAN'T SHIFT THE BLAME THAT MUCH!
I THINK THE TOWN WILL BE A-OKAY. THANK YOU.
WHAT IS THIS, SOME KINDERGARTENER'S SPEECH?!

ED

KEEP IT SIMPLE, AND YOU CAN ESCAPE!

THE STRONGEST GUARDIANS

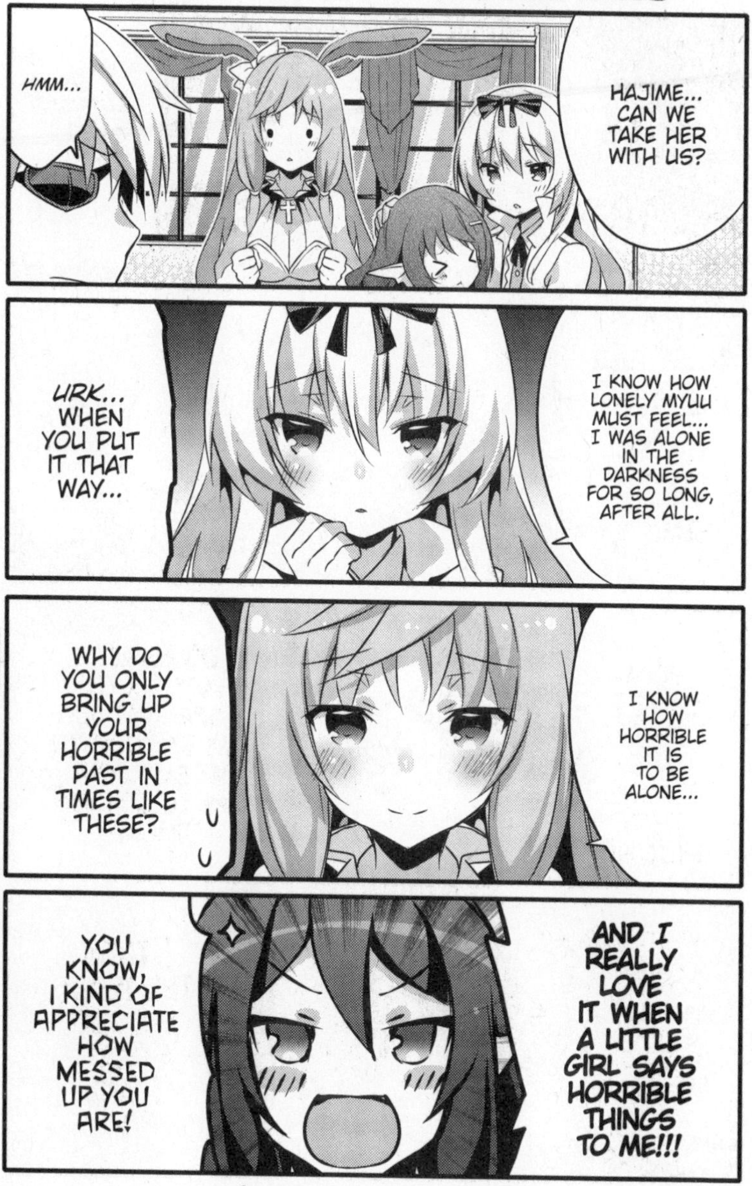

HAJIME... CAN WE TAKE HER WITH US?
HMM...
I KNOW HOW LONELY MYUU MUST FEEL... I WAS ALONE IN THE DARKNESS FOR SO LONG, AFTER ALL.
URK... WHEN YOU PUT IT THAT WAY...
I KNOW HOW HORRIBLE IT IS TO BE ALONE...
WHY DO YOU ONLY BRING UP YOUR HORRIBLE PAST IN TIMES LIKE THESE?
AND I REALLY LOVE IT WHEN A LITTLE GIRL SAYS HORRIBLE THINGS TO ME!!!
YOU KNOW, I KIND OF APPRECIATE HOW MESSED UP YOU ARE!

ED THERE GOES THE MASOCHIST!

THEY DECIDED TO BRING HER ALONG

PAPA!
?!
MYUU...
CALL ME "MAMA"!
!
POUT
POUT
PAT..
PAT..
YOU'RE NOT A MAMA...
SIIIGH...

ED

SHE'S MISSING SOMETHING...

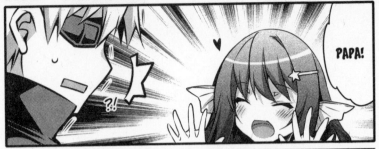

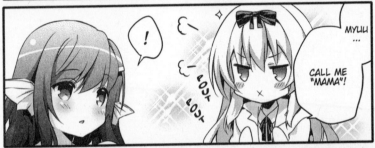

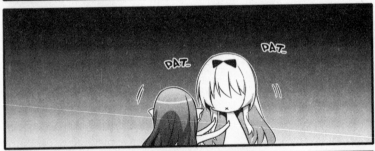

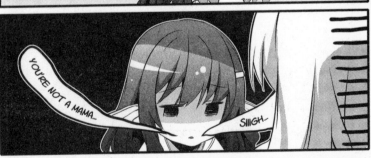

I'M NOT SUSPICIOUS!

ARIFURETA:

ARIFURETA SHOKUGYOU DE SEKAISAIKYOU

I ♥ Isekai

Being Extremely Considerate of the Little Girl

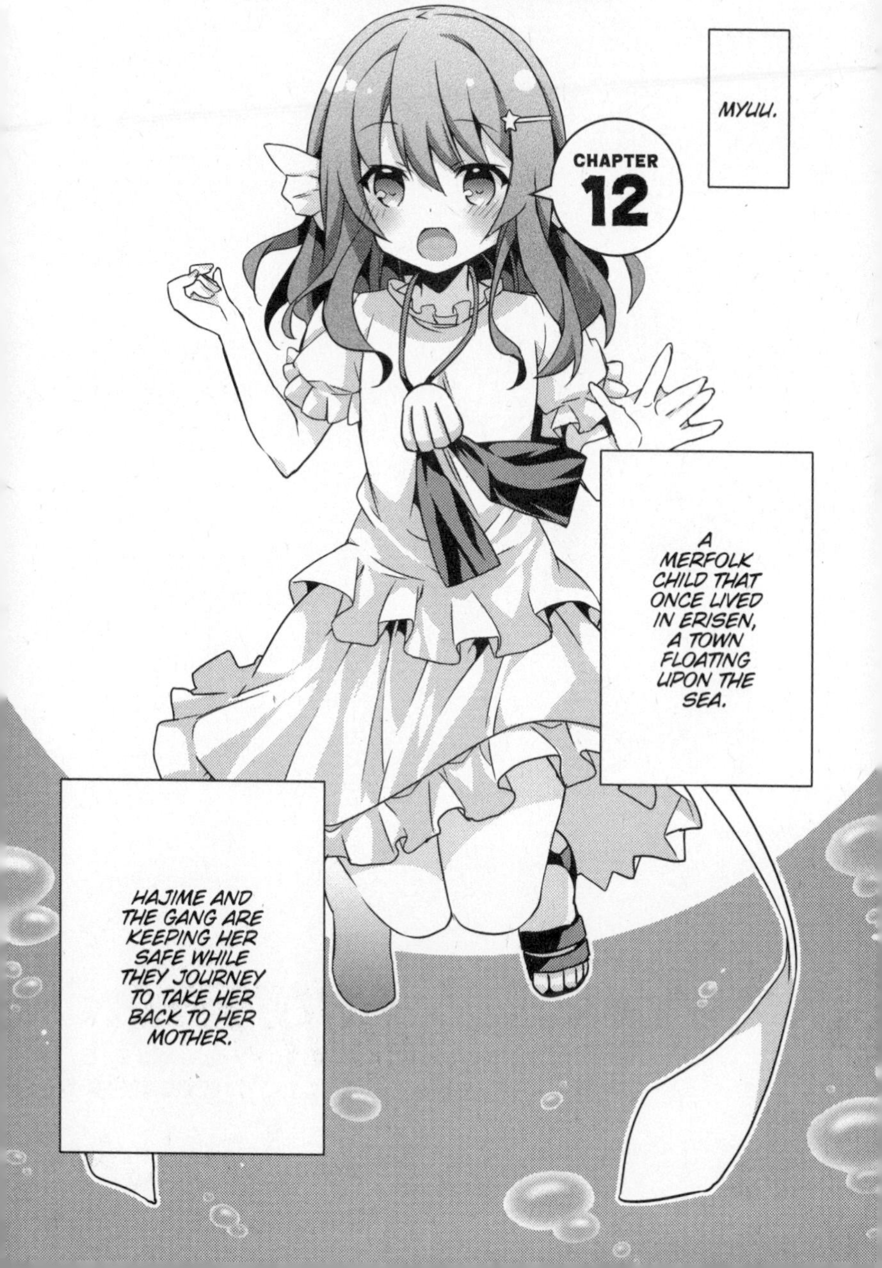
MYUU.
CHAPTER 12
A MERFOLK CHILD THAT ONCE LIVED IN ERISEN, A TOWN FLOATING UPON THE SEA.
HAJIME AND THE GANG ARE KEEPING HER SAFE WHILE THEY JOURNEY TO TAKE HER BACK TO HER MOTHER.

TRA LA LA

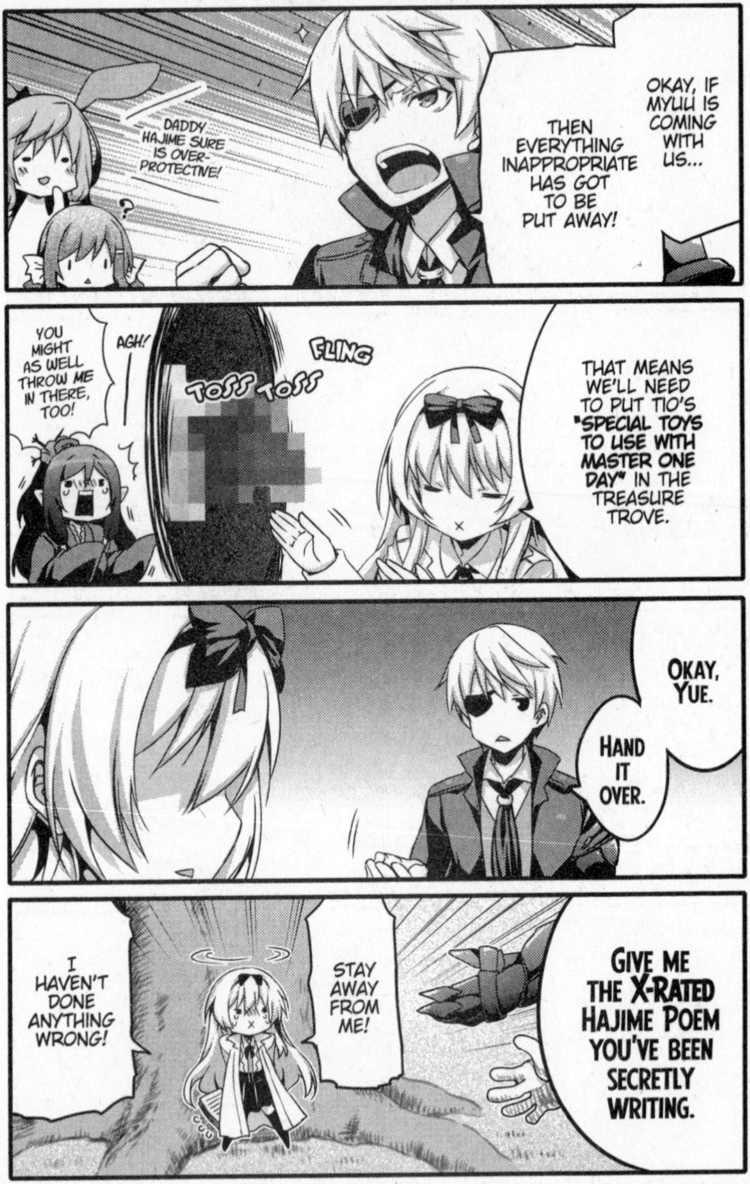
OKAY, IF MYUU IS COMING WITH US...
THEN EVERYTHING INAPPROPRIATE HAS GOT TO BE PUT AWAY!
DADDY HAJIME SURE IS OVER-PROTECTIVE!
THAT MEANS WE'LL NEED TO PUT TIO'S "SPECIAL TOYS TO USE WITH MASTER ONE DAY" IN THE TREASURE TROVE.
FLING
TOSS TOSS
AGH!
YOU MIGHT AS WELL THROW ME IN THERE, TOO!
OKAY, YUE.
HAND IT OVER.
GIVE ME THE X-RATED HAJIME POEM YOU'VE BEEN SECRETLY WRITING.
STAY AWAY FROM ME!
I HAVEN'T DONE ANYTHING WRONG!

WWW.IRASUTOYA.COM

ED IT REALLY IS...

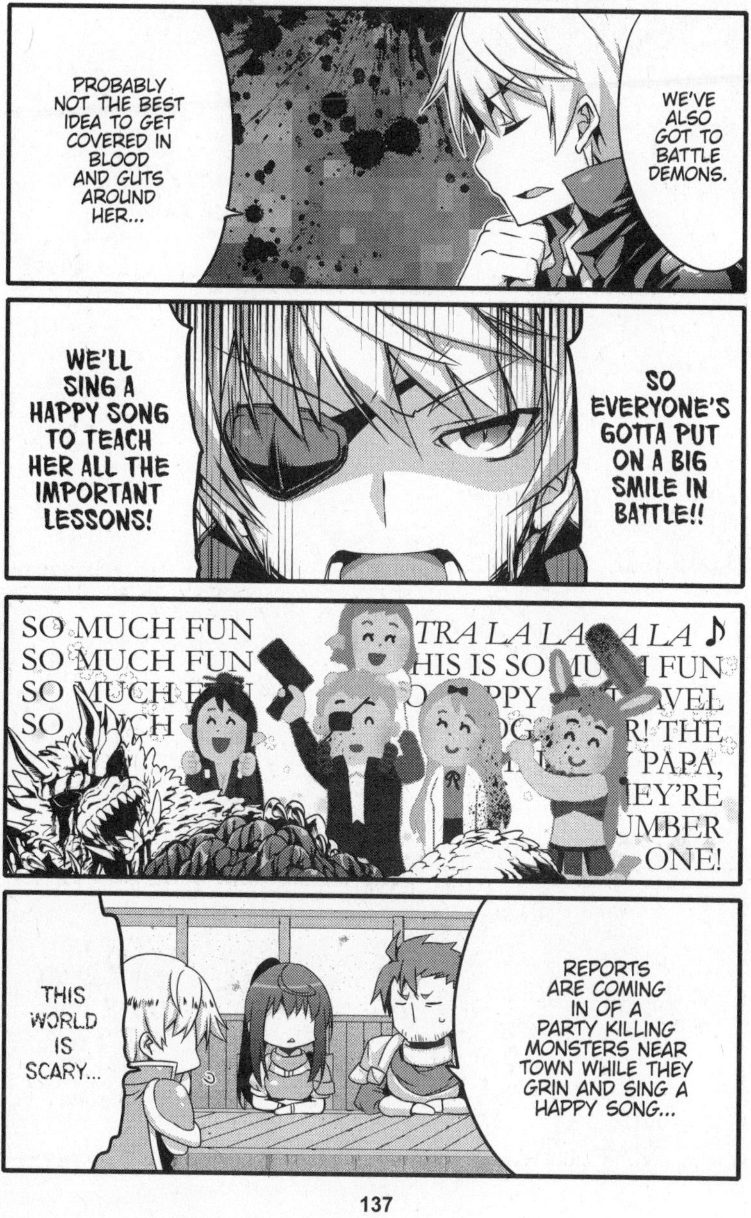
WE'VE ALSO GOT TO BATTLE DEMONS.
PROBABLY NOT THE BEST IDEA TO GET COVERED IN BLOOD AND GUTS AROUND HER...
SO EVERYONE'S GOTTA PUT ON A BIG SMILE IN BATTLE!!
WE'LL SING A HAPPY SONG TO TEACH HER ALL THE IMPORTANT LESSONS!
TRA LA LA
PAPA,
ONE!
SO MUCH FUN
SO MUCH FUN
REPORTS ARE COMING IN OF A PARTY KILLING MONSTERS NEAR TOWN WHILE THEY GRIN AND SING A HAPPY SONG...
THIS WORLD IS SCARY...

SAY IT TWICE TO MAKE IT NICE

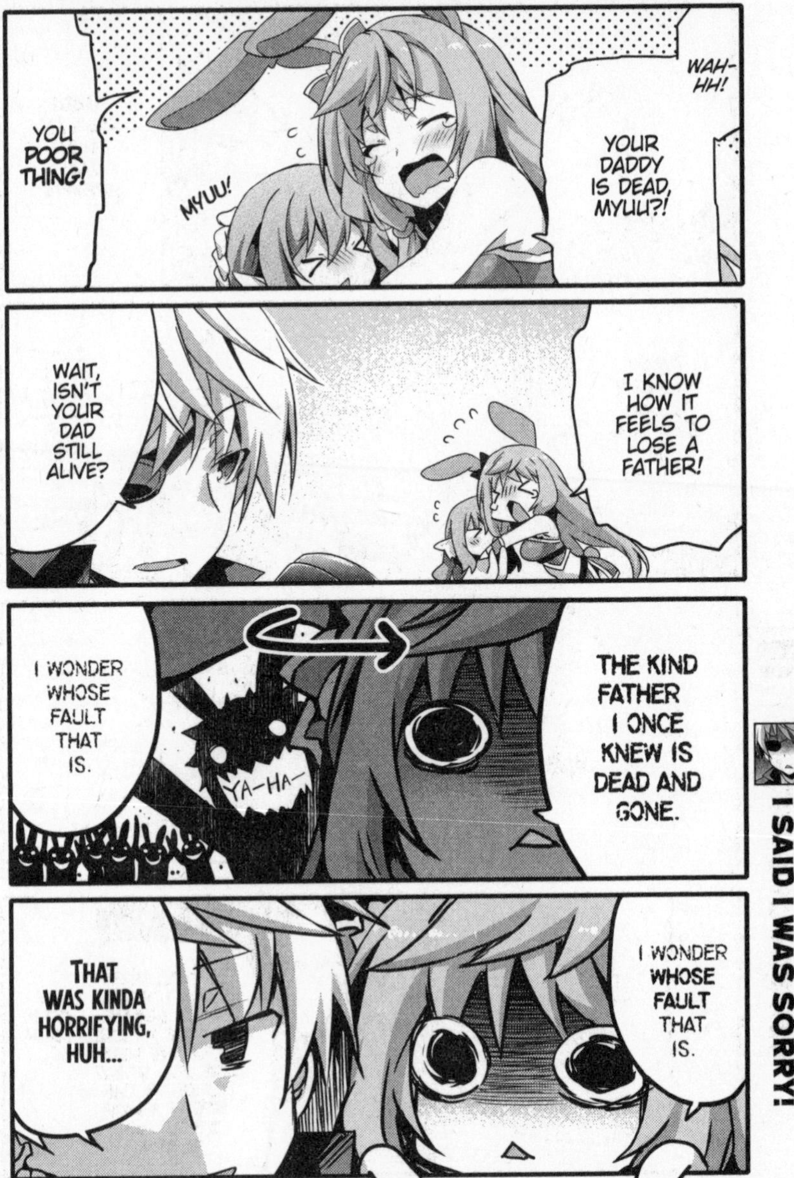
WAH-HH!
YOUR DADDY IS DEAD, MYUU?!
MYUU!
YOU POOR THING!
I KNOW HOW IT FEELS TO LOSE A FATHER!
WAIT, ISN'T YOUR DAD STILL ALIVE?
THE KIND FATHER I ONCE KNEW IS DEAD AND GONE.
YA-HA-
I WONDER WHOSE FAULT THAT IS.
I WONDER WHOSE FAULT THAT IS.
THAT WAS KINDA HORRIFYING, HUH...
I SAID I WAS SORRY!

A HAIKU: SEEING THE FUTURE / USES UP QUITE A BIT OF / MANA, HAJIME

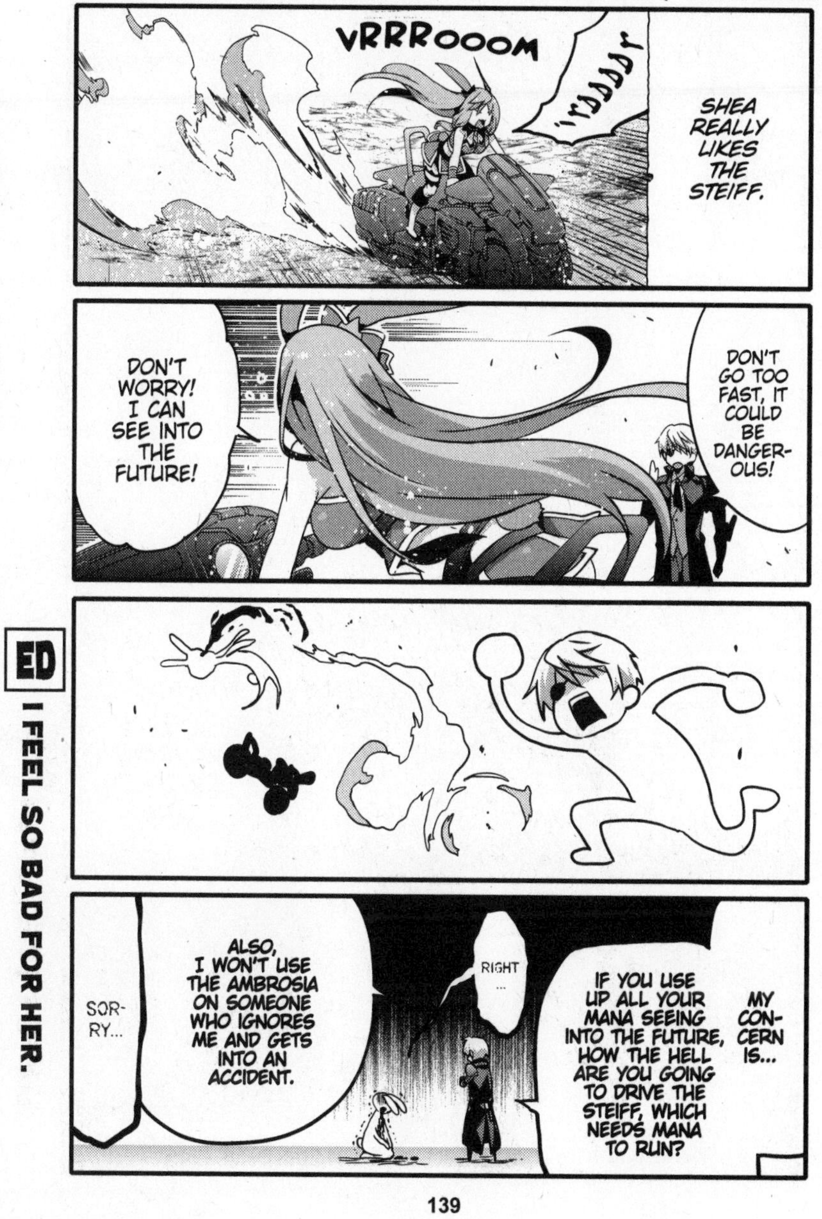
SHEA REALLY LIKES THE STEIFF.
VRRROOOM
YAAAAAY!
DON'T GO TOO FAST, IT COULD BE DANGER-OUS!
DON'T WORRY! I CAN SEE INTO THE FUTURE!
MY CON-CERN IS...
IF YOU USE UP ALL YOUR MANA SEEING INTO THE FUTURE, HOW THE HELL ARE YOU GOING TO DRIVE THE STEIFF, WHICH NEEDS MANA TO RUN?
RIGHT ...
ALSO, I WON'T USE THE AMBROSIA ON SOMEONE WHO IGNORES ME AND GETS INTO AN ACCIDENT.
SOR-RY...

ED

I FEEL SO BAD FOR HER.

IT SMELLS SO BAD

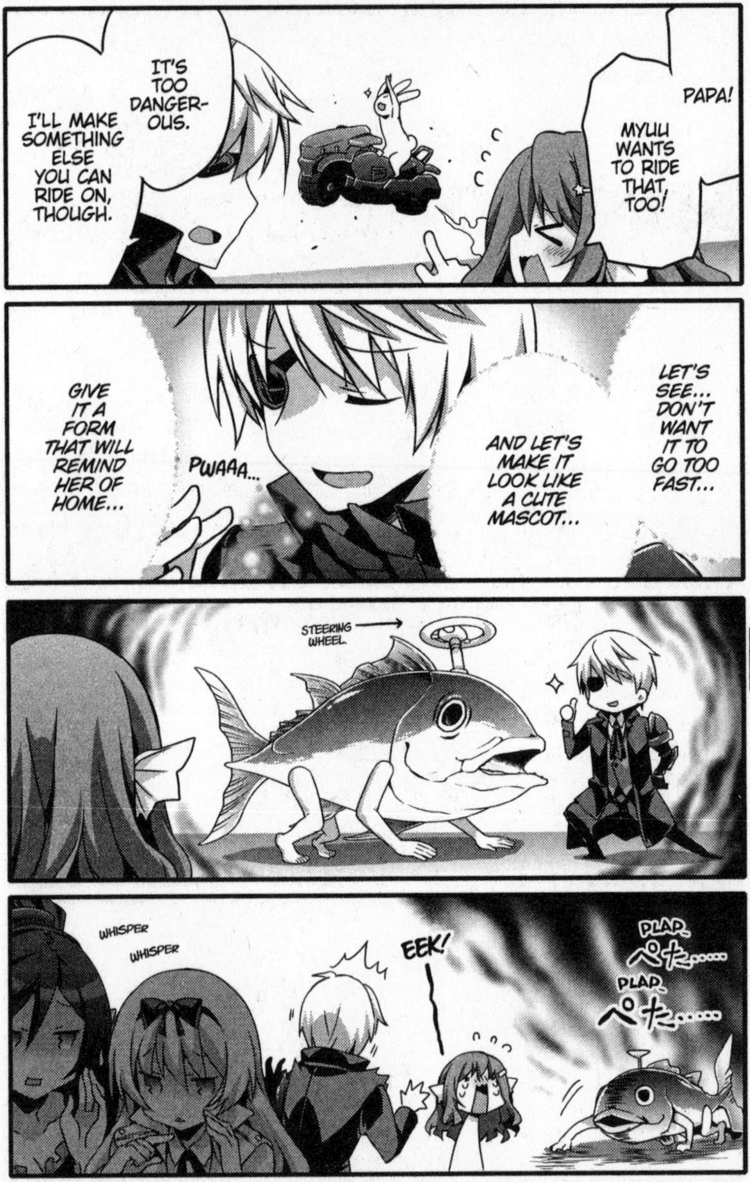
PAPA!
MYUU WANTS TO RIDE THAT, TOO!
IT'S TOO DANGER-OUS.
I'LL MAKE SOMETHING ELSE YOU CAN RIDE ON, THOUGH.
LET'S SEE... DON'T WANT IT TO GO TOO FAST...
AND LET'S MAKE IT LOOK LIKE A CUTE MASCOT...
PWAAA...
GIVE IT A FORM THAT WILL REMIND HER OF HOME...
STEERING WHEEL.
PLAP ぺた……
PLAP ぺた……
EEK!
WHISPER
WHISPER

ED

A TRAUMATIZING DEVICE...

EMBARRASSED, THEY HEADED BACK

ED WHAT A GOOD INN.

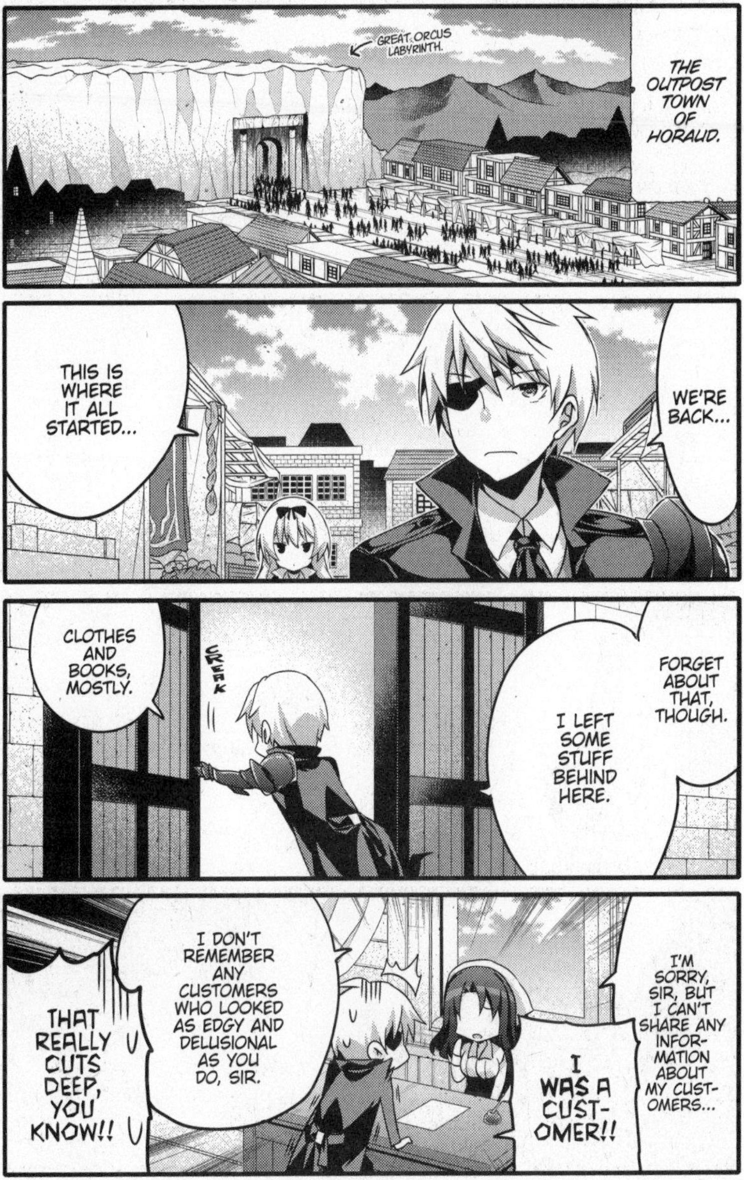
THE OUTPOST TOWN OF HORAUD.
GREAT ORCUS LABYRINTH.
WE'RE BACK...
THIS IS WHERE IT ALL STARTED...
FORGET ABOUT THAT, THOUGH.
I LEFT SOME STUFF BEHIND HERE.
CREAK
CLOTHES AND BOOKS, MOSTLY.
I'M SORRY, SIR, BUT I CAN'T SHARE ANY INFORMATION ABOUT MY CUSTOMERS...
I WAS A CUSTOMER!!
I DON'T REMEMBER ANY CUSTOMERS WHO LOOKED AS EDGY AND DELUSIONAL AS YOU DO, SIR.
THAT REALLY CUTS DEEP, YOU KNOW!!

ED

SHE STOLE THEM...

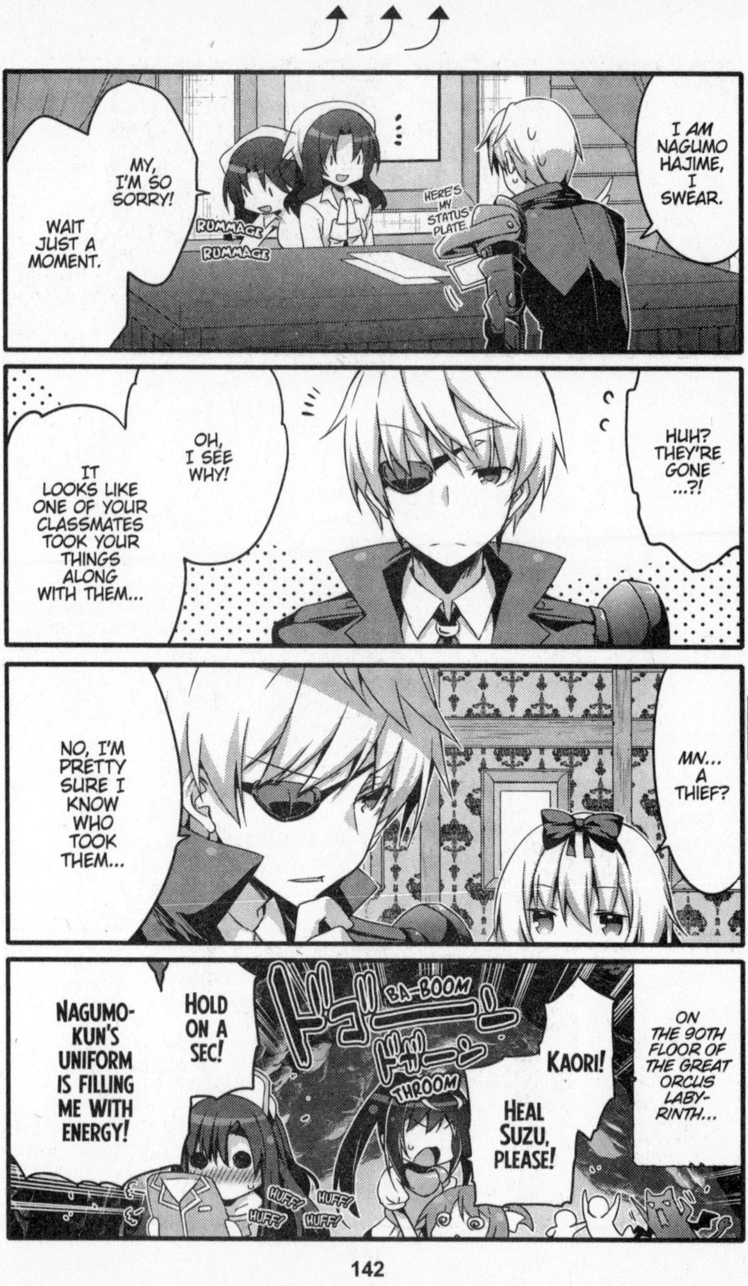

I AM NAGUMO HAJIME, I SWEAR.
HERE'S MY STATUS PLATE.
MY, I'M SO SORRY!
RUMMAGE
RUMMAGE
WAIT JUST A MOMENT.
HUH? THEY'RE GONE ...?!
OH, I SEE WHY!
IT LOOKS LIKE ONE OF YOUR CLASSMATES TOOK YOUR THINGS ALONG WITH THEM...
MN... A THIEF?
NO, I'M PRETTY SURE I KNOW WHO TOOK THEM...
ON THE 90TH FLOOR OF THE GREAT ORCUS LABY-RINTH...
KAORI!
HEAL SUZU, PLEASE!
BA-BOOM
THROOM
HOLD ON A SEC!
NAGUMO-KUN'S UNIFORM IS FILLING ME WITH ENERGY!
HUFF!
HUFF!
HUFF!
HUFF!

GUILTY

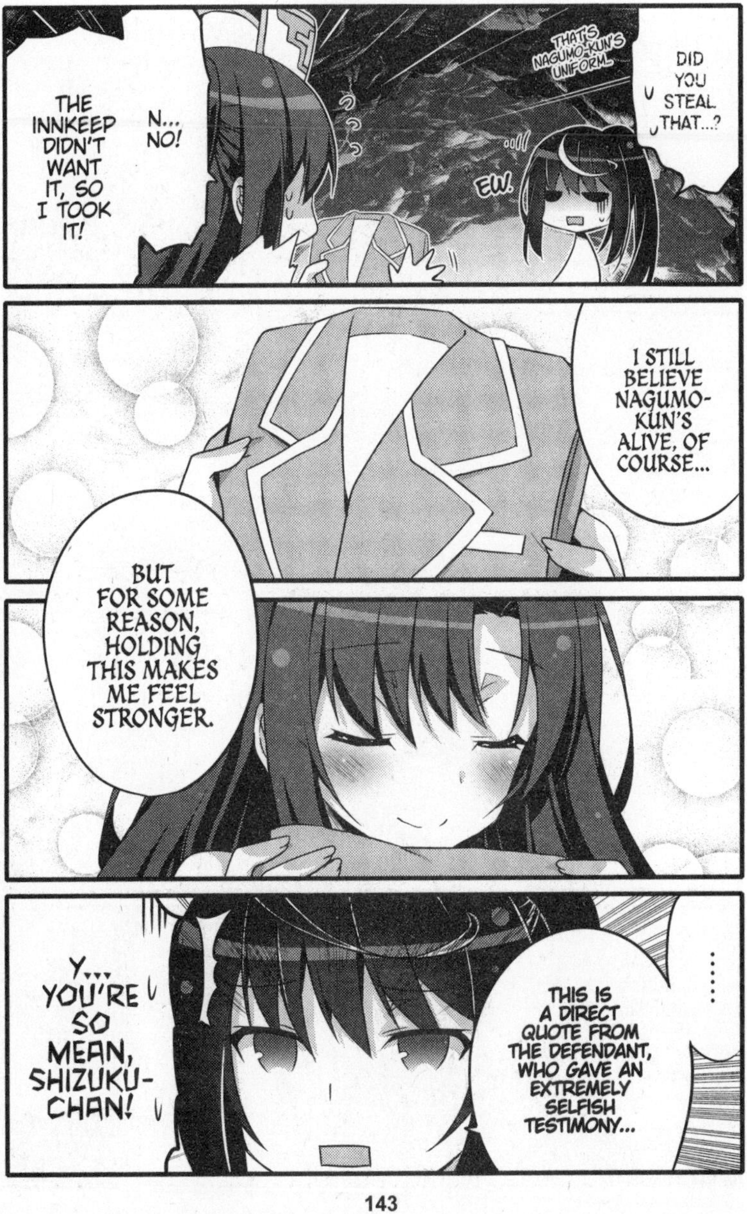
DID YOU STEAL THAT...?
THAT'S NAGUMO-KUN'S UNIFORM...
EW.
N... NO!
THE INNKEEP DIDN'T WANT IT, SO I TOOK IT!
I STILL BELIEVE NAGUMO-KUN'S ALIVE, OF COURSE...
BUT FOR SOME REASON, HOLDING THIS MAKES ME FEEL STRONGER.
......
THIS IS A DIRECT QUOTE FROM THE DEFENDANT, WHO GAVE AN EXTREMELY SELFISH TESTIMONY...
Y... YOU'RE SO MEAN, SHIZUKU-CHAN!

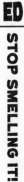

ENDOU KOUSUKE

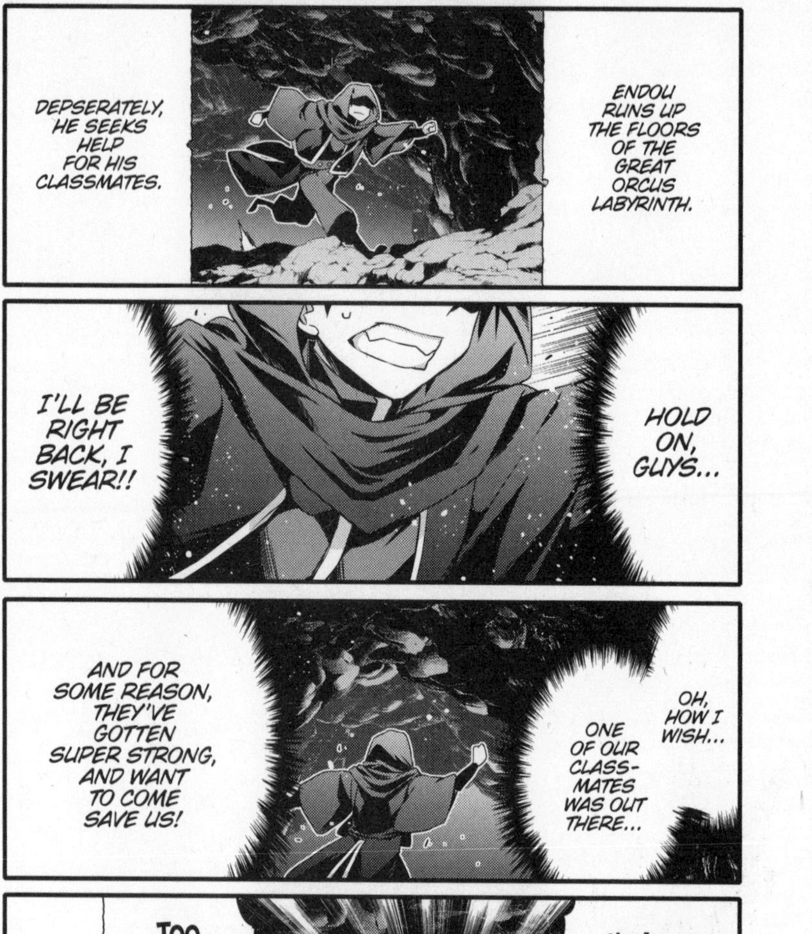
ENDOU RUNS UP THE FLOORS OF THE GREAT ORCUS LABYRINTH.
DEPSERATELY, HE SEEKS HELP FOR HIS CLASSMATES.
HOLD ON, GUYS...
I'LL BE RIGHT BACK, I SWEAR!!
OH, HOW I WISH...
ONE OF OUR CLASS-MATES WAS OUT THERE...
AND FOR SOME REASON, THEY'VE GOTTEN SUPER STRONG, AND WANT TO COME SAVE US!
HEH! MAYBE THEY'D TAKE OUT THESE ENEMIES IN ONE FELL SWOOP!
ZOOOOM
TOO BAD THAT'S NOT REAL!
IT WAS.
WOW.

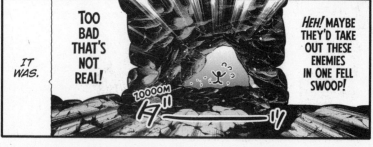

A PICTURE OF THE MAIN CHARACTER ATTACKING
THE HEROINE TO KILL THE ENEMY BEHIND HER

ARIFURETA:

ARIFURETA SHOKUGYOU DE SEKAISAIKYOU

I ♥ Isekai

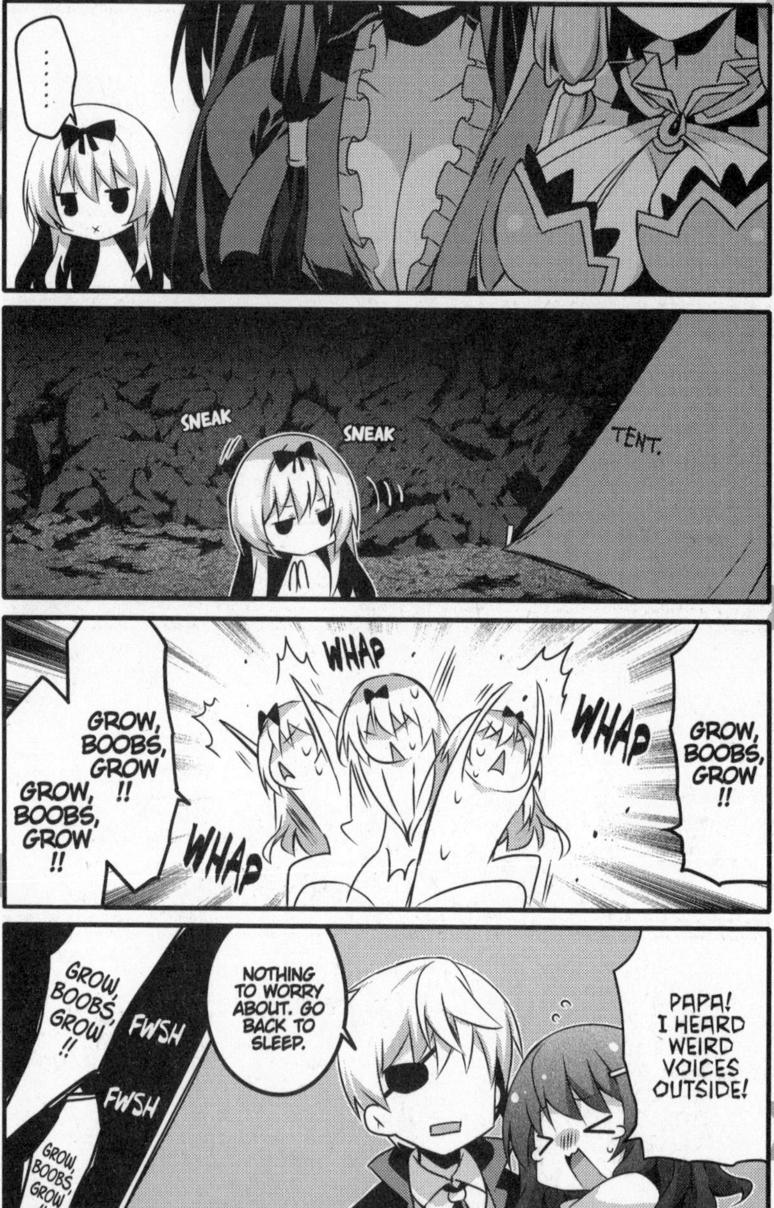
……
TENT.
SNEAK
SNEAK
GROW, BOOBS, GROW!!
WHAP
WHAP
GROW, BOOBS, GROW!!
WHAP
GROW, BOOBS, GROW!!
PAPA! I HEARD WEIRD VOICES OUTSIDE!
NOTHING TO WORRY ABOUT. GO BACK TO SLEEP.
FWSH
FWSH
GROW, BOOBS, GROW!!
GROW, BOOBS, GROW

THANKS TO -- EDITOR MNO, OUR DESIGNERS, AND STAFF MEMBERS OSAKI, HARADA, AND TSUJII!

BONUS MANGA

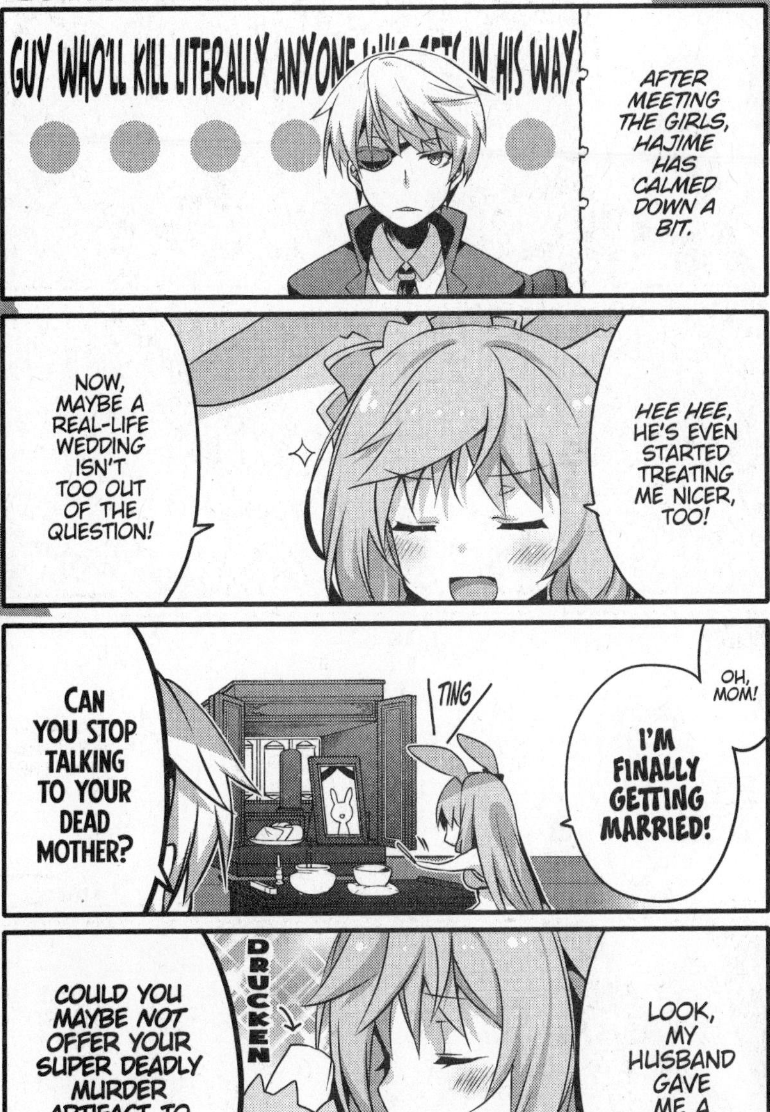
AFTER MEETING THE GIRLS, HAJIME HAS CALMED DOWN A BIT.
GUY WHO'LL KILL LITERALLY ANYONE
IN HIS WAY
HEE HEE, HE'S EVEN STARTED TREATING ME NICER, TOO!
NOW, MAYBE A REAL-LIFE WEDDING ISN'T TOO OUT OF THE QUESTION!
OH, MOM!
I'M FINALLY GETTING MARRIED!
TING
CAN YOU STOP TALKING TO YOUR DEAD MOTHER?
LOOK, MY HUSBAND GAVE ME A PRESENT.
DRUCKEN
COULD YOU MAYBE *NOT* OFFER YOUR SUPER DEADLY MURDER ARTIFACT TO THE DEARLY DEPARTED?

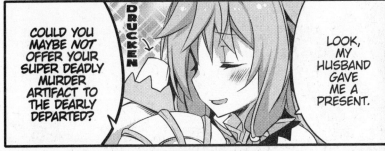

ORIGINAL WORK: RYO SHIRAKOME, TAKAYA-KI

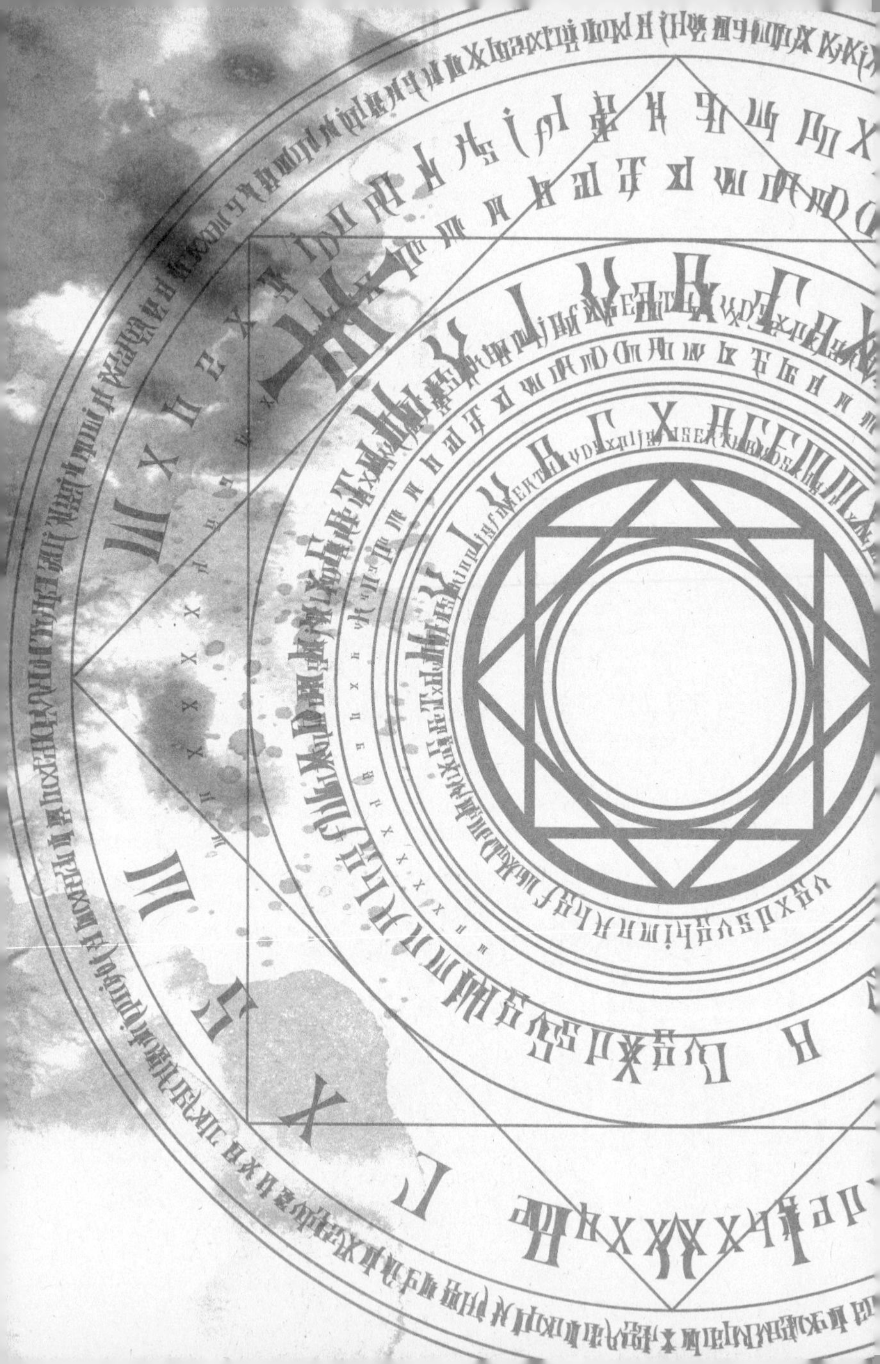

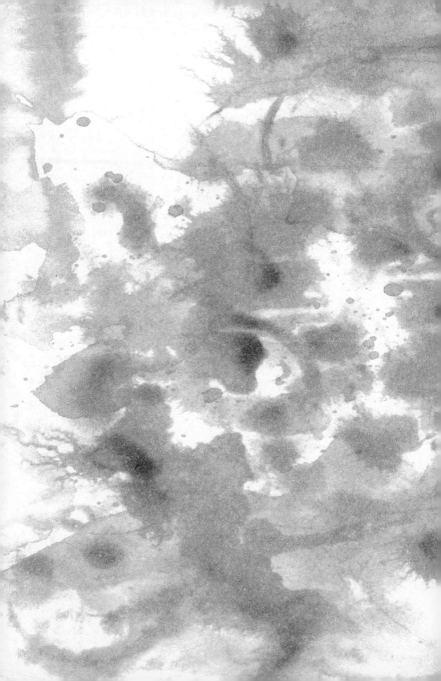

ARIFURETA:

ARIFURETA SHOKUGYOU DE SEKAISAIKYOU

I ♥ Isekai

SEVEN SEAS ENTERTAINMENT PRESENTS

ARIFURETA: I ♥ Isekai

story and art by **MISAKI MORI** / original story by **RYO SHIRAKOME**   VOLUME 1

TRANSLATION
Katrina Leonoudakis

LETTERING AND RETOUCH
Jennifer Skarupa

COVER DESIGN
KC Fabellon

PROOFREADING
Danielle King
Tom Speelman

EDITOR
J.P. Sullivan

PRODUCTION MANAGER
Lissa Pattillo

MANAGING EDITOR
Julie Davis

EDITOR-IN-CHIEF
Adam Arnold

PUBLISHER
Jason DeAngelis

ARIFURETA NICHIJOU DE SEKAI SAIKYOU VOL. 1
© 2018 Misaki Mori
©Ryo Shirakome/OVERLAP
First published in Japan in 2018 by OVERLAP Inc., Ltd., Tokyo.
English translation rights arranged with OVERLAP Inc., Ltd., Tokyo.

Seven Seas press and purchase enquiries can be sent to Marketing Manager
Lianne Sentar at press@gomanga.com. Information regarding the distribution
and purchase of digital editions is available from Digital Manager CK Russell
at digital@gomanga.com.

Seven Seas and the Seven Seas logo are trademarks of
Seven Seas Entertainment. All rights reserved.

ISBN: 978-1-64275-761-3

Printed in Canada

First Printing: December 2019

10 9 8 7 6 5 4 3 2 1

FOLLOW US ONLINE: *www.sevenseasentertainment.com*

READING DIRECTIONS

This book reads from *right to left*, Japanese style.
If this is your first time reading manga, you start
reading from the top right panel on each page and
take it from there. If you get lost, just follow the
numbered diagram here. It may seem backwards at
first, but you'll get the hang of it! Have fun!!

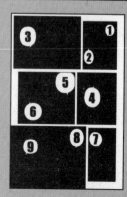